Critical Issues in

Higher
Education

for the Public Good

Critical Issues in
Higher
Education
for the Public Good

Qualitative, Quantitative, & Historical
Research Perspectives

Edited by Penny A. Pasque,
Nicholas A. Bowman, & Magdalena Martinez

Introduction by
Alexander W. & Helen S. Astin

Kennesaw State
University Press

Kennesaw State University Press
Kennesaw State University
Building 27, Suite 220, Mailbox 2701
1000 Chastain Road
Kennesaw, GA 30144

Cathleen Salsburg-Pfund, Editor
Holly S. Miller, Cover and Book Design
Michelle R. Hinson, Production Assistant

Reprinted with Permission: Green, D.O. (2004). Justice and diversity: Michigan's response to *Gratz, Grutter,* and the affirmative action debate. *Urban Education,* 39 (4), 374–393.

Reprinted with Permission: Urrieta, Jr., L. and Méndez Benavídez, L.R. (2007). Community Commitment and Activist Scholarship: Chicana/o Professors and the Practice of Consciousness. *The Journal of Hispanic Higher Education,* 6(3). 222–236.

Library of Congress Cataloging-in-Publication Data

Critical issues in higher education for the public good : qualitative, quantitative & historical research perspectives / : [editors] Penny A. Pasque, Nicholas A. Bowman, & Magdalena Martinez.
    p. cm.
 ISBN 978-1-933483-21-4 (alk. paper)
 1. Education, Higher--Research--Methodology. 2. Qualitative research. 3. Quantitative research. I. Pasque, Penny A. II. Bowman, Nicholas A., 1979- III. Martnez, Magdalena.
 LB2326.3.C75 2009
 306.43'2--dc22
                    2009045199

Printed in the United States of America

10 9 8 7 6 5 4 3 2 1

Dedication

We dedicate this book to all people working to strengthen the connections between higher education and society. We hope these myriad efforts continue to work toward equitable change regarding higher education for the public good.

Contents

SECTION II: ENGAGING STUDENTS AND THE COMMUNITY THROUGH STUDY ABROAD, SERVICE-LEARNING, AND CIVIC ENGAGEMENT

Section III: Redefining the Academy for the Public Good

Higher Education for the Public Good: Exploring New Perspectives

John C. Burkhardt, Penny A. Pasque,
Nicholas A. Bowman, and Magdalena Martínez

This book, *Critical Issues in Higher Education for the Public Good: Qualitative, Quantitative, & Historical Research Perspectives*, represents an ongoing commitment to bring new scholarly voices into a public discussion about the relationship that exists between higher education and American society. In organizing the writing project that is reflected in these chapters, we sought to provide new research which closely examines the myriad benefits between higher education and society, situated within a contemporary context. The degree to which this goal has been met is a reflection of the insight, scholarship and creativity of the authors represented in these chapters. We all owe them a debt of thanks for what they have brought to their work. It has resulted in a book that has local, state and national implications for educational practice, policy and the public. Furthermore, we hope this book builds upon and extends old frameworks that might have to be challenged, replacing them with new ideas to be explored and debated.

The concept of higher education's place in society and the assertion that college and universities are responsible for more than what is currently expected of them— more than they are giving to be sure—is one that is central to our work at the National Forum on Higher Education for the Public Good. Founded in 2000 and affiliated with the Center for the Study of Higher and Postsecondary Education at the University of Michigan, the National Forum has been in the forefront of a widening discussion that we believe is important for educators and policy makers to heed and to feed. After organizing a series of national conversations on the topic of higher education and society in 2002, the National Forum helped to shape a "Common Agenda" for fostering ongoing efforts to increase awareness, understanding, commitment and action in support of higher education's public service mission. In the years that have followed from the adoption of that goal, some progress has been made, we think, in situating this issue more centrally in the work of college presidents, policy makers and scholars. As the discussions have become more vigorous and popular, they have also become more contentious. There are more ideas available to consider; the discussions have become more nuanced, less dichotomous and more intense.

One outcome of our preliminary work at the National Forum was a realization that we needed to bring new voices into the conversation. In 2001, we initiated a series of activities to identify and encourage a generation of rising scholars at the early stages of their careers. We encouraged the scholars to participate in—and in some cases lead—the emerging scholarly debate on higher education's public role. In 2001 through 2004, we organized three symposia at which earlier career higher education scholars and established scholars convened to share perspectives on issues related to higher education for the public good. These discussions were co-sponsored with the Higher Education and Organizational Change Division of the School of Education at the University of California Los Angeles (UCLA), University of Michigan's Center for the Study of Higher and Postsecondary Education, and Michigan State University's Higher, Adult and Lifelong Education. They focused on research related to the balance between private and public benefits of higher education; the transformation of colleges and universities that was needed to achieve a better balance between private and public outcomes; the role and importance of minority-serving institutions in assuring institutional and student diversity in higher education; and the challenges facing early career researchers in maintaining a "public good" theme in their scholarly work.

In partnership with several national professional associations, we organized and funded a program to identify and promote the careers of a dozen "rising scholars" through mentoring, help with publications and support for conference attendance. The Rising Scholars were selected by and received partial funding from the Association for Institutional Research (AIR), American Association for Higher Education (AAHE), American Educational Research Association (AERA), Association for the Study of Higher Education (ASHE), and American College Personnel Association (ACPA). This initiative has contributed to the development of monographs, articles, chapters, and books, including this one.

Over the last several years, we have also nurtured the discussion on higher education's role in society through annual meetings at the Wingspread Conference Center in Racine, Wisconsin. These meetings have helped to refocus the topic of higher education's responsibilities by examining topics such as community engagement and the importance of community-institution collaboration, the nature of higher education's responsibility in a society faced with complex global challenges, and emerging frameworks for examining higher education and society. Reports on these discussions have sparked comment and generated additional new ideas, furthering the public and professional discourse (Pasque, Hendricks, & Bowman, 2006; Pasque, Smerek, Dwyer, Bowman, & Mallory, 2005).

The National Forum has also made an ambitious attempt to listen to community voices in a systematic and disciplined way. Through an effort called "Access to Democracy," we have organized structured conversations amongst the public on the question, "Who is College For?" This project has surfaced many new ways of thinking about higher education's role in the lives of the people it serves and, in particular, it has given us new insight into the subtleties that surround such concepts as "merit," "hard work" and "fairness" as they relate to perceptions of higher education access and participation. Research based on these conversations has been reported at national meetings and shared with policy makers in several state capitals, including our own (National Forum, 2007).

Across these many activities, we have made frequent and intentional references to the need for a social and professional movement that would transform the relationships we are studying in our work. The concept of a "movement" is very complicated in social science and somewhat mysterious in terms of the ways in which it is viewed by the general public. It is certainly not an idea that can be casually asserted. In our earliest gatherings of leaders to discuss these issues, the idea of a movement was discussed at some length, prompted in part by remarks made by Elizabeth Hollander at a meeting held at Wye River, Maryland. Hollander suggested that several elements must be balanced in a movement to transform higher education and society: networks of informal interaction based on a set of shared beliefs and a sense of belonging, oppositional ideas (i.e., "something to move against") and spheres of activity that operate independent of the institutions and structures that must be changed for the movement to succeed (London, 2002a; 2002b; 2002c; 2003). By these criteria, a claim that efforts to promote "higher education for the public good" have approached the status of a movement would be entirely premature. But still, there is some reason to hope that the discussion has been engaged.

In all of these efforts, and in any conversations we have had about the potential for sparking a movement across institutions and society, we have placed an intentionally high value on the inclusion of new perspectives as critical to a well-informed and productive debate. Any critical thought of changing the ways in which higher education and society inter-relate must be grounded in the experiences of young people, historically excluded populations, and community activists, and all of these partners must be engaged directly in the work of changing the status quo. The circumstances that shape how higher education and U.S. society interconnect have been evolving over nearly four centuries. Many of the distinguished scholars whose work influences our field of higher education or who provide social commentary on educational issues have seen changes over the courses of their own careers that are monumental and historic *for them*; but for younger colleagues and our community partners these same events may be perceived as less historic and more a place of departure. In this respect, this book begins an important discussion in a new place for the authors and, we hope, for the reader. Each of its chapters approaches a consideration of higher education's place in society from a vantage point that reflects not only a unique scholarly journey, but also some aspect of a collective journey.

In his chapter, Bryan McKinley Jones Brayboy explores the ways that American Indian communities, through their citizens, identify themselves in relation to ongoing struggles. Part of this examination includes the ways that American Indians and citizens of their tribal nations utilize higher education to examine and explore their complex economic, political, and social structures. The partnership described in this work may serve as a model of how other Indigenous communities and tribal nations can utilize education for their community's benefit. In this approach, academic and societal structures that have historically been oppressive can inherently serve as liberating and empowering mechanisms for tribal nations and Indigenous people.

Denise O'Neil Green examines arguments that were at the heart of a pivotal legal case. In 1997, the Center for Individual Rights filed two lawsuits against the University of Michigan on behalf of two white plaintiffs who believed they were denied admissions because of racial preferences. The diversity rationale, Michigan's counter argument, underscored the links between racial diversity and institutional mission, but rejected long standing social justice arguments of racial/ethnic equality and remediation to combat societal and institutional discrimination. Through qualitative inquiry, Denise O'Neil Green eloquently explores how Michigan shifts the focus of the affirmative action debate from racial equality to a narrower racial diversity argument, which garners broad support and neutralizes the racial preferences rhetoric.

Sara Goldrick-Rab explores patterns of student mobility between colleges and universities and its relationship with inequality. Specifically, she explains how student mobility is both a reflection of and a contributor to inequality in American higher education along social class, and to some degree, along racial and gender lines. Her goal with this research study is to move the discussion of student mobility in higher education away from its current focus on what mobility means for institutional graduation rates to a focus on the consequences of student mobility and what these consequences mean for student learning.

Nadine Dolby focuses her attention on how American students traveling abroad negotiate their national, American identity during a time of war. In particular, students became acutely aware of their American identity as they traveled outside of the United States. This realization and struggle shaped their encounter with the rest of the world. From her in-depth interviews and focus groups with approximately 100 students, Dolby describes her findings and argues that the possibility of raising students' awareness and critical reflection on their national identity, as opposed to the nebulous and diffuse stage of "global awareness," should be more clearly centered in discussions of study abroad.

Lamont A. Flowers analyzes a nationally representative dataset of college graduates to explore the relationship between volunteerism after college and a variety of college and pre-college experiences among African Americans. He shows that African Americans who graduated with degrees in social science and business were more likely to volunteer after college than were those who graduated with degrees in science, engineering, and technical/professional fields, even when controlling for previous volunteer behavior and a host of other variables. This finding supports the idea that majoring in a social science discipline can foster a sense of civic responsibility and engagement within society.

Julia Garbus examines the life of Vida Scudder, a Progressive-era academic professor and activist, and the programs she created to share her intellectual inheritance. Garbus focuses on the Circolo Italo-Americano program that led to successful cross-cultural friendship and mutual learning to enhance democracy. Her research fosters higher education for the public good as it reintroduces a woman whose life clearly embodied this principle. Garbus states that histories help chart the future by grounding current efforts which link college and community in rich traditions of similar efforts, and by showing different methods of approaching societal issues—separated by a century—but similar to those faced today.

Seanna M. Kerrigan documents college graduates' perspectives on the effect of capstone service-learning courses three years following their graduation. Her research suggests that graduates who participated in a capstone course enhanced their communication and leadership skills, community involvement, appreciation of diversity, and career development. As part of her study, Kerrigan also considers challenges faced by participants and offers suggestions for practitioners in the field of service-learning. The results of this study will contribute to the knowledge base that improves the quality and outcomes of service-learning courses, a key tool in helping higher education more effectively develop engaged individuals who are capable of leading and service in our complex and diverse communities.

In her chapter, Michele S. Moses explores how disparate opinions surrounding affirmative action and race-conscious admissions can stem from moral disagreements about conceptions of what constitutes "fairness" and "equality." Using philosophical inquiry, she argues that an understanding of these deep conceptions of moral ideals is necessary not only to understand the nature of this controversy, but also to promote policies that expand educational opportunity.

Richard L. O'Bryant looks at whether personal computing and high-speed Internet access can support community-building efforts by empowering low-income community residents to do more for themselves and each other. His study reveals that residents who have a personal computer and Internet access in their homes feel a greater sense of community, experience an increase in social contact with others, and strengthen their social ties. He asserts that academia can help create an understanding of the challenges and rich potential inherent in the formation of technological environments and use this to further effective and equitable community strategy as well as informed public discussion. Moreover, he purports that higher education plays an essential role in supporting the general expansion of knowledge, wisdom and understanding in ways that challenge traditional and often inequitable distribution of resources and opportunities, especially in terms of access to technology.

Jennifer E. Lerner investigates white students' conceptions of diversity and the potential benefits of diversity on college campuses. Through in-depth interviews, she finds that white students generally value diversity, but they do not understand the connection between diversity and racial inequality, and they reject experiences with diversity that involve issues of power and inequity. She argues that fostering an appreciation of these types of experiences should be an important step in promoting students' understanding and appreciation of "diversity."

Joshua Powers examines the ways in which university technology commercialization may result in ethical conflicts. Through his analysis of 125 licensing contracts between universities and industry, he concludes that these agreements create substantial ethical conflicts that compromise the norms of academic science and commitments to the public good. He provides several recommendations for reform, including a de-emphasis of the role of revenue generation in technology commercialization.

Luis Urrieta, Jr.'s chapter explores ten Chicana/o professors of education's sense making about their role in the academy in terms of community commitments, activist scholarship, and the practices of consciousness in their struggle for their version of the public good. Chicana/o consciousness in practice involved not only active awareness of their agency in moment-to-moment interactions, but also the responsibility to seize those moments to act for change. These Chicana/o professors consciously exercised their agency not only in reaction to white supremacy in the academy, but also in proactive, enduring ways through day-to-day practices to subvert and challenge the whitestream (i.e., traditional, Euro-centric) norms and practices of higher education. The practices of Chicana/o consciousness, Urrieta argues, can contribute to further developing a common understanding of higher education for the public good.

David J. Weerts' work examines how campus executives, faculty, and staff at large research universities articulate and demonstrate their commitment to outreach and engagement. His findings suggest that community partner perceptions of institutional engagement are informed by rhetoric and behavior of top university leaders. The study provides implications for how land grant universities might better align their leadership, organizational structures, practices and policies to be more responsive to societal needs.

Finally, Anthony Chambers and Nicholas A. Bowman synthesize the work of the Rising Scholars. In doing so, they discuss the critical themes explored in these chapters and offer suggestions for future directions for research. They also provide some specific challenges and barriers for the continuation of this work.

In essence, this book reflects the opinion that a public and professional debate about higher education's place in society is urgently needed and that the discussion must be radical in its content and process. While we acknowledge the important role that colleges and universities have had in shaping contemporary society in the United States, we also contend that what we have done to this point will not sustain us or improve our democracy long into the future. The challenges of the current century will require a system of higher learning that creates more opportunities for more people, a greater appreciation of the importance of complex knowledge and its uses, and an overall greater sense of vision.

None of this important work could have been attempted or sustained without the support of our major foundations. The W.K. Kellogg Foundation deserves special credit for establishing the work of the National Forum on Higher Education for the Public Good in 2000. The Lumina Foundation for Education has supported our efforts to promote a conversation about higher education's importance at the community level. The Charles F. Kettering Foundation has been directly involved in shaping the ways in which we have convened and conducted discussions across political, social, and cultural boundaries. The Johnson Foundation supported our work at the Wingspread Conference Center, and we have also received support from the McGregor Fund of Detroit, Atlantic Philanthropies, and many others. We are also indebted to the Horace A. Rackham Graduate School at the University of Michigan for supporting our students with fellowships and stipends, and to our colleagues at the Center for the Study of Higher and Postsecondary Education at the University of Michigan for their support and encouragement. We hold in special affection and gratitude our colleagues at the National Forum whose passion and dedication has contributed to this book and to the many other ambitious programs and activities that make that organization vital and important.

In sum, we see this book as furthering a long history of social commentary, reflection and writing on the theme of higher education and society by adding to it qualitative, quantitative, mixed methods and historical evidence that has been frequently lacking in this discussion. Quite often, higher education leaders, such as university presidents, provosts, legislators, and other decision makers, seek quality evidence that supports their perspectives regarding the roles that higher education plays in society. That evidence is crucial as they seek to motivate students, the public, and to inform policy. In an earlier book associated with the National Forum's work, *Higher Education for the Public Good* (Kezar, Chambers, & Burkhardt, 2005), various authors speak to a changing relationship between higher education and society in the hopes of strengthening perceptions of a "social charter" and call for stronger evidence for and against the arguments that book posits. We hope that with this book, we can begin to respond to that call as the authors you are about to read provide the clear and intelligible empirical evidence for which higher education leaders have been searching to build their cases.

References

Kezar, A. J., Chambers, A. C., & Burkhardt, J. C. (Eds.). (2005). *Higher education for the public good: Emerging voices from a national movement.* San Francisco: Jossey-Bass.

London, S. (2002a). *The role of public understanding, public support and public society in reflecting and shaping the covenant between higher education and society.* Ann Arbor, MI: Kellogg Forum on Higher Education for the Public Good.

London, S. (2002b). *Educating for the public good: Implications for faculty, students, administrators and community.* Ann Arbor, MI: Kellogg Forum on Higher Education for the Public Good.

London, S. (2002c). Practical strategies for institutional civic engagement and institutional leadership that reflect and shape the covenant between higher education and society. Ann Arbor, MI: Kellogg Forum on Higher Education for the Public Good.

London, S. (2003). *Higher education for the public good: A report from the national leadership dialogues.* Ann Arbor, MI: National Forum on Higher Education for the Public Good.

Martínez, M., Pasque, P. A., & Bowman, N. (Eds.). (2005). *Multidisciplinary perspectives on higher education for the public good.* Ann Arbor, MI: National Forum on Higher Education for the Public Good.

National Forum on Higher Education for the Public Good. (2007). Retrieved May 9, 2007, from http://www.thenationalforum.org/OurEfforts/Proj/A2D/index.htm

Pasque, P. A., Hendricks, L. A., & Bowman, N. A. (Eds). (2006). *Taking responsibility: A call for higher education's engagement in a society of complex global challenges.* Ann Arbor, MI: National Forum on Higher Education for the Public Good.

Pasque, P. A., Smerek, R. E., Dwyer, B., Bowman, N., & Mallory, B. (Eds.). (2005). *Higher education collaboratives for community engagement and improvement.* Ann Arbor, MI: National Forum on Higher Education for the Public Good.

Acknowledgments

There are many people to thank in conjunction with the National Rising Scholar Award and this publication of recipients' research on the topic of higher education for the public good. First, we would like to thank Tony Chambers for his original vision and efforts in initiating the Rising Scholars Program. In addition, we would like to thank the W.K. Kellogg Foundation for their initial support of the National Forum on Higher Education for the Public Good.

There are five national organizations that collaborated with the National Forum in order to select the national Rising Scholars for the 2002-2003, 2003-2004, and 2004-2005 academic years: American College Personnel Association, American Education Research Association, Association for the Study of Higher Education, American Association for Higher Education, and Association for Institutional Research. We appreciate the collaborative efforts of these associations, as they encouraged new interdisciplinary scholars whose work focuses on strengthening the relationships between higher education and society. The Rising Scholar Review Panel, which represented these six national associations and selected the scholars, included Tony Chambers (National Forum), Donna Bourassa (ACPA), Janet Lawrence (ASHE), Yolanda Moses (AAHE), Gerald E. Sroufe, (AERA) and Dawn Terkla (AIR).

We would like to thank the monograph review panel who provided scholarly feedback regarding an earlier version of the chapters from the first year of rising scholars. This group includes Lorraine Gutierrez, Barbara McFadden Allen, Linda Williams, and William Trent. Special thanks also should be shared with the assistant editors of those five chapters for their diligent work: Nancy A. Birk, Edith Fernandez, Elizabeth Fisher, Danielle Knabjian Molina and Christopher Rasmussen.

Of course, a special "thank you" goes to all of the individuals selected as rising scholars. We thank you for your persistence with this project and wish you the best with your continued scholarship on this important topic. In addition, we would like to thank the hundreds of applicants for this award whose research focuses on higher education for the public good. We encourage you to continue to conduct research and publish on this topic, as more scholarship and discussion is needed in order to strengthen the relationships between higher education and society.

Finally, we would like to thank Laura Dabundo (former director), Holly Miller, and the staff at Kennesaw State University Press for collaborating with us and making this research available to numerous constituencies. We hope this book furthers tangible research as well as current understandings of higher education for the public good.

CHAPTER 1

Introduction

Alexander W. Astin and Helen S. Astin

For most of our professional lives, the two of us have been attracted to research and writing projects that could provide us with opportunities to serve the public good. Most of these projects have involved some aspect of American higher education with a special focus on students, faculty, structure, policies, educational programs, outcomes, and the system as a whole. While a good deal of our work has been concerned with how higher education can better contribute to the lives of all students, we have been particularly concerned with issues of equity as they affect women, minorities and other underrepresented and marginalized groups.

For us, the notion of "higher education and the public good" has always involved the question of how colleges and universities can more effectively contribute to the solution of our myriad social problems and to improving the quality of life both in America as well as in the world at large. In pursuit of these goals, a central issue is how institutions and systems of institutions can "transform" themselves to become more effective instruments for serving the larger society.

An opportunity to work directly on the challenge of how to foster institutional transformation was presented to us nearly 10 years ago when John Burkhardt, then a program officer at the W.K. Kellogg Foundation and now the director of the National Forum on Higher Education for the Public Good at the University of Michigan, invited us to become part of a study group that became known as the Kellogg Forum on Higher Education Transformation (KFHET).

KFHET's main purpose was to contribute to our understanding of the institutional change process and to promote institutional transformations that enhance higher education's capacity to serve the public good. The KFHET study group's work spanned almost five years (1997–2001) and eventually led to the founding of the National Forum, currently housed at the University of Michigan.

From its inception, KFHET recognized the importance of transcending disciplinary and institutional boundaries. The study group comprised representatives from four higher education research organizations (the American Council on Education, the Center for the Study of Higher and Postsecondary Education at Michigan, the New England Resource Center for Higher Education, and UCLA's Higher Education Research Institute [HERI]) and five higher education institutions (Alverno College, the Minnesota State College System, Olivet College, Portland State University, and the University of Arizona). The group included both practitioners and scholars representing several different disciplines as well as positional roles within higher education ranging from provost to president. We were also fortunate in being able to involve a cadre of talented younger scholars, primarily doctoral students, who became partners both in the KFHET research enterprise as well as in all of the deliberations of the group as a whole.

As the work of the KFHET group evolved into what subsequently became known as the Kellogg Forum on Higher Education for the Public Good (and now the National Forum on Higher Education for the Public Good), it became increasingly apparent that younger scholars could play a critical role in furthering the work of our study group. There was, in other words, a felt need and a consensus from all quarters that mentoring our inheritors in this work was an essential and necessary next step. These considerations led to the decision to organize an Intergenerational Research Symposium on Higher Education for the Public Good. Thus, under the continuing sponsorship of the National Forum, the two of us, in collaboration with a number of colleagues from HERI and from the Michigan Center, organized such a symposium that took place in November of 2002. In many ways, this volume of scholarly papers has its origins to that symposium that took place almost four years ago.

The symposium comprised 45 participants, including 14 senior scholars, six mid-career scholars, 23 emerging/rising scholars and two representatives of philanthropic foundations. The four areas of scholarly inquiry identified as the most critical ones for analysis and discussion were: Access and Equity, Faculty Roles and Performance, Student Development, and University-Community Partnerships. Our deliberations centered around five questions:

1. What do we know about each area?
2. How do we facilitate further research in each area?
3. What is the role of funding in shaping research agendas?
4. How do we most effectively disseminate findings from the research in each area?
5. How do we best develop the next generation of scholars?

The two primary goals of the symposium were to create a research agenda that could serve the public good and to develop mentoring relationships and collaborations between senior scholars and emerging/rising scholars.

The two-and-a-half days of animated deliberations generated a great deal of creative thinking, enthusiasm, and optimism. We were able to learn from each other and to identify creative research questions and strategies but, most importantly, we succeeded in nurturing new connections and relationships that transcended the boundaries of age and status. Many of the professional and personal relationships among those who were part of the intergenerational symposium have persisted and evolved over the past four years.

Several of us, for example, organized and participated in sessions held as part of the national conferences of the Association for the Study of Higher Education (2002) and the American Educational Research Association (2005). A number of us also prepared research proposals for funding, and even though the proposals did not get funded, they served the purpose of further nurturing cross-generational relationships. We know of a number of stories that can be told of how the symposium served as the starting point for intergenerational connections among scholars that persist today.

This volume, which represents another outcome of those early efforts to ensure that the legacy is passed on, is further testimony to the importance of encouraging and supporting our inheritors to continue research and writing that serves the public good.

All fourteen contributors to this volume represent the new generation of scholars who are not only very talented, but who also care to do research and to write about critical issues facing higher education and society at large.

We salute each of you for your creative thinking, for the diligence and dedication with which you carried out this work, and for your passion and caring.

Alexander W. Astin and Helen S. Astin
Higher Education Research Institute
University of California, Los Angeles

Addressing Class, Gender, and Race in Higher Education

CHAPTER 2

Climbing Up and Over the Ivy:

EXAMINING THE EXPERIENCES OF
AMERICAN INDIAN IVY LEAGUE GRADUATES

Bryan McKinley Jones Brayboy

Abstract: In this chapter, I am interested in exploring the ways that American Indian communities, through their citizens, identify themselves in relation to ongoing struggles. Part of this examination includes the ways that American Indians, and citizens of their tribal nations, utilize higher education to examine and explore their complex economic, political, and social structures. I examine how higher education for the public good informs and is informed by the struggles of these communities and what it may mean for institutions of higher education in a world that continues to change. I argue that all education at these institutions should be higher education for the public good.

In the last year, I have often wondered about what "higher education for the public good" meant and how it might be useful for American Indian peoples and tribal nations. I[1] was particularly interested in making sense of the connection between college and our lives on reservations or in communities with large American Indian populations. An elder in a community in which I have worked for almost ten years best articulated the connection between higher education for the public good and our communities. I was interested in knowing why community elders were continuing to encourage their young people to attend college, even though the retention rates were low for Indigenous students. Institutions were marginalizing, oppressive, and failed to understand the needs of its Indigenous students. In response to my question and concern he told me, "We send you all there [institutions of higher education] as a way of acknowledging where we come from. We have to fight fire with fire and use the natural relationships that might be counterintuitive to some [people] in order to win this war....Make no mistake that we are at war for our lives, cultures, and rights to be independent nations." This quote and the thinking behind it offer new ways to examine higher education for the public good for American Indian communities. It also offers a challenge to institutions of higher education to think about what their roles are for different communities and for the larger public.

In this chapter, I am interested in exploring the ways that American Indian communities, through their citizens, identify themselves in relation to ongoing struggles. Part of this examination includes the ways that they utilize higher education to examine and explore their complex economic, political, and social structures. I intend to examine how higher education for the public good informs and is informed by the struggles of these communities and what it may mean for institutions of higher education in a world that continues to change.

This chapter is informed by three guiding questions:

1. How and in what ways do tribal nations utilize institutions of higher education to address local and enduring struggles?
2. How and in what ways does higher education for the public good inform these struggles?
3. How is higher education informed by the struggles themselves?

These questions force institutions of higher education to (re)consider their own roles within society and particular communities.

Before proceeding further, I offer a brief discussion of my methods used for data collection and analyses. I then offer a theoretical overview of both higher education for the public good and the idea of local and enduring struggles as they are couched in Holland and Lave's (2001) notion of history in person. I make connections between these two concepts before presenting data collected and its subsequent analysis. Finally, I conclude with the importance of higher education for the public good for both institutions of higher education and marginalized communities; I argue that all education at these institutions should be higher education for the public good.

METHODS[2]

The original data for this monograph come from a two-year ethnography conducted with seven American Indian undergraduate students at two Ivy League universities between 1995 and 1997. In the original study (Brayboy, 1999) I was interested in examining the cultural, educational, political, emotional, and psychological costs and benefits of being an academically successful American Indian undergraduate student at an Ivy League university. In the original study, I found that individual students established strategies to assist them in being both "good Indians" and "good students" simultaneously. Being a good Indian meant that they were individuals who saw themselves as members of a tribal community and the community likewise saw them as an integral part of their community. In several of these instances, the individuals chose to attend an Ivy institution because they believed that the skills and credentials earned there would assist their tribal communities in their quest for sovereignty. These individuals all work in their communities and have, in fact, assisted their communities toward larger political ends.

In the years since, I have collected data from the original participants in the study in their roles as students and professionals. I also conducted participant observation in their homes away from the university during school summer breaks. I conducted interviews with community and tribal leaders, analyzed documents, and conducted focus groups. I have, since 1996, visited each community once a year and interviewed community and tribal leaders. Additionally, I have maintained telephone and electronic mail correspondence with the original participants and many of the tribal and community members. For this particular chapter, I rely on the original participant observations and interviews, as well as on follow-up interviews with the participant and their tribal elders.[3] The long-term nature of this research is important for addressing notions of both local and enduring struggles. I have seen the ways in which the geographical, political, economic, and cultural landscapes have changed over a relatively short period of time. The time is significant enough to make some judgments based on the changes in the landscape. Ultimately, I recognize that these communities are always in a state of being and becoming; they are—like all communities—liminal (or in a temporary state) because of the fact that they change constantly.

For the purposes of this chapter, I focus on the experiences of one student, Heather. Her case is instructive for many of the other students with whom I have worked. Like other students in the study she came to Sherwood in order to assist her community's political agenda. Heather put her community before herself in terms of academic achievement; she formulated strategies, in some cases with the assistance of her Indigenous classmates, to enhance her achievement and her ability to be both a good Indian and a good student. Heather encountered severe personal costs for her work.[4] The methods are informed by the theoretical frame that is grounded in the notion that higher education can be—and has been—utilized by marginalized communities to address their enduring struggles. It is to this framework that I now turn.

Higher Education for the Public Good and History in Practice

Two related theoretical frames organize this chapter. Higher education for the public good is an integral part of how I envision the role of institutions of higher education in our society. Additionally, "history in practice" frames the struggles of local communities as they find and define their places in the world. Together, these concepts outline a vision of how communities rely on and make sense of themselves and their struggles in relation to the services provided by institutions of higher education.

The Kellogg Commission (2000) has argued:

> The irreducible fact is that we exist to advance the common good. As a new millennium dawns, the fundamental challenge with which we struggle is how to reshape our historic agreement with the American people so that it fits the times that are emerging instead of the times that have passed (p. 9).

In this vision of higher education, the Commission alludes to an arrangement "with the American people." The Commission also points to the idea that agreements have to change to meet the present needs. The vision that I articulate below seeks to extend and complicate this vision. For what happens when the agreements between universities and American people may be contradictory to the needs of other people of the Americas? That is, what happens when larger society has policies in place that are destructive for particular communities? Whose agreements are honored when American Indian communities have disputes with the federal, state, and local governments that are hundreds of years old? At this point, I argue that the common good may be both debatable and contextual. By this, I mean what some see as a "common good" may, in fact, be uncommonly bad for others. At this point of departure, how do we as a society decide whose good is met at the expense of others?

Additionally, I will argue that the times that are emerging are, in the case of many marginalized communities, tied to the past and our enduring struggles. Given this argument, what then is the agreement and whom does it serve? Can the agreement serve both sides in a disagreement or struggle? If so, what does that mean for the agreement? I believe the agreement can—and must—be contradictory because there are enduring struggles between particular communities and society at large or governmental structures. It is not the role of institutions of higher education to necessarily better prepare one side of the struggle, but to seek equity and justice for all segments of society.[5] It is in this vein that a search for the common good must begin. My point here is not to disagree with the Commission for they have offered a useful vision; my intent is to push and extend that vision to be wider and more encompassing with a particular focus on the struggles of marginalized communities.

In this chapter, I use higher education for the public good to convey a multi-faceted idea that is rooted in notions of activism. My definition includes two in-depth components: how higher education serves society, and how higher education prepares active, vibrant citizens. Importantly, institutions of higher education do not do these things in a vacuum; they are not the source of all knowledge or the center of society. Rather, they are a part of a larger whole for a global community, and for specific local communities. Higher education clearly plays a role in larger society. In a vision of public good the University must ask the question: How is society best served? Generating new, creative, and inventive ideas, universities can begin to address ways to assist local communities as they continue to face struggles. More importantly, higher education for the public good has a reciprocal relationship with society where it serves society, but also finds many of its guiding principles from community members. By teaching students and encouraging faculty, staff, and administration to be active citizens and community oriented, higher education for the public good offers expertise and creativity to address societal issues in constructive, proactive, innovative and interesting ways. For communities who have enduring struggles, innovation and creativity become an integral part of addressing their struggles, and working toward creating a solution that works for a specific community.

It is important that the citizens graduating from and working in institutions of higher education be activists in our society. Individuals are, and become, parts of local, national, and global communities that they wish to serve actively. These individuals also recognize that a core of people working together are able to generate responses to societal and community needs. Importantly, these citizens also form proactive strategies for activist-oriented roles in society. Ultimately, higher education must create affirmative contexts of self-determination for communities within larger society. In the case of this chapter, American Indian students, and the community members that guide them into specific colleges for specific purposes, highlight the role of higher education for the public good. Returning to the elder with which this chapter started, higher education for the public good allows communities to fight fire with fire. Essentially, this community has legal and societal struggles with the local, state, and federal governments. They have essentially put young people in place to gain education, skills, and credentials in order to fight the governmental structures using the government's language and tactics. The Indigenous communities are buoyed by their cultural knowledges and epistemologies and a vision of the fact that the past continues to influence the present and future. They are attempting to redefine the new rules by playing by the old ones.

Higher education for the public good has at least two potential weaknesses. First, there is the danger of having too much focus on individuals and not enough on the communities from which they come. When institutions of higher education tend to focus on individuals as such, communities may get lost in the process. Can we build a strong community one member at a time without a coherent strategy or philosophy of activism in place? Institutions of higher education must focus on community values and priorities in order to truly carry out higher education for the public good. It is important to note that individuals will not be lost in the process; rather, they will be seen as belonging to something and coming from some place. I do not mean, however, to minimize the inherent danger associated with fighting fire with fire. Individuals who take up fire or the tools of dominant institutions then become co-opted by the institutions and by society. There is always a danger of this occurring and it is harmful to both the individual and the community. It is a risk those communities facing enduring local struggles must make. I do not minimize the fact these communities have other strategies in place in order to meet the needs of their communities. They are not solely relying on institutions to assist them in their political goals. They have instituted their own culture and language revitalization programs, pursued their own economic endeavors, and created educational institutions that serve the needs of many of their members who live in areas of reservations or other tribally based areas.

The second weakness may be that institutions of higher education cannot clearly articulate their place within society. Too often, those of us in the academy have been criticized for not being connected to communities. What, after all, do we have to contribute to society? How much of our research and theorizing can be linked to community improvement or espouse ideas that communities can take and make their own? Too often, it seems, we attempt to dictate to communities how their communities "should" live by instituting programs that go into communities to "improve" them or by bringing our expertise to communities without recognizing that communities have knowledge and skills of their own. Is there a coherent message of our contributions, and if so, what is it? If we listen to and hear communities,[6] as institutions of higher education, we can begin to articulate our place within society in meaningful ways. These threats must be acknowledged and strategically and effectively addressed by a higher education for the public good.

History in practice is a theoretical concept posited by Holland and Lave (2001). This idea explores the "mutually constitutive nature of long and complex social, political, and economic struggles and the historically fashioned identities-in-practice and subjectivities they produce" (p. 3). History in practice is a combination of two concepts that Holland and Lave outline as "history in person" and "enduring struggles" (pp. 5–6). History in person refers to a "constellation of relations... between subjects' intimate self-making and their participation in contentious local practice" (p. 5). In other words, how do individuals make sense of who they are in relation to and because of events that occur in their immediate surrounding community? Enduring struggles is a "constellation of relations...between contentious local practice and broader more enduring (historical, processual, and open ended) struggles" (Holland & Lave, p. 6). Together, enduring struggles and history in person make up history in practice.

It is important to know that this process begins with local struggles or those struggles in specific times and places that extend into enduring struggles. These enduring struggles are often situated in explicit local conflict. For the Indigenous community that I discuss in this chapter, those explicit local conflicts are with the local, state, and federal governments.[7] They are rooted in treaty rights or those promises made by treaties that are being ignored by municipalities and private businesses. For the case study, the tribal nation's conflict occurs over the ownership and uses of natural resources that are indigenous to their own lands. Because treaties promised all monetary rewards to the tribal nation, they are fighting with the federal government and a private natural resources company over working conditions and profit sharing. Many of the discussions occur in legalese and are written against the tribal nation. Many of the original agreements are in direct conflict with the treaties, but the federal government refuses to enforce the law in spite of its official position as trustee of the tribal nation.

The conflict is both local and enduring. The results will inform how communities are making sense of who they are in relation to the contentious practices. Holland and Lave (2001) write, "struggles produce occasions on which participants are 'addressed' with great intensity and 'answer' intensely in their turn" (p. 10). The community discussed in this chapter is being addressed and answering with great intensity. I am particularly concerned with the role of higher education for the public good's role in the manner in which these communities are now answering.

The following sections and analysis will take up the ideas and questions stated at the beginning of this chapter. There is a particular focus on the connections between higher education for the public good and the local and enduring struggles of the Indigenous community. I argue that this community specifically sends young people to institutions of higher education in order to meet its need to solve particular struggles.

THE PLACE, SPACE, AND PEOPLE: MOVING TOWARD HIGHER EDUCATION FOR THE PUBLIC GOOD

In the following section, I discuss a community in which I have worked for ten years as a researcher. The community is located in the southwestern part of the United

States. It is, like many reservation communities, removed from highly traveled roads and interstates and can be described as rural. The community is about 110 minutes from the closest large city. Many members of the community make bi-weekly or monthly trips to the city to stock up on goods that are hard to find on the reservation. There are places in the community that do not have running water or electricity. The state of living in some corners is "third world like," according to one community member who has traveled the world extensively. The community is rich in natural resources with an abundance of uranium, natural gas, and oil. The community is divided over how to utilize these resources. It is believed that some of the most valuable resources are found in the ground, but many in the community refuse to bother because of its spiritual and sacred importance.

In the community, there is a clear vision held by some community members that institutions of higher education offer a place to develop "modern day warriors." When I asked one community leader what he meant by modern day warriors, he told me:

> These are our people who know how to fight using computers, books, law, and book smarts....We must reach a point where we have balanced young people who understand who they are and the importance of fighting for who we are, but...they have to be able to talk to white people...the government...the BIA...these businesses who want our [natural resources], but don't want to pay for them.

He went on to tell me, "We make a deliberate attempt to have those schools [universities] train you people to fight for our rights and for us." In this community, there have been struggles over the use of natural resources and education for the tribal nation's bilingual or monolingual (tribal language-only) students.

The fight with the private company stems back over 100 years and is directly tied to a treaty that proclaimed that all natural resources and the resulting monies or profits would go directly to the tribal nation. The private company, according to tribal elders, used the lack of English and legal knowledge of tribal leaders, and signed a 150-year lease that essentially gave the tribe eight percent of the profits and leased the land to the company for less than one dollar per month. To add insult to injury, the collection of the natural resource is dangerous and toxic. The company has used tribal labor to extract the resources and failed to implement proper safety measures. As a result, the incidence of cancer is almost quadruple the natural rate found among communities outside of the reservation. This is clearly an example of both an enduring struggle and one that is, at any given time, local and focused for this community. This struggle has become part of everyone's life on the reservation because the industry influences individuals and families on an everyday basis either through the incidence of cancer or as a form of economic survival.

While individuals in the community are aware of the health problems they are also aware that, by reservation standards, the industry pays well. In spite of the hazards, individuals from the local community go to the site to work on a daily basis. Holland and Lave (2001) remind us that local and enduring struggles can be contradictory. Essentially, the pay clouds the dangers of the industry and individuals must decide if they will starve today, leave their home for a low paying job in the urban area two hours south of the reservation, or potentially die of cancer later. These choices finally led a community of leaders to consider how they might send their children and young warriors to college in an effort to address the struggles.

Heather is a young woman from this reservation, and one of the warriors sent out to do battle for her community. She grew up in a home that borders the reservation; both of her parents have been active in tribal politics for several decades, and they are viewed as leaders in the community. Both are professionals whose work takes them on and off the reservation. Heather attended high school in the local town where the student body was a mixture of members from her tribal nation, surrounding tribal nations, and local Anglos. There was a small percentage of Latina/os. The school was almost evenly split between Indigenous students and Anglos.

Recognizing that the tribal nation needed good, strong Indigenous leaders, they began to look for young people who were adept thinkers and verbally skilled. They found one such student in Heather. One leader in the community, in reference to this informal program, commented, "We actually modeled some of what we did from the old East German bloc countries and from the Chinese in that we looked for kids—really young kids—who displayed a particular talent that we thought would be useful."[8] He went on to say, "If kids seem to be healers, we thought of them as doctors; if they could teach or seemed like good teachers, then we would steer them in that direction....I know this seems a bit extreme, but we live in extreme times."[9] Heather was a student who showed promise as a potential lawyer in the community. When I met her during her first semester as a college student, she told me, "I have always wanted to be a lawyer. My father and mother and my elders told me that's what I was going to be, so I wanted it....I do this because it will mean a better life for my people, my siblings, my cousins and nieces and nephews....I can handle anything for those reasons; and I have."

Heather did endure insults and psychological and racist attacks in college and in law school in order to meet her goals. In college, she was actively involved in the campus American Indian student group and began the process of building an Ivy League coalition of American Indian students. Along the way she found staff and professors in whom she placed trust and confidence in her ultimate goals. These individuals assisted her in developing skills that they believed would be useful for her life long endeavors. She worked as a research librarian's assistant during her time at her university where she acquired the requisite skills to be a thorough creative researcher. These skills would serve her well in the future in law school and as a tribal attorney. She took this job after a professor found out about her aspirations and made arrangements to have her campus job be in the library. The professor knew a reference librarian who was interested in American Indian issues. Together they helped Heather become an able reference librarian and a capable researcher before she finished college. Another area in which professors served as mentors for her included her summer jobs. Each summer break, Heather would spend a month working in an internship in Washington, D.C., that helped her become more familiar with the role of Washington in her tribal nation's affairs. Over the summers she worked for the Department of Interior, Department of Energy, Smithsonian Institute, and served as intern in the Department of Justice. In addition, she interned for the tribal nation's law firm and different tribal governmental offices. This conscious, well-rounded experience made her aware of what was happening on a national level with in the United States and her tribal nation. She was well informed of the issues and potential solutions before entering law school.

In her academic work, a cohort of professors and staff members assisted her in creative research projects. She implemented a study of water rights and natural resources for a political science course. For a geology course, she examined the impact of mining on different lands and communities, including her own. Her work was focused toward addressing the enduring struggle in which her home community was engaged.

In turn, her professors traveled to her home community and conducted life histories; took soil samples; examined the intricate weaving, pottery, and jewelry designs of her nation's artisans; and formed computer simulations of the impact of certain events on the water supply. This research assisted the professors in their own research and course offerings and the findings were turned back to the tribal nation for their own uses. It was, in the goal of higher education for the public good, a reciprocal relationship that benefited all parties. The tribal nation's understandings of particular issues were greatly enhanced in these partnerships. Heather played a key role in introducing these faculty and staff members to community members and in articulating the community's desired needs to the scholars. The fact that scholars and community could discuss these issues and establish partnerships is remarkable in and of itself. This is one of the creative ways communities can be proactive in addressing their needs and creating solutions to particular struggles, both local and enduring.

In this process, communities are attempting to address their enduring struggles in innovative ways. For the institution's part there was a group of committed scholars that took up the mantle of higher education for the public good. In order for this relationship to be truly effective, institutions, as a whole, must assume components of this work to address the needs of particular communities as defined by the community. The connection in these cases was one student sent to a specific university for a particular end. This leads to the natural question: How do institutions of higher education begin to form relationships with communities that are both local and enduring? How do these institutions form collaborative partnerships with communities to address enduring struggles?

One important piece of the case just outlined has to do with the fact that members of the institutional community were activists. If higher education for the public good has an activist component, members of an institution's community must be committed to activism. Activism can be, as illustrated above, rooted in an individual's research agenda. In this case a professor of geology interested in the impact of particular practices on soils and water resources led him to conduct research that assisted the community. In the process his own research agenda was fulfilled. The point here is that professors can meet their professional requirements and be activists simultaneously.[10] Additionally, institutions cannot create groups of activists if they do not have experienced activists in their midst.

Another important piece of this case is that the institution, or its constituent members, respected the knowledge of the community and became aware of its struggles. Unlike many cases in which an institution or its members may try to dictate a solution or path of action to a community, these members listened to community leaders and elders, observed what was occurring, and acted according to the wishes of community members. They saw their place within the community as they served the community's needs and by extension the university became part of a larger whole as part of a solution to an enduring and local struggle.

In beginning to ask the question, "How is society best served?" these faculty members are asking the community, "How can we best serve you?" The faculty members did not attempt to take over the situation or the struggle; rather, they took their lead from the community who had their own ideas about what would best serve their needs. Eventually, the community leaders asked faculty members for ideas. One community leader told me:

> We needed to see if his [a faculty member] heart was true. Did he want to work with us, or did he want to use us? What was in it for us? Did he have our interests at heart or his own?...As soon as we knew that he wanted to work with us, it changed things completely.

This leader went on to say, "We realized that he could really help us and give us the kind of information we needed to make our case. Of course, he was able to get what he needed, but we got what we needed first."

Answering these questions offers a connection between higher education for the public good and history in practice. History in practice encompasses the struggles of communities in their local practices and the ways that individuals make sense of themselves. By becoming activists to address the enduring struggles and by resisting the overwhelming power of the local, state, and federal government in the affairs of American Indians, these communities engage in history in practice. Importantly, higher education for the public good becomes a source of power for them as they engage in the struggles. The solution includes more than simple skills and credentials earned at an institution of higher education; there are components of using these skills toward a particular end and by particular people. The institution is aware that it plays a role in the process of addressing the struggle and that the local community determines how it uses the institution to meet the struggle head on.

Heather graduated from college and was admitted to another Ivy League university's law school. The tutoring and mentoring continued, as did her focus on serving her community. During the summer of each year between law school, Heather interned in the law firm that served her tribal nation. The firm was in a large urban area several hours away from the community. Heather traveled between her community and the law firm and became actively engaged in the process of serving the community. Her coursework focused on tribal law, contracts, and federal cases. It was a program developed to best serve her community. Immediately upon graduation, Heather returned to her home community, studied for the bar exam, and passed it four months later. She also began working for the community's law firm immediately upon graduation.

Heather's work focused on addressing the natural resources on her reservation's land. She conducted extensive research using her knowledge of the law and the skills developed as a reference librarian and attorney. Her thorough research, in connection with her intimate knowledge of the enduring and local struggles, was an incisive and integral part of an ensuing lawsuit. I cannot overstate the connections that individuals have with local and enduring struggles as they begin to address them. She told me, after her first year in law school, "This [company] has eaten our tribe alive; they continue to behave in ways that are unconscionable. How can they continue to deny links between these cancer rates and their [work]? I'm going to help end this." In Heather's case, she was focused for seven years on these struggles, and clearly working toward a solution to the problem. She knew families who had lost family members to cancer. She saw how the management of the private company treated those in the community who looked like her. She saw the dependence of the community on an industry that was simultaneously destroying it. Heather's words are also those of an activist. She understands that a group of individuals with the right training and preparation may have an opportunity to take up the struggle and change its direction. Higher education for the public good is particularly important here because members of the institution of higher education asked themselves, "What is best for this society?" as they assisted Heather in her role in the struggle. In the process they helped feed Heather's activist's motivations.

Two years after she finished her law degree, Heather was part of a team of attorneys that represented her tribal nation in a lawsuit against the private natural resources company. In a series of negotiations—lasting over an eighteen-month period—much of the data that Heather had compiled were presented. The company and the tribal nation negotiated a new contract. The contract included better compensation for the resources' worth. The new contract also created safer and better working conditions, a comprehensive health insurance plan for employees, and ensured the employment of members of her tribe in management positions. Higher education for the public good also played a key role in this process. On behalf of her tribal nation, Heather was the key researcher of the case. She successfully held her own in the negotiations and relied on her knowledge and skills gained at the institution of higher education.

I met with her recently to discuss the negotiations and to catch up on her life. Dressed in a gray suit with cream pinstripes, black pumps, and carrying a worn, leather briefcase, Heather looked very much like an attorney. She sat in an old chair in her office that overlooked a scenic vista. Her diplomas were on the wall. Her office was scattered with law cases, legal folders, pink telephone messages, and bookcases stacked with books and folders. Other than her diplomas, she has not "had time to do anything with [my] office." I felt like I was in a busy attorney's office. About the negotiations, she told me, "I was the only woman in the negotiation process, but many of the people with whom I negotiated were alumni [from her undergraduate and law schools]. We connected on that and I think they had more of a sense of respect for me." She went on to tell me, "I knew that data from one end to another, so I was comfortable. It quickly became apparent to them that I was the one with the knowledge, so I felt good about my role." Heather also mentioned the fact that "I also knew some of these people from my time in Washington; so that worked out well." Heather's presence was made more powerful because she had graduated from two prestigious institutions of higher education, and had served internships in departments in Washington, D.C. She was well rounded, and had credentials that are impressive. The role of higher education for the public good is important here. The entire process of creating and assisting an activist came together as the tribal nation was addressing an enduring struggle. With her education, Heather has helped create a "better life for [her] people, [her] siblings, [her] cousins and nieces and nephews." This is a story of empowerment and liberation both for Heather and for her tribal group.

Heather is what Deyhle and Swisher (1997) have called "adapters." Heather knew that the structures of the classroom and social environment were not completely comfortable for her, so "[she] accept[ed] this segment of [her life] as a short interruption on [her] way to meeting life goals" (p. 167). These interruptions were, in Heather's case, expected and planned in order to gain specific skills and credentials from elite institutions of higher education for personal and/or tribal betterment, self-determination, and tribal autonomy. Her adaptation makes her one of the new tribal warriors. But what are the costs for individuals like Heather who adapt and commit their lives to the tribal nation?

While this is an interesting story and one that ended well for the tribal nation, I do not want to romanticize this process. Heather's work was important to the process, and she has devoted her life to making life better for her tribal nation. At the same time, the enduring struggles over treaty rights continue; unemployment, alcohol, and domestic abuse rates remain high, and the poverty level of the tribal nation ranks in the lowest tenth in the United States. Formal higher education is still a rarity in this community, and Heather is one of a few attorneys from her tribal nation. Health care is abysmal, and cancer and diabetes claim lives every week in this small, intimate community. Heather's connection with elite institutions of higher education has not removed the enduring or local struggles. As each is addressed, another replaces it on the scale of importance. These enduring local struggles will continue as long as the community remains at the mercy of the United States Federal Government in many decisions.

There are personal costs for Heather as well. Heather wants to have a family and raise children on the reservation. Due to her education and her prominent role in the community, she is inundated with work. Additionally, she is a controversial figure in the community. She left the community for seven years and wears fancy clothes; as a result, many are intimidated by her. She has struggled with relationships. She has also encountered jealousy from those in the community who do not fully understand her motivations. She has moved off the reservation and into the local town. She has an unlisted phone number and is often concerned about how others will receive her on the street. She is a bit of an outcast even as she has helped her community. This is a complicated role for her and a complicated one for the community as they address their local and enduring struggles.[11]

The manners in which tribal leaders and elders have addressed this enduring struggle are not fully supported by the entire tribal nation. There are some leaders and elders who believe that institutions of higher education have nothing to offer these communities. Many of their beliefs are rooted in another enduring struggle between the tribal nation and schools. It is important to note that these struggles can and do conflict with each other. Marginalized communities, in their quest to address these struggles, are forced to be creative and strategic in ways that may not be approved by everyone in the community.

In response to the objections outlined by community members who want to steer clear of institutions of higher education, one of the weaknesses of higher education for the public good is highlighted. These institutions are not clearly articulating their own places within society. Much of this is connected to the fact that institutions of education have for centuries been used to assimilate American Indian communities (e.g., Child, 2000; Lomawaima, 1995, 1996). In many ways, the purpose was to "kill the Indian and save the man." In the process, American Indian communities have come to distrust these institutions. How are institutions of higher education articulating the ways that they are different now than they have been in the past? How do these institutions show enough humility to listen to a community and offer a piece of themselves to address these enduring struggles? How do these institutions make amends for the work they has done to create monolingual speakers or citizens who do not return home to tribal communities? What measures are being put into place to make the institutions more welcoming and to become better hearers of the communities? Are institutions capable of practicing humility when their structures are rooted in elitism? If so, what will the humility look like, and how will institutional cultures adapt to allow for the humility? Institutions of higher education must participate in the process of addressing the enduring struggles of which they are a part for many American Indian communities. It is to that potential vision that I now turn in the conclusion, and I offer remedies for institutions of higher education that want to participate in higher education for the public good.

CONCLUSION: TOWARD A HIGHER EDUCATION FOR THE PUBLIC GOOD

Holland and Lave (2001) argue:

> In the course of local struggles, marginalized groups create their own practices. Participants in these groups both are identified by these practices and often identify themselves as "owners" of them. These practices thus provide the means by which subjectivities in the margins of power thicken and become more developed and so more determinant in shaping local struggles (p. 19).

The response to the tribal nations' local and enduring struggles put forth above is creative and rooted in a tribal belief that the community must adapt and adjust to meet the issues their citizens face. I have outlined one such response, and how different members in the same community countered it. Still, higher education for the public good must articulate its place in society, and become a viable option for communities that have been marginalized and are engaged in enduring struggles.

The vision of higher education for the public good is one that must be symbiotic between institutions of higher education and marginalized communities. Institutions of higher education, in order to articulate their place in society, must be not only useful to society, but also viewed that way by many of their detractors. What, then, can these institutions do to make themselves seem as useful as they can be? First, higher education for the public good must be based in a philosophy of humility. As important as we, as academics, think our institutions are, we must recognize that there are forms of knowledge that are thousands of years old that communities rely on for guidance and operation. We cannot think that because we have knowledge based in "scientific" understanding, that our knowledge is better or superior. What can we learn from these communities and their knowledge sets? How do we ask questions as learners to improve our own ability to teach others? I believe that higher education for the public good must be rooted in both teaching and learning. Returning to the argument I made earlier in this chapter, institutions must develop the ability to hear communities and to address the needs in ways that make sense for the communities. Institutions of higher education must become hearers *and* learners in order to promote higher education for the public good.

Communities too must see that institutions of higher education can be successfully used to assist them in their enduring and local struggles. Utilizing "scientific knowledge" in ways that make sense for these communities is an effective tool in fighting for justice. In the example involving Heather's community, the use of soil samples, geological studies, computer simulations, and medical references was invaluable for the new negotiations of a contract. Importantly, the institution of higher education—and its staff—was guided by the community in its search. The focused nature of the studies and the fact that they were rooted in community-oriented ideas and agendas is one key aspect of higher education for the public good. Community epistemologies and ontologies must be the driving force behind the work that is accomplished. I do not mean here to argue that institutions of higher education lose their sense of independence and ability to drive their own agendas. I mean to argue that higher education for the public good must be a negotiation between communities and institutions that focuses on specific goals outlined by the communities.

Finally, institutions of higher education and communities need to see that some of their goals are more congruous than originally imagined. In this case, Heather's issues of justice and scholarship drove the community, the institution and its faculty. Justice and scholarship need not be incongruous. In fact, higher education for the public good recognizes that scholarship should incorporate components of justice, and be focused on serving the public and community good.

Ultimately, local and enduring struggles can be addressed through community sets of knowledge and those coming from institutions of higher education. Higher education for the public good is the entity through which many of these struggles are addressed and managed.

Heather's case is one example of how the connections between scholarship and justice coalesce toward a common good. The next steps for this conversation are rooted in institutions of higher education recognizing their role in the oppression of many marginalized communities and focusing on ways to end the marginalization. This admission, along with a plan toward working with communities to end enduring struggles, is the future of higher education for the public good.

Endnotes

1. I am an enrolled member of the Lumbee tribe of North Carolina.
2. Due to space constraints, I do not offer an extensive overview of my methods and methodology. For a more detailed treatment, please see Brayboy, 1999 and Brayboy, 2000.
3. Since 1996, I have conducted over 100 interviews, and conducted hundreds of observations. I also have several hundred e-mail correspondences with the participants in the study. In this chapter, I am relying on interviews, observations and electronic mail correspondence with the former student and several tribal members.
4. Reviewers have pushed me to think about whether students who attended Ivy League institutions are indicative of other students who may have attended schools that are not considered "Ivy League" or "elite." In response, it is important to point to the fact that a study that focused on the experiences of seven students is limited in its scope and generalizability; however, these students struggled with how to make sense of who they were both as cultural beings and as students in a rigorous academic environment. I believe that many marginalized students at all institutions, including Historically Black Institutions, Hispanic Serving Institutions, and Tribal Colleges and Universities, must—at some point—make sense of how to connect these issues. The work of scholars of color point to the fact that faculty of color, at all types of institutions must also try to make sense of similar issues (Smith, 2004; Turner & Meyers, 2001). I am left with the question: Are the experiences the same? Certainly not; however, there are some similarities that connect many of the participants.
5. One issue with this vision, clearly, is that it may be in and of itself contradictory, yet I do not believe it must be this way. Like privilege, justice is not necessarily a zero sum game. That is, in order for one person or group to gain privilege or justice, it must come from another person who holds it. On the contrary, concepts like privilege and justice must be less like a limited amount of goods and services, and more like an endless bounty of items from which to choose. In the case of equity and justice, I believe that institutions and society must take a long, hard look at these issues and, in conjunction with those communities who have been oppressed, marginalized, and disempowered, work through a plan to help them empower themselves. Institutions and society have long been at the heart of reinforcing social stratification and segregation; higher education for the public good calls for society and institutions to cease these reinforcements and move toward more equity and justice throughout our communities.

6. The concept of hearing is an important one that researchers and academics may not consider as carefully as we should. For well-conceptualized notions of hearing see Williams (1991), Delgado-Bernal (1997), and Solorzano and Delgado Bernal (2001).

7. At the request of the communities, I do not identify them. One leader in a community told me, "Many nations have similar problems. The point is that we have ways that we are trying to deal with this. Other nations may or may not use these strategies, but the struggles and the war is the same." I honor the request for these nations to remain anonymous to the larger public.

8. This case is clearly different than creating a national team of elite athletes; in this case, this is a desperate measure at ensuring survival for a community under siege.

9. Not every child was looked at this way. Another person involved in the process told me, "We need people who can do many things, so having a good mechanic is just as important as having a good doctor is just as important as having people who can do many things." The tribal council and elders chose a few young students every year to engage in the process; importantly, many who they thought would be good at one occupation, chose to do something entirely different. This is not a process that is embraced by everyone on the community, and not all young people are willing to do what they are steered toward. My intention here is to focus on a few students who are engaged in this process toward meeting the enduring and local struggles head on.

10. It is important to note here that the work was well received by academic colleagues and was published in a variety of scholarly journals. On the surface, the professor is a well respected academic in his field; underneath the surface, the work served to assist the community in its enduring struggles.

11. The personal costs are not uncommon for individuals like Heather who serve their communities, but do so in such a controversial manner. Having degrees from elite institutions, coupled with the sense of what that means for her, has been personally crippling. This has been true for several other individuals who participated in my original study. Each has "mortgaged" him or herself for the good of the community. By mortgaging, I mean that they pay, in self interest, much more personally so that the community can face its struggles head on. The personal costs are tremendous; yet, the community benefits.

References

Brayboy, B. Mc.K. (1999). *Climbing the ivy: Examining the experiences of academically successful Native American Indian students in two Ivy League universities.* Unpublished doctoral dissertation, University of Pennsylvania.

Brayboy, B. Mc.K. (2000). The Indian and the researcher: Tales from the field." *International Journal of Qualitative Studies in Education, 13,* 415–426.

Child, B. (2000). *Boarding school season: American Indian families, 1900–1940.* Lincoln, NE: Bison Books.

Delgado Bernal, D. (1997). *Chicana school resistance and grassroots leadership: Providing an alternative history of the 1968 East Los Angeles blowouts.* Unpublished doctoral dissertation, University of California at Los Angeles.

Deyhle, D. & Swisher, K. (1997). Research in American Indian and Alaska Native education: From assimilation to self-determination. In M. Apple (Ed.), *Review of Research in Education* (Vol. 22, pp. 113–194). American Educational Research Association: Washington,

DC.Holland, D., & Lave, J. (2001). History in person: An introduction. In D. Holland & J. Lave (Eds.), *History in person: Enduring struggles, contentious practice, intimate identities* (pp. 3–33). Santa Fe, NM: School of American Research Press.

Kellogg Commission. (2000). *Renewing the covenant: Learning, discovery, and engagement in a new age and different world.* Kellogg Commission on the Future of State and Land-Grant Universities. Retrieved February 15, 2004, from http://www.kelloggforum.org/vision.html

Lomawaima, T. (1995). *They called it prairie light: The story of Chillocco Indian Boarding School.* Lincoln, NE: University of Nebraska Press.

Lomawaima, T. (1996). Educating Native Americans. In J. Banks & C. M. Banks (Eds.), *Handbook of research on multicultural education.* New York: Simon & Schuster MacMillan.

Lomawaima, K. T. (2000). Tribal sovereigns: Reframing research in American Indian education. *Harvard Educational Review, 70,* 1–21.

Solorzano, D. G., & Delgado Bernal, D. (2001). Examining transformational resistance through a Critical Race Theory and LatCrit Theory framework: Chicana and Chicano students in an urban context. *Urban Education, 36,* 308–342.

Smith, W. A. (2004). Black faculty coping with racial battle fatigue: The campus racial climate in a Post-Civil Rights era. In D. Cleveland (Ed.), *A long way to go: Conversations about race by African American faculty and graduate students* (pp. 171–190). New York: Peter Lang Publishers.

Turner, C. S., & Myers, S. L., Jr. (2000). *Faculty of color in academe: Bittersweet success.* Needham Heights, MA: Allyn & Bacon.

Williams, R. (1997). Vampires anonymous and critical race practice. *95 Michigan Law Review, 2,* 741–765.

CHAPTER 3

Shifting from Racial Equality to Racial Diversity:

MICHIGAN'S ANSWER TO THE AFFIRMATIVE ACTION COLLEGE ADMISSIONS DEBATE

Denise O'Neil Green

Abstract: In 1997, the Center for Individual Rights filed two lawsuits against the University of Michigan on behalf of two White plaintiffs who believed they were denied admissions because of racial preferences. The diversity rationale, Michigan's counter argument, underscored the links between racial diversity and institutional mission, but rejected long standing social justice arguments of racial/ethnic equality and remediation to combat societal and institutional discrimination. Through qualitative inquiry, this study explores how Michigan shifts the focus of the affirmative action debate from racial equality to a narrower racial diversity argument, which garners broad support and neutralizes the racial preferences rhetoric.

In 1997, the Center for Individual Rights (CIR) filed two lawsuits on behalf of Jennifer Gratz and Barbara Grutter, White plaintiffs who believed they were denied admission solely because of their race. CIR argued that the University of Michigan awarded racial preferences to African Americans, as well as other underrepresented minorities, by considering their racial/ethnic background as a plus factor in the admissions process. But, CIR deemed consideration of race a violation of the 14th amendment's equal protection clause.

When the *Gratz v. Bollinger* and *Grutter v. Bollinger* cases were filed, Michigan's chances of winning were very questionable. Considering the fact that these two cases were filed by the same organization that, in 1996, successfully represented plaintiffs in the *Hopwood* case, supporters of affirmative action had reason to be concerned. With *Gratz* challenging Michigan's race-conscious undergraduate admissions policies and *Grutter* doing the same at the law school, the valued notions of equal opportunity and educational access for African Americans and other minority groups were also challenged. But more importantly, these lawsuits exposed how our country's selective public institutions are gateways to upward mobility, elite social networks, and prime educational resources.

Unfortunately, only a chosen few have an opportunity to attend a selective, public institution and therein lies the source of the conflict and debate regarding access and affirmative action. Given the increased competition for acceptance to elite, public institutions and legal challenges to race-conscious admissions policies in the 1990s, the debate intensified. Though traditionally arguments of racial equality and remediation were used in defense of affirmative action, the University of Michigan, taking the lead, shifted the debate from racial preferences versus racial equality to racial preferences versus racial diversity. Through qualitative inquiry, this study explores how Michigan shifted the focus from equity to a narrower diversity argument, mobilizing broad support and neutralizing the racial preferences rhetoric. However, before one can discuss how Michigan changed the debate, a discussion of race neutral and race-conscious positions is needed.

Race Neutral versus Race-Conscious

Establishing affirmative action as a legitimate policy has been one of the most difficult and divisive issues in our nation (McPherson, 1983). Since the policy was initiated, race-conscious affirmative action measures have generated debate in the nation and in the higher education community (Fleming, Gill, & Swinton, 1978; Garcia, 1997; Tierney, 1997). During the course of this contentious and emotional debate, proponents and opponents have broached numerous positions and perspectives to denounce or bolster the importance of maintaining affirmative action. The compensatory, corrective, and redistributive arguments are integral to the race-conscious rationale (Brest & Oshige, 1995; Bullington & Ponterotto, 1990; Edley, 1996; Francis, 1993; Swanson, 1981; Tierney, 1997; Wolf-Devine, 1997). The moral and color-blind arguments are also central to the debate (Edley, 1996; Tierney, 1997). The core thesis of each perspective is discussed below.

Compensatory arguments rely on the central idea that damages should only be awarded to victims who were harmed or injured (Edley, 1996; Francis, 1993;

Tierney, 1997). Acknowledging that past forms of discrimination, including slavery, de jure segregation, and Jim Crow, have a lingering, negative affect on present day African Americans in the arena of employment and education, supporters argue that affirmative action, though insufficient, serves to compensate for past forms of societal discrimination (Bergmann, 1996; Eastland, 1996; Simmons, 1982).

Though compensatory perspectives focus on past injustices, corrective arguments place an emphasis on contemporary, societal wrongs and efforts to rectify them (Francis, 1993; Tierney, 1996). Proponents of this position focus on organizational policies and structures which disparately impact particular groups, especially African Americans and other underrepresented minorities. If such disparities exist in an education or business organization, then corrective measures, such as affirmative action, would operate to discontinue discriminatory practices. By exposing and eliminating unjustifiable barriers to minority groups, future discrimination is minimized (Edley, 1996). Hence, this remedy focuses on outcomes (Francis, 1993).

Redistributive arguments assume society is unjust in its distribution of social rewards, power, and resources. Given this assumption, steps must be taken to equalize the extreme imbalance of the haves and have-nots (Francis, 1993), who most often comprise underrepresented minority groups and the poor. To rectify this injustice, affirmative action serves as a redistributive measure to redirect social rewards, resources, and power to minority groups that historically have been excluded from receiving such societal benefits (Swanson, 1981), thereby reducing the disparities that persist.

Although the corrective, redistributive, and compensatory arguments were prominent in the debate, the moral position remained central to both advocates' and opponents' sense of justice with respect to affirmative action. Often, proponents argued that affirmative action was simply the right policy to implement (Edley, 1996; Francis, 1993). Their moral stance was fortified by the understanding that past racial discrimination has not been adequately addressed in this country and continues to influence racial inequities between Whites and racial/ethnic minorities (Bowen & Bok, 1998; Chang, Witt-Sandis, & Hakuta, 1999; Tierney, 1996). In many cases the moral position was intertwined with other supportive rationales, such as corrective and compensatory.

Rivals of affirmative action have stated that the policy is unfair, immoral, and discriminatory (Cohen, 1996; Clegg, 2000; D'Souza, 1991; Edley, 1996). The policy is considered wrong because losers are easily identifiable along racial/ethnic lines—namely Whites who lose due to racial preferences believed to be embedded in the policy (Clegg, 2000; D'Souza, 1991; Edley, 1996; Francis, 1993). Opponents also argue that affirmative action changes the rules of the game, and therefore undermines trust and principles of fairness (Edley, 1996; Francis, 1993).

The race-neutral or color-blind argument directly opposes affirmative action's premise. That is, opponents see the policy as discriminatory, regardless of intent, and therefore will not support a policy that they believe promotes government-sponsored discrimination (Clegg, 1998). Color-blind advocates recommend that government entities should aggressively enforce anti-discrimination laws that are on the books (Clegg, 1998; Edley, 1996). Ironically, opponents to affirmative action acknowledge that racial discrimination exists but do not agree that race-conscious measures are the answer (Betzold, 2000; Clegg, 2000; D'Souza, 1991). Class-based measures or percent plans, which intentionally de-emphasize race, have been deemed as appropriate solutions by the race-neutral camp (Bowen & Bok, 1998; D'Souza, 1991; Edley, 1996; Herrnstein & Murray, 1994; Wilson, 1995) because some assume that class-based affirmative action, for instance, would redistribute awards to the most needy and deserving (Duster, 1996; Lucas, 1996; Malamud, 1997). Supporters of affirmative action have had mixed responses to various race-neutral strategies; however, the central retort has been that race cannot be ignored, given the historical legacy of racial discrimination and segregation in this country. Overall, race-conscious, moral, and color-blind arguments were prevalent in the affirmative action debate. Opponents to affirmative action often used the color-blind stance, while others argued from different racial equity vantage points. The moral argument was used on both sides.

AFFIRMATIVE ACTION AND HIGHER EDUCATION

Prior to the Michigan cases, the debate regarding the use of race-conscious or race-sensitive policies to promote greater access for African Americans and other under-represented groups was not new to higher education. Since *Bakke*, the debate has essentially been framed by those in opposition to race-conscious admissions strategies, with supporters in higher education struggling to articulate why such strategies are acceptable. Because various higher education constituencies, including White parents and their prospective students, believe the admissions process should be race-neutral and based solely on merit, opponents advanced a system that only considers students' talents and skills, as well as other individual characteristics (i.e., socio-economic status), but not racial background. If race was a part of the formula, the admissions process was characterized as unfair and discriminatory.

While constituents who opposed consideration of race argued that utilization of race as a factor is unfair to White applicants; those who advocated for racial consideration argued that accounting for race helps to minimize the unfair advantages White applicants are automatically afforded in the process.

Although many perspectives have been expressed on this issue, essentially two different camps have emerged and weighed into the debate. On one side, there was the racial preferences camp that insisted policies and practices should be race-neutral. On the opposite side, the race-conscious camp argued that using race-sensitive policies was needed to provide equal access, educational opportunity, and a remedy for recent past and present day discrimination. Defenders of the race-conscious position also argue that elite, public institutions have historically excluded and discriminated against minority student applicants by implementing policies and practices that favor White applicants. Therefore, affirmative action in admissions must be used to remedy present institutional and societal discrimination.

Unfortunately, the courts have turned away from this position as a remedy for societal discrimination (*Bakke*, 1978; *Podberesky*, 1994). Since the courts no longer legitimized race-conscious remedies as a means of correcting societal discrimination, the racial diversity camp surfaced and argued that within the context of higher education, diversity was important to educational excellence and a democratic society. Before the diversity rationale gained notoriety, however, the University of Michigan had to engage strategically in the debate to defend its mission, institutional integrity, and race-conscious policy.

DESIGN OF THE STUDY

The University of Michigan was selected for a detailed case study analysis to explore the phenomenon of institutional engagement in a public policy debate in which race was the central issue. More specifically, this study sought to understand how Michigan defended its race-conscious policies, while shifting the debate. In order to examine this phenomenon, institutional responses were examined to determine which approaches were used to defend Michigan against charges made by plaintiffs in both *Gratz* and *Grutter* cases. A case study design was most appropriate for three reasons:

1. a case study design enables the researcher to investigate the phenomenon at the macro level while also examining units of analysis that may be pertinent to the phenomenon but are not identified at the outset of the study;
2. this approach allows the researcher to investigate "a contemporary phenomenon within its real-life context" (Yin, 1994, p. 13); and
3. a case study allows the researcher to examine a single unique case in-depth, especially if the "boundaries between the phenomenon and its context" (Yin, 1994, p. 13) are seemingly unclear.

Purposive sampling guided the selection of informants in order to acquire participants who had the greatest potential to provide information for case development (Creswell, 1998). A total of 26 informants were chosen due to their high levels of engagement with either the law school or undergraduate lawsuits. Informants included former President, Lee Bollinger; former Law School Dean, Jeffrey Lehman; former Associate Vice President and Deputy General Counsel, Elizabeth Barry; and former Provost, Nancy Cantor. These informants, along with others, including representatives of the Center for Individual Rights, the American Council on Education, and legal council for the student defendant intervenors of the *Grutter* case, were critical to providing substantive data that described the interplay between the parties most intimately engaged in crafting and implementing the institution's response strategies from 1997, when the cases were filed, to 2003, when the United States Supreme Court ruled on both cases.

Guiding all interviews were four major questions that probed for response strategies during the course of litigation. The questions were:

1. What is the organization's position with respect to the legal challenges?
2. What strategies and tactics have been used to advance the organization's position?
3. How has the organization handled roadblocks or challenges? and
4. What role has the organization played in this entire litigation process?

Questions were broad to avoid imposing any relationships or directionality (negative or positive) to any aspects of the phenomenon to allow unanticipated themes or constructs to emerge (Creswell, 1998).

Overall, data were collected over a six year period (1997 to 2003) from four sources:

1. 26 audio-taped interviews of informants—the primary data source, which was collected by 2001;
2. over 100 primary and secondary sources in the form of legal documents, internal reports, memos, electronic messages, web sites, and newspaper articles;
3. participant observations of campus events related to the lawsuits; and
4. the researcher's periodic journaling of reflections and impressions of interviews and campus events from 1997 to 2002.

Interviews ranged from 20 minutes to 2 hours, averaging one hour in length. All interviews were audio-taped and completely transcribed.

Data Analysis and Verification

For the first stage of analysis, rich, thick case descriptions were developed pertaining to the chronology of events. In case descriptions, pertinent facts, major players, events, interactions, and outcomes related to particular aspects of the case were highlighted (Creswell, 1998). Following the development of case descriptions, open coding was conducted. According to Strauss and Corbin (1990), "open coding is the process of breaking down, examining, comparing, conceptualizing, and categorizing data" (p. 61). During open coding, the interview data and selected documents were reviewed for "discrete happenings, events, or other instances of phenomena" (p. 61) and classified under coding categories. If these categories seemed to possess similarities, they were grouped into higher-order categories and conceptually identified under a label that captured their shared characteristic(s) (Miles & Huberman, 1994).

With the completion of case descriptions and coding, direct interpretation was applied (Creswell, 1998; Stake, 1995). Interpretation involved examining the descriptive narrative and categories, drawing meaning to develop emergent themes. Interpretation, in this form, required that the data be taken apart and put back together again in more meaningful ways (Creswell, 1998). Categories from open coding aided this interpretive process with the constant comparing of data for conceptual patterns of meaning (Strauss & Corbin, 1990).

While the data was written in a narrative form to capture the "truth" or accuracy of the accounts described, several verification procedures were followed to ensure credibility and trustworthiness of the study (Merriam, 1998). First, different data sources were used to provide corroborating evidence (triangulation). Second, feedback from specific informants was solicited to verify the study's findings and interpretations (member checks). Furthermore, a rich and detailed description of the phenomenon was provided to allow the reader an opportunity to examine the characteristics of the phenomenon and determine the plausibility of the findings (rich, thick description) (Creswell, 1998).

FINDINGS

From the case study data five strategies emerged that were critical to formulating Michigan's answer to the affirmative action dilemma:

1. establishing a critical position in the debate,
2. framing the message,
3. going public,
4. addressing the media, and
5. recruiting allies.

Each organizational response enabled Michigan to strengthen its national position as a defendant of race-conscious policies.

Establishing a Critical Position in the Debate

To establish a critical position in the affirmative action debate, the University of Michigan had to confront the polarizing language of the race neutral camp. The rhetoric was staggering, convoluted, and emotionally charged. The interplay between terms, such as racial preferences, reverse discrimination, angry White males, merit, fairness, class remedies, intelligence, testing, racial conflict, and individual rights, conjured heated debates among the higher education community, as demonstrated in the hundreds of news articles, editorials, and op-ed pieces printed in the national press (Green, 2003a). To oppose the racial preferences camp and its rhetoric, Michigan had to respond strategically to the Center for Individual Rights, one of the conservative organizations publicly advancing an anti-affirmative action campaign (Schmidt, 2003).

The Center for Individuals Rights completely denounced the use of racial preferences in admissions; however, other types of preferences were not ruled out. For example, students who were economically disadvantaged could be given additional consideration in the admissions process. CIR's assumption is that socio-economic status can place one at a disadvantage in the admission process whereas race does not necessarily do so. Mr. Levey, Director of Legal and Public Affairs, explained CIR's position before the cases reached the United States Supreme Court:

> Our position, and we believe it's also the position of the Supreme Court, is that racial preferences, explicit racial preferences can only be justified as a remedy for an institution's own past discrimination. And they can't use it to achieve the right racial balance on campus; …they can only be used to remedy the effects of the institution's own past discrimination. That said though,

we have nothing against true diversity. In other words, if a University is seeking true diversity, diversity of ideas, experiences, backgrounds, philosophy, and racial diversity happens to be a side effect of seeking that, that's fine. We're not against giving preferences based on social economic disadvantages or any other kind of demonstrated disadvantage. But we are against the blind awarding of preferences based simply on skin color.

While CIR spoke against racial preferences, campus diversity was a concept the organization did support in principle. CIR argued that racial diversity was not an outcome that should be forced or contrived but should come naturally as a result of using other factors, such as social economic status. According to CIR, racial balancing among student populations should not be the goal.

Since the Center for Individual Rights had won *Hopwood* (1996), a case which struck down the use of race in admissions for the states within the jurisdiction of the 5th Circuit Court of Appeals, and no other public university had won a case based on the diversity rationale, the University of Michigan faced a difficult set of circumstances. Nonetheless, Michigan relied upon a narrow diversity argument to counter CIR's position, highlighting three critical points: the importance of race in American society, the need to expand educational opportunities, and the goal of an integrated society. In 1998, former President Lee Bollinger and former Provost Nancy Cantor wrote an opinion piece that appeared in the Washington Post titled, "The Educational Importance of Race." It reads:

Our public universities have always cast a wide net in admitting students. Selecting a student body is not a simple matter of drawing a line though [sic] some rank ordering of individual applications. Universities have been especially watchful for merit wherever it is found. They have been alert to the potential of those who may not have had full opportunity to manifest their talent....CIR's challenge to "affirmative action" in higher education is a challenge to our philosophy of education and to the historical purposes of our great public universities....They [CIR's objectives] also rest on a profoundly mistaken conception of education and the role of race in a modern education.

CIR seeks to eliminate all consideration of race in college admissions. If it is successful, as it was in an earlier lawsuit against the University of Texas, we will in all probability soon return to a largely segregated system—de facto rather than de jure, to be sure, but segregated nonetheless....The country cannot afford to deprive institutions of higher education of the ability to educate generations of young Americans—minority and nonminority—in an environment that enables all to flourish, and understand each other, in a truly integrated society (Bollinger & Cantor, 1998, p. A17).

The University of Michigan's counter argument underscored the links between race, the institution's educational mission, a racially diversity student body, and social integration. The emphasis was not on racial preferences, but on providing opportunities to those who otherwise would have been excluded. In addition to rejecting the racial preferences position, Michigan also rejected explanations that placed an emphasis on racial equality and remediation. Hence, according to Michigan, neither racial balancing nor correcting for past discrimination were the intended goals of a racially diverse student population; diversity was simply a means through which selective institutions could move American society closer to "a truly integrated society" by educating "minority and non-minority" in diverse environments for all to achieve their educational and social potential.

Framing the Message

Taking a critical position divorced from traditional race-conscious arguments and adopting the diversity rationale was an important step for Michigan, since it provided a starting point with which the institution could frame a diversity message and promote what it does best: research. Because Supreme Court Justice Powell's decision in *Bakke* (1978) affirmed that diversity had an essential and compelling role in colleges and universities, many institutions voluntarily implemented race-based affirmative action admissions policies to be more inclusive of under-represented minority groups (Bowen & Bok, 1998; Eastland, 1996; Hurtado, 1999; Synnott, 1979). They argued that a diverse student population benefited the learning environment (Astin, 1993; Brest & Oshige, 1995; Moses, 1994). Others, however, disagreed with this assertion and argued that diversity compromised standards of excellence (Astin, 1993; D'Souza, 1991; Edley, 1996; Smith, 1989). Given the lack of evidence to support diversity claims, framing the message was an important strategy. Elizabeth M. Barry, former Associate Vice President and Deputy General Counsel at the University of Michigan, who had a great deal of responsibility for directing the communication effort connected to the lawsuits, indicated that "empirical proof" was necessary to reinforce the institution's diversity defense:

> We were going to defend this suit comprehensively by reliance on the law, in this case mainly the Supreme Court decision in 1978, the *Bakke* case, and buttressing that reliance on the law, with empirical proof that racial and ethnic diversity enhances

education. [Because] there was a proper foundation in educational theory and practice for that view of the law,…we embarked upon creating the record that we have with respect to empirical proof.

To establish the research record, an abundance of data was collected from within and outside of the institution. Both campus-level and national studies became a part of the record to defend the importance of diversity in a campus environment and the need for affirmative action policies to achieve diversity. Former Provost Nancy Cantor, who played a major role in directing the research record's development, added that the University of Michigan had embarked upon a strategy and research agenda that had not been accomplished by any other institution:

> We clearly felt that it was important to gather as much data or to use as much data as possible in making that case, since it wasn't a case that had been made with data that much before. I think we felt it was important to both draw on data that our own faculty and staff had collected and also to pull in relevant studies nationally. The Harvard Civil Rights Project had done a fair amount and there were others. We developed a set of expert witnesses that could address the educational value from a number of perspectives.

Before arguing the benefits of racial diversity, Michigan's strategy was to establish that race still mattered and influenced the lives and experiences of Americans in this country. Several expert witness testimonies were dedicated to establishing this connection (University of Michigan, 1999b). Patricia Gurin, Professor Emerita of Psychology at the University of Michigan and former Interim Dean of the School of Literature, Science, and the Arts, submitted the leading expert witness report on the institution's behalf. In discussing the legal strategies of both cases, Gurin indicated that, "because it's [race] the fault line in our society, it's the most important basis of diversity. So, a number of the expert reports were about that, especially Segrue's."

With the salience of race established, Michigan, in collaboration with national scholars, developed an emerging body of research. Seminal publications, such as *Diversity and Higher Education* (Gurin, Dey, Hurtado, & Gurin, 2002), *Shape of the River* (Bowen & Bok, 1998), *Diversity Challenged* (Orfield & Kurlaender, 2001), and *Compelling Interest* (Chang, Witt, Jones, & Hakuta, 2003), were critical in framing the narrative now used to justify the need for racial diversity on college campuses (Green, 2003b). Ultimately, these works fortified the position that diversity benefits all students, majority and minority alike, and demonstrated that interactions between peers of racially diverse backgrounds yield positive educational outcomes for both minority and non-minority students such that "students learn more and think in deeper, more complex ways" (University of Michigan, 1999a, p. 6).

The research record and its connection to the diversity rationale were symbiotic in that each existed for the purpose of aiding the other. While the research record was guided by underlying assumptions of Justice Powell's diversity rationale, the diversity rationale was bolstered by research in a manner that the racial equality argument could not. Because the research record placed the need for diversity in a concrete, tangible educational context versus a broader, racial equality and remediation context, the diversity rationale was framed as a sound and justifiable legal argument that legitimized the use of race in admissions decisions. With a new approach and cutting-edge research to articulate the educational importance of diversity, the University of Michigan asserted itself as a leader in two arenas, diversity research and the affirmative action debate. As history bears out in the *Grutter* (2003) decision, establishing a research record was a vital undertaking that ultimately tipped the balance in Michigan's favor.

Going Public and Addressing the Press

The University of Michigan's fight for maintaining racial diversity, though devoid of traditional race-conscious positions, still faced criticism from faculty, alumni, and students. In an effort to address criticisms and explain the institution's stance on affirmative action to the campus community, constituent groups, and the nation, Michigan's leadership voiced the institution's position on multiple occasions, in different arenas, and through different venues. The number of venues where Michigan's leadership articulated reasons for defending affirmative action included the courtroom, campus, and higher education community. Because it was important to disseminate this information to multiple stakeholders, a two-pronged communication strategy of going public and addressing the press was devised to best serve the institution's interest.

Elizabeth Barry expressed that typically when parties are involved in litigation, there is a tendency to release as little information as possible or to say nothing at all. But, given the importance of these cases, senior leadership determined that taking the silent approach was not a viable strategy. On the contrary, being open with the press and the public through meeting with editorial boards of newspapers and maintaining a Website on the lawsuits moved the University of Michigan from a defensive stance to an offensive position. According to both Barry and Jeffery Lehman, former Dean of the University of Michigan Law School, opening the lines of communication was a significant step. Barry emphasized going public through the internet:

> So, for instance, we created the Website that we have about the case. We put everything up there. We put the legal stuff up there, the legal proceedings, our positions, Q&A; we told people how we do admissions; and, it seems, four years later, that was a no-

brainer to do the Website. But, to be that open is really unique in the context of litigation. And, it was a significant step.

Lehman underscored working with the media:

> In terms of the public view, I think the key moment, and I don't know whether this was nine months in or a year in, was when we decided it was time to start taking the offensive and to recognize that the reporters and media people that they're just reporters and media people; they're people with a job. They don't live and work and study in a University; they are doing their jobs. So, about a year into the trial, we started taking our message out on the road and went to visit with editorial boards at newspapers.

To move from a defensive position to a more offensive one, the senior leadership had to become increasingly media savvy and learn to better convey the institution's complex and complicated legal position. Former Dean Lehman best articulated what was needed:

> That's part of what put us on the defensive early on after the lawsuits were filed. We were sort of back on our heels for six to eight months trying to figure out why the newspapers were so unkind to us; why they were saying things that weren't true. We did not have the experience in working with the media that we have now and, CIR did....I think our own lack of sophistication with respect to the media was a significant challenge for us to overcome. And I think we've had to work really hard to get better at it.

Using the media to the institution's advantage was an important lesson to be learned. As Lehman implied, CIR had more experience, but those who spoke on the institution's behalf, including the President, Provost, Dean of the Law School, and General Counsel, had to develop a message that took the focus off of CIR's story of the victims and draw attention to Michigan's story of a prominent public institution that was striving to maintain racial diversity for the purpose of educational excellence, its educational mission, and democracy, in spite of opposing forces.

Recruiting Allies

While communicating the diversity message, Michigan's leaders also sought to develop coalitions and mobilize allies, which was a major undertaking. Involving to a great degree the attention of former President Bollinger, this public institution went to higher education associations, government leaders, and large corporations for public support. Armed with a diversity message and research to substantiate institutional claims, Michigan's efforts brought prominent people to its side and developed a broad-based coalition of supporters that expanded when both cases reached the Supreme Court in 2003.

Constituent groups on campus and beyond voiced their positions. Alumni, faculty, students, higher education associations, businesses, interest groups, and political figures were all compelled to enter the debate. Through many press releases, opinion pieces to the editor, resolutions, declarations, and statements that were published in newspapers, organizational correspondence, and Websites, opposing constituent groups communicated their respective messages. Most often, press releases announced submission of briefs to the court and/or results of new studies or polls that demonstrated public support or dissatisfaction with affirmative action in the form of racial preferences. Though mounting support was demonstrated for both camps during this six-year period, the University of Michigan was able to recruit key players to the diversity camp, including Former President Gerald R. Ford, the American Association of Universities (AAU), the American Council on Education (ACE), the General Motors Corporation, and the United States military.

Former President Gerald R. Ford, also an alumnus of the University of Michigan, wrote in support of affirmative action and the use of race as a factor in the admissions process. In a 1999 New York Times letter to the editor, Ford stated:

> At its core, affirmative action should try to offset past injustices by fashioning a campus population more truly reflective of modern America and our hopes for the future. Unfortunately, a pair of lawsuits brought against my alma mater pose a threat to such diversity. Not content to oppose formal quotas, plaintiffs suing the University of Michigan would prohibit that and other universities from even considering race as one of many factors weighed by admission counselors.
>
> So drastic a ban would scuttle Michigan's current system, one that takes into account nearly a dozen elements—race, economic standing, geographic origin, athletic and artistic achievement among them—to create the finest educational environment for all students (Ford, 1999, p. 15).

Ford's statement clearly does not endorse quotas but does support the type of affirmative action policies that enable institutions to provide an educational environment for students of all different racial backgrounds in order to promote a more diverse and integrated society. But, Ford also points out that "affirmative action should off set past injustices"—racial injustices. Acknowledging that past racial injustices have occurred and need to be addressed, Ford hints at a race-conscious, equity perspective while incorporating the educational importance of race, which is "to create the finest educational environment for all students."

Because threats of a lawsuit were made well before the petitions were filed in 1997, former President Bollinger initiated conversations with prominent higher education associations in order to mobilize the higher education community. President Bollinger said, "I felt that we needed to enlist unanimous support of all higher education....And so a lot of work early on was on making sure that AAU, ACE, and other educational institutions were very supportive, publicly supportive." As a result of these dialogues, in an unprecedented move, AAU and ACE declared their support for diversity. In a 1997 statement on the "Importance of Diversity in University Admissions," AAU reaffirmed its commitment to diversity and its support for the use of race as one of many factors:

> We therefore reaffirm our commitment to diversity as a value that is central to the very concept of education in our institutions. And we strongly reaffirm our support for the continuation of admissions policies, consistent with the broad principles of equal opportunity and equal protection, that take many factors and characteristics into account—including ethnicity, race, and gender—in the selection of those individuals who will be students today, and leaders in the years to come (American Association of Universities, 1997, par. 10).

About one year later the American Council on Education also issued a statement "On the Importance of Diversity in Higher Education" that was endorsed by approximately 60 national associations with higher education affiliations. However, this statement, which appeared in the *Chronicle of Higher Education*, did not squarely confront the issue of using race-conscious admissions policies. After providing a litany of positive outcomes connected to educating a diverse college student population, the statement concluded with the educational purpose of diversity:

> Each of our more than 3,000 colleges and universities has its own specific and distinct mission. This collective diversity among institutions is one of the great strengths of America's higher education system, and has helped make it the best in the world. Preserving that diversity is essential if we hope to serve the needs of our democratic society....Diversity enriches the educational experience....It promotes personal growth and a healthy society.... It strengthens communities and the workplace....It enhances America's economic competitiveness.

Achieving diversity on college campuses does not require quotas. Nor does diversity warrant admission of unqualified applicants. However, the diversity we seek, and the future of the nation, do require that colleges and universities continue to be able to reach out and make a conscious effort to build healthy and diverse learning environments appropriate for their missions. The success of higher education and the strength of our democracy depend on it (American Council on Education, 1998, par. 1–8).

Although higher education associations, such as ACE and AAU, joined Michigan, former President Bollinger noted that "in order to make the case to the broader public, we needed more than higher education, because people are suspicious of higher education on this and other issues." Understanding that support was needed from the corporate world and the military, the University of Michigan sought their support. Early in the litigation process, as Bollinger and other university leaders presented their case, support was not forthcoming; however, with the willingness of key individuals, Michigan gradually secured support from General Motors (GM) and other corporations. By the time these cases were accepted by the U.S. Supreme Court, the diversity rationale was solidified and validated by segments of society that seemed to matter most: corporate America and the military.

The GM brief indicated that the "nation's interest in safeguarding the freedom of academic institutions to select racially and ethnically diverse student bodies is indeed compelling: the future of American business and, in some measure, of the American economy depends upon it" (General Motors, 2003, p. 2). The GM brief further stated:

Diversity in academic institutions is essential to teaching students the human relations and analytic skills they need to succeed and lead in the work environments of the twenty-first century. These skills include the abilities to work well with colleagues and subordinates from diverse backgrounds; to view issues from multiple perspectives; and to anticipate and to respond with sensitivity to the cultural differences of highly diverse customers, colleagues, employees, and global business partners (p. 2).

In addition to General Motors, 65 other leading businesses concurred that diversity is a compelling interest and aids students in learning how to lead and work with others from different backgrounds:

Diversity in higher education is therefore a compelling government interest not only because of its positive effects on the educational environment itself, but also because of the crucial role diversity in higher education plays in preparing students to be the leaders this country needs in business, law, and all other pursuits that affect the public interest (Fortune 500 Companies, 2003, p. 2).

Retired military leaders, who included all former chairmen of the Joint Chiefs of Staff and Gen. H. Norman Schwarzkopf, the commander in the Persian Gulf War, also filed a brief which echoed similar statements of support, declaring that consideration of race is critical to integrating the military and ensuring national security.

> Like numerous selective educational institutions, the military already engages in aggressive minority recruiting programs and utilizes the service preparatory academies and other programs to increase the pool of qualified minority candidates. These important steps are vital to the continuing integration of the officer corps. The fact remains: Today, there is no race-neutral alternative that will fulfill the military's, and thus the nation's compelling national security need for a cohesive military led by a diverse officer corps of the highest quality to serve and protect the country (Retired Military Leaders, 2003, pp. 9–10).

These very important briefs were noted in the *Grutter* Supreme Court decision. Each brief in its distinct way reiterated that diversity was a compelling government interest for our society. Exhibiting evidence from earlier court rulings, internal reports, historical accounts, and empirical research, each party agreed that the use of race-conscious policies was needed to allow the organization, whether educational, corporate, or military, to fulfill its respective mission and purpose.

With higher education associations, businesses, government officials, and military academies steadily coming to the support of Michigan throughout the litigation process, it appears the diversity rationale was the critical piece needed to galvanize support from higher education and different sectors of American life. If Michigan had adopted a racial equity orientation, it is very unlikely that these same players would have come to the institution's aid. Former President Bollinger reflected on these dynamics and expressed as he saw it, their implications:

> I think we went from a world in which it was one or two universities to all of higher education, to major political figures and major corporations and unions. And that made the point that this is central to America's identity and its purposes. And it's intertwined. It comes out of *Brown vs. Board of Education*

and the historic commitment of this country to promote racial integration and the role of education, in that process. It has really been a heartwarming and encouraging process for me. I think both Gerald Ford and General Motors and the editorial boards, I think everybody saw it from their own particular angle, but they all looked at education as the source of a kind of melting pot, bringing this society together, making good citizens, making good workers, making good policy. It just resonates with people as something that is so desirable, so important that we don't want to reverse course.

Discussion

Racial discrimination in education has always been a problem for African Americans in this country, with the courts mediating this problem to the advantage of African Americans in some cases (e.g., *Brown v. Board of Education*, 1954), and to the disadvantage of African Americans in others (e.g., *Hopwood v. University of Texas*, 1996). In the University of Michigan cases, the U.S. Supreme Court had an opportunity to issue a ruling that would benefit or further disadvantage African Americans and other historically under-represented minorities. As indicated above, there were a range of equity arguments that could have been made in support of race-conscious policies. In light of this fact, racial equality arguments seemed the obvious choice for the University of Michigan; however, the institution chose to argue the racial diversity rationale in its defense.

Since Michigan decided to stick strictly with the diversity rationale, it had the support of an earlier Supreme Court decision in *Bakke*. Because *Bakke* upheld racial student diversity in the educational context but ruled against correcting past racial discrimination as a viable argument, one could assume Michigan's leadership believed the institution had greater legal standing if it argued the diversity rationale. What is unique about Michigan taking a narrow diversity focus and rejecting compensatory, corrective, or redistributive arguments is Michigan's method for establishing racial diversity as a compelling, societal interest. While the diversity rationale does not advance the position that race-conscious policies are needed to correct racial inequities, Michigan's research record incorporated evidence to document past and present racial inequities in American life, particularly in the state of Michigan. This type of documentation was needed to substantiate the importance of racial/ethnic student diversity in higher education.

Given the need to establish the glaring racial/ethnic inequities that still remain in the state of Michigan and the country, why reject traditional racial equity arguments? Using any of these claims would have required the University of

Michigan to disclose and document past and present discrimination—not desirable for institutional image, especially if the university desires to increase its enrollment of minority students. Furthermore, the institution had a better chance of winning in court with the diversity rationale. One could also interpret Michigan's actions as a compromise, in that the institution went as far as it could in the research record demonstrating the need for corrective measures without explicitly arguing for them. As an outcome of this legal strategy, many important and prominent constituents came forward and publicly supported the University of Michigan's position by expressing their support for the diversity rationale.

Michigan's diversity message acknowledged that race facilitates difference in our experiences and backgrounds, but also reminds us that at one point in our nation's history, we were legally segregated by race and, as a country, we should not return to that period in our history. With that point made, Michigan framed racial/ethnic differences as an asset to educational environments rather than a liability. The logic is that racial diversity or difference:

1. benefits all students in an educational environment,
2. enhances learning, and
3. in the long run, helps the democratic enterprise.

In addition, linking racial diversity to democracy and educational excellence positively framed affirmative action such that others could and did support the policy. Lastly, the rejection of traditional equity arguments does not preclude advocates who strongly promote racial equality and race-conscious policies from supporting the University of Michigan's position. In light of these conclusions, the narrower diversity argument mobilized broader support, while neutralizing racial preferences, color-blind, and race-neutral rhetoric because racial fairness and racial equity were not central to Michigan's focus. Educational excellence was the focus. By shifting the focus, a significant change is demonstrated in the course of the debate.

Even though the Supreme Court with a 5-to-4 decision deemed the diversity rationale as a legitimate argument for maintaining affirmative action policies (*Grutter*, 2003), the affirmative action debate continues. Our nation's progression from *Brown v. Board of Education* to *Bakke v. University of California, Davis* to *Grutter v. Bollinger* demonstrates that racial equity for African Americans and other under-represented minority groups in education remains tenuous and riddled with conflict, debate, and compromise. If institutions truly wish to advance the status of African Americans and other under-represented minority groups in this country, then this case study provides five important lessons pertaining to institutional engagement over issues of race:

1. frame a clear, distinct message;
2. establish a critical position that clearly connects with the institutional mission;
3. substantiate message claims with sound educational research;
4. recruit prominent allies from within and outside the higher education community; and
5. through different venues, communicate the institution's message to the public and the press.

Ultimately, the shift from racial equality to racial diversity may have lessened the potency of traditional race-conscious arguments, but the shift has not lessened the level of advocacy and institutional engagement needed to address issues of racial/ethnic discrimination for groups that continue to be impacted by this country's legacy of segregation and discrimination.

Reprinted with permission: Green, D.O. (2004). Justice and diversity: Michigan's response to *Gratz, Grutter,* and the affirmative action debate. *Urban Education,* 39 (4), 374–393.

References

Association of American Universities. (1997, April 14). *AAU Diversity Statement on the Importance of Diversity in University Admissions.* Retrieved December 11, 2003, from http://www.aau.edu/issues/diversity4.14.97.html

American Council on Education. (1998, February 13). *On the Importance of Diversity in Higher Education.* Retrieved December 11, 2003, from http://www.acenet.edu/bookstore/descriptions/making_the_case/works/importance.cfm

Attinasi, L. (1996). Getting in: Mexican Americans' perceptions of university attendance and the implications for freshman year persistence. In B. Townsend (ASHE Reader Series Ed.) & C. Turner, M. Garcia, A. Nora, & L. Rendón (Vol. Eds.), *Racial and ethnic diversity in higher education* (1st ed., pp. 189–209). Needham Heights, MA: Simon and Schuster Custom Publishing.

Astin, A. W. (1993). Assessment for excellence: The philosophy and practice of assessment and evaluation in higher education. Phoenix, AZ: Oryx Press.

Bergmann, B. (1996). *In defense of affirmative action.* New York: Basic Books.

Betzold, M. (2000, May). Showdown: Affirmative action. *Ann Arbor Observer, 24,* 33.

Bollinger, L., & Cantor, N. (1998, April 28). The educational importance of race. *Washington Post,* p. A17.

Bowen, W., & Bok, D. (1998). *The shape of the river: Long-term consequences of considering race in college and university admissions.* Princeton, NJ: Princeton University Press.

Brest, P., & Oshige, M. (1995). Affirmative action for whom? *Stanford Law Review, 47,* 855–900.

Bullington, R., & Ponterotto, J. G. (1990). Affirmative action: Definitions and philosophy. In J. G. Ponterotto, D. E. Lewis, & R. Bullington (Eds.), *Affirmative action on campus* (Vol. 52). San Francisco: Jossey-Bass.

Chang, M., Witt-Sandis, D, & Hakuta, K. (1999). The dynamics of race in higher education: An examination of the evidence. *Equity and Excellence in Education, 32*(2), 12–16.

Chang, M. J., Witt, D., Jones, J. & Hakuta, K. (Eds.). (2003). *Compelling interest: Examining the evidence on racial dynamics in colleges and universities.* Stanford, CA: Stanford University Press.

Chesler, M. (1987). Professionals' views of the "dangers" of self-help groups (CRSO Paper 345). Ann Arbor, MI: University of Michigan, Center for Research on Social Organization.

Clegg, R. (1998, May/June). Beyond quotas: A color-blind vision for affirmation action. *Policy Review, 89,* 12–20.

Clegg, R. (2000, July 14). Why I'm sick of the praise for diversity on campuses. *The Chronicle of Higher Education, 46,* p. B8.

Cohen, C. (1996, February 25). Race in University of Michigan admissions. *The University Record.* [On-line]. Available: http://www.umich.edu/~urecord/9697/Feb25_27/faculty.htm

Creswell, J. (1998). *Qualitative inquiry and research design: Choosing among five traditions.* Thousand Oaks, CA: Sage.

D'souza, D. (1991). *Illiberal education.* New York: Vintage Books.

Duster, T. (1996). Individual fairness, group preferences, and the California strategy. *Representations, 55,* 41–58.

Eastland, T. (1996). *Ending affirmative action: The case for colorblind justice.* New York: Basic Books.

Edley, C., Jr. (1996). *Not all Black and White: Affirmative action and American values.* New York: Hill and Wang.

Fleming, J. E., Gill, G. R., & Swinton, D. H. (1978). *The case for affirmative action for blacks in higher education.* Washington, DC: Howard University Press.

Ford, G. (1999, August 8). Inclusive America, under attack. *The New York Times,* p. A15. Fortune 500 Corporations. (2003, February 18). *Brief for Amici Curiae 65 Leading American Businesses in Support of Respondents (Nos. 02-241 and 02-516).* Retrieved November 3, 2003, from http://www.umich.edu/~urel/admissions/legal/gru_amicus-ussc/um/Fortune500-both.pdf

Francis, L. P. (1993). In defense of affirmative action. In S. M. Cahn (Ed.), *Affirmative action and the university* (pp. 9–47). Philadelphia: Temple University Press.

Garcia, M. (1997). The statement of affirmative action at the threshold of a new millennium. In M. Garcia (Ed.), *Affirmative action's testament of hope: Strategies for a new era in higher education* (pp. 1–17). Albany, NY: State University of New York Press.

General Motors Corporation. (2003, February 18). *Brief of General Motors Corporation as Amicus Curiae in Support of Respondents (Nos. 02-241 and 02-516).* Retrieved November 3, 2003, from http://www.umich.edu/~urel/admissions/legal/gru_amicus-ussc/um/GM-both.pdf

Gratz v. Bollinger, 539 U.S. 244 (2003).

Green, D. (2003a, October). *Articulating the benefits of racial diversity to the national press: Triumphs, challenges, and lessons learned from* Gratz *and* Grutter. Presentation conducted at the biannual meeting of the American Council on Education, Office of Minorities in Higher Education, Educating All of One Nation (EAON), Atlanta, GA.

Green, D. (2003b, Fall). Creating a new narrative for racial diversity. *Association of the Study of Higher Education Newsletter, 16*(3), 9–10.

Grutter v. Bollinger, 539 U.S. 306 (2003).

Gurin, P., Dey, E., Hurtado, S., & Gurin, G. (2002). Diversity and higher education: Theory and impact on educational outcomes. *Harvard Educational Review, 72,* 330–366.

Herrnstein, R. J., & Murray, C. (1994). *The bell curve: Intelligence and class structure in American life.* New York: The Free Press.

Hopwood v. State of Texas, 78 F.3d. 932; 1996 U.S. App. Lexis 4719 (5th Circuit 1996).

Hurtado, S. (1999, Spring). Reaffirming educators' judgment: Educational value of diversity.

Liberal Education, 85(2), 24–31.

Lucas, C. J. (1996). *Crisis in the academy: Rethinking higher education in America.* New York: St. Martin's Press.

Malamud, D. (1997). Affirmative action, diversity, and the black middle class. *University of Colorado Law Review, 68*, 939–1000.

McPherson, M. (1983). Value conflicts in American higher education. *Journal of Higher Education, 54*, 243–278.

Merriam, S. (1998). *Qualitative research and case study applications in education: Revised and expanded from case study research in education.* San Francisco: Jossey-Bass.

Miles, M. B., & Huberman, A. M. (1994). *Qualitative data analysis.* (2nd ed.). Thousand Oaks, CA: Sage.

Moses, Y. T. (1994). Quality, excellence, and diversity. In D. G. Smith, L. E. Wolf, & T. Levitan (Eds.), *Studying diversity in higher education* (pp. 9–20). San Francisco: Jossey-Bass.

Orfield, G. & Kurlaender, M. (Eds.) (1999). *Diversity challenged: Evidence on the impact of affirmative action.* Cambridge, MA: Harvard Education Publishing Group.

Podberesky v. Kirwan, 38 F.3d. 147 (4th Cir. 1994).

Retired Military Leaders. (2003, February 3). *Consolidated Brief of Lt. Gen. Julius W. Becton, Jr., et al. as Amici Curiae in Support of Respondents (No. 02-241, 02-516).* Retrieved November 3, 2003, from http://www.umich.edu/~urel/admissions/legal/gru_amicus-ussc/um/MilitaryL-both.pdf

Schmdt, P. (2003, April 4). Behind the fight over race-conscious admissions. *The Chronicle of Higher Education, 49,* pp. A22–A25.

Simmons, R. (1982). *Affirmative action: Conflict and change in higher education after Bakke.* Cambridge: Schenkman.

Smith, D. G. (1989). *The challenge of diversity: Involvement or alienation* (Vol. 5). Washington, DC: The George Washington University.

Stake, R. (1995). *The art of case study research.* Thousand Oaks, CA: Sage.

Strauss, A., & Corbin, J. (1990). *Basics of qualitative research: Grounded theory procedures and techniques.* Newbury Park, CA: Sage.

Swanson, K. (1981). *Affirmative action and preferential admissions in higher education: An annotated bibliography.* Metuchen, NJ: The Scarecrow Press.

Synnott, M. G. (1979). *The half-opened door: Discrimination and admissions at Harvard, Yale, and Princeton, 1900–1970.* Westport, CT: Greenwood Press.

Tierney, W. (1997). The parameters of affirmative action: Equity and excellence in the academy. *Review of Educational Research, 67,* 165–196.

Tierney, W. G. (1996). Affirmative action in California: Looking back, looking forward in public academe. *Journal of Negro Education, 65,* 122–132.

University of California Regents v. Bakke, 438 U.S. 265 (1978).

University of Michigan. (1999a). *Compelling need for diversity in higher education, expert reports in defense of the University of Michigan.* Retrieved Dec. 10, 2003, from http://www.umich.edu/~urel/admissions/research/

University of Michigan. (1999b). Selections from the compelling need for diversity in higher education, expert reports in defense of the University of Michigan. *Equity and Excellence in Education, 32*(2), 36–72.

Wilson, J. K. (1995). *The myth of political correctness: The conservative attack on higher education.* Durham, NC: Duke University Press.

Wolf-Devine, C. (1997). Which side are the angels on? *Academe, 83*(1), 24–28.

Yin, R. K. (1994). *Case study research: Design and methods* (2nd ed.). Thousand Oaks, CA: Sage.

Chapter 4

The Puzzle and Paradox of Student Mobility in Higher Education

Sara Goldrick-Rab

American students have never attended college in a straightforward and linear fashion. In 1946, fresh out of the Navy, my grandfather began his pursuit of a bachelor's degree in New York City (NYC), at Hunter College's Bronx Lehman campus. After a year he decided to move to the University of Miami for the warmer weather. One year later, he changed again, moving to back to NYC to attend New York University. He went back to care for his mother, who was living alone. Incredibly, he graduated in 1950—right on time.

My grandfather was not an anomaly then, nor would his decisions be considered terribly odd now. Since the time the federal government began keeping track of students changing schools, the number of students attending more than one college has steadily grown. In 1972, nearly half (47.5 percent) of undergraduates attended more than one college; by 1982 it was 51.3 percent, and in 1992 it was 56.5 percent. In fact, nearly one-fifth (18.9 percent) of 1992 high school seniors went on to attend more than two colleges (Adelman, Daniel, & Berkovits, 2003; Adelman, 2004).

Yet throughout its history, American higher education has been a system of individual institutions that pride themselves on being distinctive and innovative, and invest heavily in their own success. The core learning of higher education does not rely on a common curriculum across schools, it is not organized around common timelines, nor does it utilize a common student record system. In this sense, it is rather miraculous that students manage to be mobile at all. Transfer and articulation agreements, designed to facilitate the flow of credits among schools, are a relatively new phenomenon. These agreements have yet to demonstrate their effectiveness on improving student outcomes (Roksa, 2006).

But students continue to move. Should higher education be concerned? How should policymakers and practitioners respond, if at all? As a sociologist, I approach these questions by first posing an additional one: Does student mobility reflect and/or create inequality? Based on my empirical studies of national longitudinal college transcript data, the answer to this question is "yes." Student mobility is both a reflection of and a contributor to inequality in American higher education along social class, and to some degree, along racial and gender lines. Student mobility should be treated as a concern and grappled with thoughtfully. In this paper, I briefly review my research on inequality in student mobility and formulate some suggestions for both policy and future research. My goal is to move the discussion of student mobility in higher education away from its current focus on what mobility means for institutional graduation rates to a focus on what mobility means for student outcomes and, in particular, student learning.

STRATIFICATION AND STUDENT MOBILITY

Rigorous study of student mobility requires the use of college transcript data collected for thousands of students across hundreds of schools. Relying on a sample of students who all end up at one institution will produced biased findings (Kearney, Warner, & Kearney, 1995), as will a sample of students from schools only in one region or state (Bach, Banks, Kinnick, Ricks, Stoering, & Walleri, 2000). There are two national datasets created by the National Center for Education Statistics that are particularly useful for this purpose, as they track students from middle or high school until early adulthood, and collect transcripts from all of the schools students attend: High School and Beyond of 1982 (HSB) and the National Educational Longitudinal Study of 1988 (NELS).

My research thus far has examined the more contemporary cohort of students found in the NELS data. In particular, I have focused on the group of NELS students who graduated from high school 1n or around 1992 and began college at a four-year institution prior to the year 2000. Unlike students who start at two-year schools, these students are not required—in order to earn a bachelor's degree—to be mobile. Thus their mobility presents additional puzzles and challenges.

TYPES OF MOBILITY

There are numerous ways in which students can change schools. Like my grandfather, they can do so fluidly and continuously, simply by leaving one school and then immediately enrolling in another. They can move while taking some time off between attending schools, interrupting their movement. Students can move from one four-year school to another, or they can move from a four-year to a two-year institution. They can combine enrollment options, doing a so-called "reverse transfer" interrupted by a stopout (or discontinuous enrollment). The possibilities are extensive.

Of the 2,135 NELS students who started their postsecondary education at a four-year institution and went on to attend at least one other college, 20 percent also experienced an interruption in their enrollment. I term this pattern "interrupted movement," and compare it to "fluid movement" across schools (Goldrick-Rab, 2006a). Sixty percent of NELS students who changed schools moved laterally, from one four-year school to another; the other 40 percent made a 'reverse transfer' to a two-year institution (Goldrick-Rab & Pfeffer, 2007).

Characteristics of Mobile Students

The students engaged in different types of mobility are distinguishable by other characteristics as well. Students who interrupt their movement among schools are more often male, nonwhite, and from the bottom 20 percent of the U.S. socioeconomic status (SES) distribution. They also have lower high school test scores, lower high school grade point averages, and engage in less rigorous high school curricula than students who do not change schools. The relationship between a student's family socioeconomic status and their propensity for "interrupted movement" is significant, such that students from the bottom 20 percent of the socioeconomic distribution are more than three times more likely to engage in that pattern, compared to students in the top 20 percent. This is true even when controlling for gender, race, and high school preparation (Goldrick-Rab, 2006a).

On the other hand, students engaged in fluid movement are disproportionately female and well-off (in the top 20 percent of the SES distribution). They are average high school students with test scores and high school GPAs in the middle of the distribution who participated in slightly challenging high school courses. Somehow—or for some reason—when they change schools, they manage to do so continuously (Goldrick-Rab, 2006a).

Students who "reverse transfer" from a four-year to a two-year school are more likely to have parents in working-class occupations who did not attend college. Controlling for other ascriptive characteristics and high school background, the odds of reverse transfer are 35 percent higher for first-generation students (compared to students with college-educated parents) (Goldrick-Rab, 2006b).

Consequences of Student Mobility

These differences in how students change schools are not benign; instead they result in highly disparate outcomes in terms of degree completion. Students who move to a two-year institution greatly reduce their chances for completing a bachelor's degree (BA), perhaps because most two-year institutions do not grant four-year degrees. As a result, the probability of completing a bachelor's degree is 119 percent lower if a student does a reverse transfer, even when controlling for other determinants of completion including: demographic characteristics, high school achievement, degree expectations, selectivity and control of the initial institution attended, timing of college entry, enrollment intensity, and college GPA (Goldrick-Rab & Pfeffer, 2007).

Moreover, my preliminary analyses also indicate two additional reasons to be concerned with mobility. First, each institutional change a student makes during college appears to be associated with reduced chances for bachelor's degree completion. For example, changing schools between the first and second years of college enrollment reduces the odds of completion of a degree by 49 percent; a change between years two and three reduces completion by 73 percent and; a change between years three and four reduces the odds of completion by 60 percent. These effects are above and beyond the negative impact of taking time off between any of those years of enrollment, even when controlling for a student's college grade point average.

Second, there is some evidence of interaction effects between parental education and institutional change, such that first-generation students incur a greater penalty for their mobility. This means that the effect of mobility seems to be most detrimental precisely for those students most likely to move.

The Mobility Quandary

If changing schools subsequent to starting college reduces the chances for degree completion for the majority of mobile students, why do they do it? Are these irrational decisions made by uninformed actors? Or are we failing to see the *benefits* of student mobility not captured by a focus on degree completion?

My thoughts on this puzzle are informed by two additional findings from my research. First, while family background is a significant predictor of a student's attendance pattern, high school achievement is of greater importance. This could mean that poor students may be more likely to follow disadvantageous pathways, partly because they have less money and less information about how to effectively navigate college, but also because they had lower grades in both high school and college (Goldrick-Rab, 2006b).

Second, college is a path-dependent process. Students who successfully complete their first year of enrollment are more likely than those who do not to go on to a second successful year, and so on. Success begets success, failure begets failure—numerous little decisions begin to add up. Students from low-SES backgrounds are less likely to experience success in college early on and as a result, they quickly end up "off-track," changing schools, or taking time off. In the end, poor students also have lower completion rates (Goldrick-Rab, 2006c).

So what matters more: the money and resources students bring to college with them, via their parental income, education and occupation; or their past and present academic achievement? Are students changing schools because they are under-resourced, or because they are failing their classes? Are their outcomes smaller because changing schools disrupts college learning in such significant ways, or because students who change schools lose their credits, financial aid, and social support?

These are important questions, and unfortunately we still have far too few answers. Our otherwise rich national surveys include very few questions probing into the causes of student mobility, other than to ask rather simply, "Why did you leave the last school you attended?" Further, the surveys do not include sufficient financial aid data to test the impact of different forms of aid packages on student mobility, or even to examine the loss of aid following or preceding a move. Finally, because they draw on national samples, these surveys do not include sufficient numbers of low-income or minority students, or students from individual states. In addition, the surveys do not allow for deep, contextualized studies. If the federal government were to successfully create a student unit-record system for the entire system of higher education *and* allow non-governmental researchers access to the data, our knowledge about the equity implications of student mobility would greatly improve.

The limited body of qualitative research in this area suffers from small sample sizes and sample bias, but what it does suggest is that mobility is only partially about academics (Bach et al., 2000; Kearney et al., 1995). Students change schools to be closer to home or family, to take a new job, or to start a new life. Major parts of an adult's life course intersect in important ways with a college education, and this needs to be better understood.

In an effort to improve our knowledge base, I am working to identify high schools in one urban area (Chicago) that disproportionately graduate students who go on to be mobile in college. I may begin to observe them while in high school and interview them as they move into and through college. This sort of in-depth longitudinal research is intensive and costly, but fruitful. Perhaps we will learn about the ways in which being able to change institutions helps to keep students enrolled in college at all. Some questions this research will pursue include: If students can no longer afford to attend their first school, and therefore move to another one, are they better off? If the choice is between losing a husband to a work transfer, or staying at the initial college you attended, is it better to move?

HELP OR HINDER MOBILITY?

One of the most vexing questions facing higher education policymakers and practitioners concerned with mobility is whether they should to try to stop students from changing schools, or whether they should facilitate the process. As my research has shown, my grandfather was unusual—he was a poor kid who changed schools numerous times and still managed to earn a degree in four years, thanks in large part to the G.I. Bill, which gave him financial security throughout his postsecondary education. Few students in his position today manage to make it that far.

Borden (2004) has argued persuasively to institutional administrators that we should do what we can to help, including enhancing articulation agreements and agreeing on common core courses. But the institutional incentives in many ways push in the other direction. An environment of accountability focused on graduation rates serves to reinforce the notion that students belong to institutions and are best retained there. The most elite institutions work very hard to prevent their students from transferring, even if it is in students' best interests. For example, faced with a miserable freshmen year at the College of William and Mary in 1995, I was told by the advisor that transferring simply would not be allowed; indeed, *"No One Has Ever Left William and Mary!"* No fewer than five administrators (and my mother) tried to prevent my departure—albeit to no avail. When I arrived at my destination institution, George Washington University, there was no one to greet me or help me transition into my new environs.

While the average non-selective four-year institution lacks the resources to put forth such a concerted effort to retain students, it still has every incentive *not* to facilitate the easy flow of students across schools. Evidence that students with fewer resources are especially disadvantaged when they move among schools suggests that institutions should be encouraged to make help mobility a more transparent, simpler process.

Perhaps most importantly, the unequal outcomes of student mobility indicate that we must do more to hold institutions accountable for helping all students achieve their goals. Success for some students comes in the form of graduation from the first school they attended right out of high school. But for others, completing a degree may necessarily take time, and changing schools may be evidence of steps in the right direction. Recently, an African American friend reminded me of this when telling his college tale. William's (a pseudonym) story goes something like this:

> After barely finishing high school in a poor North Carolina district, William began college at a two-year school with little clue of what to expect. College life stimulated his interest in learning, and he soon realized he had to go elsewhere to get a "real" education—so he moved to a non-selective four-year college in Kansas. After one year he refined his academic interests and realized that the opportunities he desired required attending a major research university. Two transfers later, William found himself enrolled

at Cornell University where he earned his bachelor's and master's degrees. William then went on to finish a law degree at Western New England College School of Law, a one-year executive program at Harvard Law, and a second master's degree at Harvard.

Unquestionably an educational and professional success, William needed required courses, as they provided him the opportunity and time to learn as much about himself as about the subjects he studied.

STEPS TOWARD MOBILITY

The first step for institutions must be to define the goals and outcomes in higher education as broadly as students themselves define them. In addition, success ought to be measured wherever it occurs. For example, we can measure how well institutions facilitate successful mobility by looking at how many students who transfer out eventually graduate at their next institution. Or we could examine many incoming transfer students and their experience with interruption (or no interruption) in their financial aid package.

Second, all schools should create significant institutional capacity to support transfer, so any student wishing to leave campus can do so, but through well-informed decision making. The ability to transfer effectively is currently predicated on a student having the know-how that comes from having college-educated, financially secure parents. This advantage could be ameliorated by an effective advising system.

Third, states should get involved to provide fiscal incentives for both two- and four-year public institutions to engage in this work. Such an approach will encourage schools to help students succeed, wherever and whenever it suits them. In this sense, the focus becomes the student—my father, William, me—and student success.

References

Adelman, C. (2004). *Principal indicators of student academic histories in postsecondary education, 1972–2000.* Washington, DC: U.S. Department of Education.

Adelman, C., Daniel, B., and Berkovits, I. (2003). *Postsecondary attainment, attendance, curriculum, and performance: Selected results from the NELS:88/2000 postsecondary education transcript study* (NCES 2003–394). Washington DC: U.S. Department of Education, National Center for Education Statistics.

Bach, S. K., Banks, M. T., Kinnick, M. K., Ricks, M. F., Stoering, J. M., & Walleri, R. D. (2000). Student attendance patterns and performance in an urban postsecondary environment. *Research in Higher Education, 41,* 315–330.

Borden, V. M. H. (2004, March/April). Accommodating student swirl. *Change, 36*(2), 10–17.

Goldrick-Rab, S. (2006a). Following their every move: How social class shapes postsecondary pathways. *Sociology of Education, 79,* 61–79.

Goldrick-Rab, S. (2006b). *Pushed into jumping? The context of "choice" in college pathways.* Manuscript submitted for publication.

Goldrick-Rab, S. (2006c). *Getting off track: Path dependence and socioeconomic inequality in college completion.* Paper presented at the annual meeting of the Association for Institutional Research, Chicago, IL.

Goldrick-Rab, S. and F. Pfeffer (2007). *Second Chances: Student Mobility, Institutional Differentiation, and Stratification in College Completion.* Paper presented at the annual meeting of the American Sociological Association, New York City.

Kearney, G. W., Townsend, B., & Kearney, T. (1995). Multiple-transfer students in a public urban university: Background characteristics and interinstitutional movements. *Research in Higher Education, 36,* 323–344.

Roksa, J. (2006). *States, schools and students: Contextualizing community college outcomes.* Unpublished doctoral dissertation, New York University.

Engaging Students and the Community through Study Abroad, Service-Learning, and Civic Engagement

CHAPTER 5

Reflections on War, Nation, and Identity:

AMERICAN UNDERGRADUATES ABROAD

Nadine Dolby

Abstract: Study abroad is increasingly a key component of U.S. universities' efforts to both create and solidify their commitments to international education. Often positioned as part of an effort to expand students' worldview, study abroad is also seen as a way to improve American undergraduates' ability to negotiate a global workplace. This chapter takes a different approach to analyzing American students' experiences abroad, by focusing attention on how they negotiate their national, American identity during a time of war. In doing so, I argue that for the students who participated in this research, making sense of their national identity was of considerable more importance than attempting to form a global consciousness. While this aspect of the study abroad experience is often neglected or overlooked in the rush to "sell" students on the benefits of a global outlook, I assert that from an educational perspective, the possibility of raising students' awareness and critical reflection on their national identity—particularly in the relatively nationalistic and isolationist context of the United States—should be more clearly centered in discussions of study abroad.

S tudy abroad is increasingly a key component of U.S. universities' efforts to both create and solidify their commitments to international education.[1] Often positioned as part of an effort to expand students' worldview, study abroad is also seen as a way to improve American undergraduates' ability to negotiate a global workplace. For example, Northwestern University promotes study abroad as a way to become a "global citizen," while the University of Georgia suggests that students study abroad to broaden their horizons and "gain a new perspective."[2]

This essay, and the research project on which it is based, takes a different perspective on analyzing how American undergraduates give meaning to their experiences outside of the United States. Instead of trying to understand whether and how American students' outlooks become more global, I focus attention on how they negotiate their national, American identity during a time of war. In doing so, I argue that, for the students who participated in this research, making sense of their national identity was of considerably more importance than attempting to form a global consciousness (see McCabe, 2001). Students became acutely aware of their American identity as they traveled outside of the United States and this realization, and struggle, shaped their encounter with the rest of the world (Dolby, 2004). While this aspect of the study abroad experience is often neglected or overlooked in the rush to "sell" students on the benefits of a global outlook (Bolen, 2001), I assert that from an educational perspective, the possibility of raising students' awareness and critical reflection on their national identity—particularly in the relatively nationalistic and isolationist context of the United States—should be more clearly centered in discussions of study abroad.

In the balance of this essay, I first briefly review the current context of study abroad in the United States and the relevant literature on nation and national identity. I describe the research study on which this essay is based, giving details of data collection and analysis. I then present qualitative data from interviews with returned study abroad students that examines how the negotiation of their American identity was at the center of their experience abroad. I reflect on how this phase of the research study is connected to an earlier phase of the study that explored similar questions, yet in a different context. Finally, I suggest future directions for research in this area.

STUDY ABROAD IN THE UNITED STATES: THE CURRENT CONTEXT

Though growing in popularity in recent years, study abroad is still unlikely to be a part of the typical U.S. student's undergraduate experience. In academic year 2005–2006 (the most recent year for which figures are available), 223,534 students at American universities studied abroad (Institute of International Education, 2007). While this number is 150 percent the number who studied abroad a decade ago, it still represents only a tiny percentage of all undergraduates. Over one-third (37 percent) of U.S. students who study abroad do so for one semester. Enrollment in short term programs has grown dramatically in the past few years, with 52 percent of students who study abroad doing so for a period less than eight weeks. Only 5.5 percent of students who study abroad do so for an entire academic year; thus most students who study abroad (approximately 94.5 percent) are abroad for only a relatively short period of time (Institute of International Education, 2007).

Much of the growth in the number of students studying abroad can be attributed to increased institutional support of such initiatives under the larger rubric of international education (American Council on Education, 2003). Federal government initiatives have also been significant factors in the growth of study abroad: the availability of federal financial aid for study abroad in 1992, President Bill Clinton's executive memorandum encouraging international experience and awareness in 2000, and more recently, the formation of the Bipartisan Commission on the Abraham Lincoln Study Abroad Fellowship Program. Proposed by the late Senator Paul Simon in 2003 and passed in January 2004—a month after his death in December 2003—the commission is charged with recommending "a program to greatly expand the opportunity for students at institutions of higher education in the United States to study abroad, with special emphasis on studying in developing nations" and which "meets the growing need of the United States to become more sensitive to the cultures of other countries" (HR 2673, Section 104). In November 2005, the Commission released a report calling on the United States to send one million students abroad annually by 2016–2017 (Commission on the Abraham Lincoln Study Abroad Fellowship Program, 2005), and the United States Senate declared 2006 the "Year of Study Abroad."

The Commission highlighted two core reasons why American undergraduates should study abroad: "global competence" and "national needs." Specifically, the Commission pointed towards multiple factors prompting it to call for a dramatic expansion of studying abroad including: globalization and economic competitiveness, national security, U.S. leadership, active engagement in the international community, and the educational value of study abroad (pp. v–vi). Independent organizations such as NAFSA: Association of International Educators (2003), the American Council on Education (2003), and the Forum on Education Abroad have also been at the forefront of initiating efforts to increase the number of American undergraduates studying abroad.

In comparison to other areas of higher education, research on study abroad policy, programs, and student participants is relatively limited. Much of the literature is concerned with outcomes for individual students, including language acquisition, personal growth, academic outcomes, and professional development (Allen & Herron, 2003; Bacon, 2002; Freed, 1995; Jurasak, Lamson, & O'Maley, 1996; Shannon, 1995; Van Hoof & Verbeeten, 2005; Wagner & Magistrale, 1995; Whalen, 1996).[3] Additional studies examine the impact on students' and alumnae's global and international perspectives (Akande & Slawson, 2000; Douglas & Jones-Rikkers, 2001). Theoretical work on the relationship between study abroad and identity is underdeveloped. On one hand, given the practical and applied focus of the field, such emphases are understandable. However, this underdevelopment is still curious, given the explosion of scholarly interest in the humanities and social sciences in globalization, transnationalism, post-colonialism, and nation. In one of the few exceptions, Mell Bolen (2001) situates study abroad within the larger shift to a consumption-based, post-Fordist economy, and examines the implications of such shifts for study abroad as a cultural practice. Bolen's analysis underscores that research on study abroad must include efforts that move beyond the evaluation or "what works" paradigm to interrogate the fundamental assumptions that shape our pedagogical approach to the study abroad experience, and the ways in which study abroad produces identities. In this research project, I respond to Bolen's analysis through investigating how students make meaning of their national, American identity while outside of the United States—a critical, yet rarely discussed aspect of study abroad.

NATIONAL IDENTITY:
A FRAMEWORK FOR ANALYSIS

Why nation? It may seem to be common sense (Gramsci, 1971) that research on study abroad be grounded in paradigms that privilege the "global" and "international" as key educational objectives of the study abroad experience. Yet, the recent surge of patriotism and nationalism in the United States post 9/11 should alert us that national sentiments and identity are a fundamental element of how Americans see and position themselves vis-à-vis the world (Apple, 2002). Furthermore, the aftermath of September 11th, along with the United States' occupation of Afghanistan and then Iraq, led to intensified public interest and debate on the contours of American identity, which heightened awareness of the relationship between nation and self among students who were preparing to travel abroad.

The construct of "nation" is invested with an illusion of certainty. Yet, at the core, nations are nothing more than artificial constructs created, Arjun Appadurai argues, as "a product of the collective imagination" (1993, p. 414). As Benedict Anderson (1983) has detailed, nations were originally born through print media, which allowed individuals who were geographically dispersed to imagine themselves linked by an affective attachment to an imagined, abstract entity: the nation. Such affective ties are not natural in a biological sense, but are created and then continually nurtured through particular practices which are necessary to sustain the continuation of the nation. Eric Hobshawn (1994), for example, argues that such "invented traditions" as the Pledge of Allegiance; the ceremonial raising, lowering, and displaying of the flag; and the ritualistic singing of the national anthem at sports events are at the core of the perpetuation of national identity.

Politicians from various nations often face contradictory impulses to maintain national borders and national identities for political purposes, and simultaneously to erode or ignore these borders when it suits a nation's economic objectives. For example, the border between the United States and Mexico is both rigid and fluid. On one hand, U.S. border patrol agents capture dozens of Mexican citizens each night, as they attempt to cross the "no man's land" between Mexico and Texas. Simultaneously, American corporations, such as Tyson, are accused of actively recruiting and facilitating illegal migration to fill low-paying, hazardous jobs in poultry processing plants, jobs that Americans do not want.

Increasingly, there are also forces that are beyond the control of nation-states, both rich and poor. For example, as Saskia Sassen (2001) observes, the "global cities" of New York, London, and Tokyo are situated in, but are not wholly of, their corresponding nation-states of the United States, Britain, and Japan. Thus, New York is not necessarily the quintessential "American" city, but is, in fact, the exact opposite.

Less economically advantaged states are also forced to respond to global forces and rework their ideas of national identity. Peggy Levitt's (2001) research on the Dominican Republic exemplifies the way that states reshape their notions of citizenship to accommodate new global realities. Dominican communities are increasingly transnational and diasporic, and the economic health of the Dominican Republic depends on the movement of its citizens residing abroad. In response, the state is rethinking its idea of "citizenship" and parliamentary representation to ensure the continuation of close national ties between the state, the nation, and Dominican nationals living abroad. Many other nation-states, including Mexico, Brazil, Ecuador, Portugal, and India are similarly revamping and broadening the way the "nation" is imagined to embrace people beyond the physical borders of the nation (Appadurai 1993, 1996; Levitt, 2001). Aiwha Ong's (1999) writing similarly documents the way that Chinese nationals deploy "flexible citizenship" to develop new spaces of attachment that defy traditional national borders. As Appadurai (1996) observes, there are increasing patterns of "sovereignty without territoriality" where the assumed connection between a geographical locale and a "people" is fractured.

The above developments, among many others, suggest that the "nation" increasingly contradicts the space of identification. For example, Martha Nussbaum (1996) advances the idea of a "cosmopolitan" identity, premised on a common human bond that exceeds and transcends the nation-state. Bruce Robbins (1998), also concerned with cosmopolitan identities, stresses the significance of local attachments and calls for the proliferation of ties that work both above and below the level of the nation-states. Amy Gutmann (1996), critical of Nussbaum's stance, asserts that the notion of a common human bond is too abstract, and that no global polity has attempted such a project. Clearly, few people feel emotional attachment to global bodies such as the United Nations, and other global entities (such as the World Trade Organization, the International Monetary Fund and the G-8) inspire solidarity only in opposition. Arjun Appadurai (1993) suggests the model of "new patriotisms" (such as the now defunct Queer Nation) that evolve from multiple, local attachments and move, octopus-like, throughout the world.

Despite the above contradictions and challenges, this destabilization of "nation" has not weakened its power to shape American identities, but has instead created a space in which the taken-for-granted assumptions about the unity, singularity, and solidity of nation and national identity are questioned. As I will discuss, American undergraduates abroad do not reject their national identity, but reshape it so that their identity becomes more flexible, malleable, and open to multiple articulations. Craig Calhoun (2002) notes the continually reforming nature of national identity when he writes:

> To treat nationalism as a relic of an earlier order, a sort of irrational expression, or a kind of moral mistake is to fail to see both the continuing power of nationalism as a discursive formation and the work—sometimes positive—that nationalist solidarities continue to do in the world. As a result nationalism is not easily abandoned, even if its myths, contents, and excesses are easily debunked (p. 150).

As Calhoun (2002) suggests, the choice is not simply between a "thin" cosmopolitan identity detached from nation, and a "thick" ethnocentric identity. As I demonstrate, student encounters with nation exceed such dualistic models. Instead, students actively produce new forms of national belonging.

METHODOLOGY, DATA COLLECTION, AND ANALYSIS

The research discussed in this chapter is from the second phase of an on-going research project on study abroad and social identities (Dolby, 2004, 2005). In 2000–2001, I conducted the first phase of this research where I analyzed the study abroad experiences of 26 American and 20 Australian students. The American undergraduates, from a large Midwestern university I referred to as "University of the Midwest," all studied abroad in Australia in (the U.S.) spring semester 2001. Likewise, the Australian students all studied in the United States in 2001, though their actual periods abroad were staggered through the year. Both groups of students were interviewed before they left their home country and upon their return (see Dolby, 2004; 2005, for a complete discussion of these studies).

In this second phase of the research, American undergraduates from three large research universities in the Midwest were interviewed in 2004, after their return from studying abroad. Of the 50 students interviewed, most had studied abroad the previous semester and all had returned within the previous year. Students who participated in this second phase of the research studied in countries all over the world for a time period of one semester. Forty-eight students who participated in this research were White students and two were African American students. One of the White students was a native of Poland and a U.S. permanent resident; the rest of the participants were Americans by birth. Nationally, 83 percent of students who study abroad are White, 6.3 percent Asian American, 5.4 percent Hispanic, 3.5 percent African American, 1.2 percent multiracial, and .6 percent Native American (Institute of International Education, 2007). As this research sample is self-selected, it is not representative, though clearly White students are both the majority of students who study abroad, and the majority of my sample. Students' majors varied widely and included disciplines in the humanities, social sciences, and sciences and engineering. With few exceptions, most students studied abroad their junior year, which is also typical; nationally, 38 percent of students who study abroad are juniors. My sample included 28 women (56 percent) and 22 men (44 percent); nationally the majority of study abroad students are female (65.5 percent; Institute of International Education, 2007).

Students were interviewed in small focus groups of 3–6 students. In total, 14 focus groups were conducted during calendar year 2004.[4] The focus groups allowed for interaction and discussion that can differ dramatically from a conversation between a researcher and a single participant. For example, George Kamberelis and Greg Dimitriadis (2005) assert focus groups' emphasis on collective inquiry has the potential to create:

> synergy among participants that often leads to the unearthing of information seldom ready-to-hand in individual memory. Focus groups also facilitate the exploration of collective memories and shared stocks of knowledge that may seem trivial and unimportant to individuals but come to the fore as crucial when like-minded groups begin to revel in the everyday (p. 903).

Thus, in a focus group, the process of inquiry is to some extent controlled by participants and is, in this way, an instance of collective pedagogy and meaning-making.

Focus group discussions lasted approximately 1 1/2 hours and were audio-taped, transcribed, and coded (Strauss & Corbin, 1998). During the focus group, students were asked to reflect on their study abroad experiences, what they had learned about themselves as Americans, what they had learned about the nation where they had lived, and whether/how their perspectives on the world had changed as a result of studying abroad. All of the students who participated in this phase of the research had studied abroad in 2003 or 2004, as the United States was preparing for and entering a war in Iraq. This reality dramatically shaped students' experiences outside of the United States. In some cases, the war affected their choice of destinations (e.g., several chose London because the British were "America's strongest ally"); in other instances, it cut short their study abroad experience (one student had to leave Turkey after only a few weeks), and in all cases the war was a compelling, unavoidable influence that shaped their study abroad experience. Despite the official end of the war in May 2003, the ongoing conflict and violence in Iraq continued to be a factor in students' experiences abroad throughout 2003 and 2004, and was a central issue of discussion during the focus groups.

My analysis in this essay is qualitative and interpretive (Denzin, 2000). I am interested in how students construct meaning from their experience, particularly how they negotiate national identity at a time when the definition and contours of being an American are publicly and loudly debated in the United States and abroad. As a small, qualitative study, my objective is not to form generalizable hypotheses, but to understand how the participants in this study made sense of being American abroad during troubled times. My methodological approach situates the data within a critical framework that is sociologically based and contextual. Thus, in this essay, I do not simply report and describe the data collected during this research, but use specific analytical frameworks. Lois Weis and Michelle Fine (2004) refer to this process—this "theory" of method—as compositional studies. In this approach, "analyses of public and private institutions, groups, and lives are lodged in relation to key social and economic structures" (p. xvi). I analyze how students' identities as American citizens are shaped within (not determined by) the historic and troubled times in which they find themselves.

NEGOTIATING "AMERICA": UNDERGRADUATES ABROAD

For the students who participated in this research, understanding themselves as Americans was a significant component of the experience of studying abroad. Because of the current political context of the United States and its relationship to the rest of the world, students who participated in this phase of the research were acutely aware of their national identity, even before departing. This finding contrasts markedly with the earlier phase of this study (Dolby, 2004), which examined students who studied abroad in spring semester 2001. Those students, who were interviewed initially in December 2000, had little understanding or knowledge of the United States' position in the world.[5] In contrast, in this phase of the study, students frequently mentioned their concerns about being an American abroad—whether in the context of worries about safety, or their ability to meet and form friendships with locals. And, of course, study abroad programs are themselves addressing concerns about being American in a post September 11th world. Most students reported that their pre-departure orientation had included instructions not to wear university sweatshirts and baseball caps in public, not to congregate in a visible manner in a large group of Americans, and not to draw attention to oneself through boisterous behavior.

Many students began to associate these behaviors with the stereotypical "bad" American and attempted to distance themselves from such conduct. For example, Rachel, who spent a semester in London, recalled:

> I also found myself looking more critically at Americans who were there. Americans who came to England. Like if I was at a restaurant, and I heard Americans being loud, and just not being culturally sensitive, I would get really mad.

For some students, it became important not only to criticize Americans who were displaying "bad" behavior, but to actively try to counter the American stereotypes. Students proudly reported incidents where they were positioned as atypical Americans. Joanne, who studied in Spain, commented:

> All the [Spanish] students were pretty much receptive. They were a little shocked that we didn't act like constantly drunk and really idiotic Americans like they expected, that we were actually intelligent. I think they were impressed that we actually knew Spanish.

Similarly, Ian, who spent several weeks in Turkey before being forced to leave in advance of the U.S. invasion of Iraq in March 2003, reflected:

> We met a group of Turkish students…basically all they knew about the U.S. was from movies and stuff, stereotypically negative. And so we were like the first people that they kind of liked that were from here. They had [American] exchange students from the past that they thought were annoying.

The majority of students who were interviewed stated that it was important not be seen as a typical American (i.e., to display behaviors which were considered boorish and insensitive). For example, Tim, who studied in Italy, expressed being embarrassed about typical American behavior:

> Americans go into a place, and they decide this is mine, the wall's mine, the silverware is mine. So as a group of Americans wherever we would go we'd be just, yep, this is ours now. No, you can't talk to me that way. I've decided to speak English, you're going to speak English, you're going to play this type of music....It was so embarrassing.

Here, student participants reject what Craig Calhoun (2002) describes as a "thick" national identity, or one which is exclusionary and ethnocentric. However, it is also important to note that students do not adopt what Calhoun refers to as a "thin" national identity, one which is detached from any affiliation to a nation. Thus, students do not say, "I do not want to be an American"; they very clearly posit that they do not want to be "that type" of American, or the bad or "ugly" American (Lederer & Burdick, 1958/1999). Students are not rejecting their national identity or affiliation, but seeing it as something that is flexible, open to re-articulation, and perhaps even improvement.

Though most students rejected the personae of the bad or "ugly" American, there were a few exceptions. One student, Alan, who studied abroad in Amsterdam, conceded that he actively embraced behavior that the other students considered inappropriate. He related this story of his experience buying tickets for the Paris Metro:

> None of us spoke French. It was funny because my friend went up there and the only thing we knew was like "bonjour." So he goes up there and he says, "Bonjour. Hi there." The lady looked at us and she started to speak the little bit of English that she could and then as we tried to like, not be as grateful to her, then she stopped and pretended not to speak any English at all, and just wouldn't help us.

Alan admits that he and his friends were, in his words, "messing around." While Alan is unapologetic about his behavior, he also does not display the arrogance that I often witnessed in the earlier phase of this research. Alan does not see a need to be penitent for his rudeness, and he is also aware that others may not approve. He is able to understand—if not wholly accept—the perspective of the ticket agent at the Paris Metro station.

The U.S. at War: Complicating National Identity

Being abroad during wartime presented another layer of challenges for these American students. Few, if any, students found themselves in nations where the general population supported the United States' actions in Iraq. While some students (e.g., those in Britain and Spain) were technically studying abroad in nations that were allies, there was often a considerable gap between government policy and public opinion. Thus, almost all of the students faced difficult questions about their support of or opposition to the war.

Few students felt that the correct approach to this dilemma was to assert unquestioned American superiority or wholehearted support for the war. Some, like Debbie who studied in Italy, clearly tried to separate themselves from the actions of the U.S. government:

> A lot of people that I talked to, they didn't like the American government. And they were like, "How do you feel about this and why did you go into the war?" And it's months later but they're like, "Why'd you guys do this?" I'm like, I didn't go there.

Sam, who also studied in Italy, also encountered this challenge early in his stay:

> One of the first things that happened when I got there is my French roommate, we—in broken English—got into discussing about Bush, and I was like, eh, I don't agree with everything my country does, and he was like, okay, and sort of just ended the conversation. Because I didn't want to be arguing about that, at least not when you first meet someone. Later in the year we had full-blown discussions for hours on end about the United States and what it does, and often it was me against five or six other people. But sometimes people, they'd help me out, and sometimes I'd have to admit that we were wrong. I don't know, it was nice to hear what other people thought about things.

Students realized that their national identity, in this context, was necessarily adaptable, as they negotiate a middle path between Calhoun's "thin" and "thick" national identities. They found a way to hold on to their sense of a national identity and an affinity for people and place, but at the same time make room for others' opinions and perspectives. Students actively constructed and strove to personify this "good" American, who is respectful of other cultures and people, open-minded, and willing to be critical of the United States' role in the world. Yet, students did not actively articulate the idea of global or international citizenship as they tried to understand how to behave as an American in a situation where they were guests in someone else's nation. Thus, for example, Martha Nussbaum's (1996) idea of a "cosmopolitan" citizenship or identity would not have particular resonance for the students who participated in this research study. Instead, students were invested in understanding their identity within a national (in this case, United States) paradigm, but one which is more reflective and self-conscious, and moves away from the narrow, ethnocentric, exclusive ideas of nation that are commonly associated with the United States (Jack, 2002).

National Identity and Study Abroad: Pedagogical Implications

Despite the rhetoric of study abroad providing a "global experience," the students who participated in this research were predominantly concerned with negotiating their national (American) identities. Certainly, these students were abroad at a relatively unique moment in U.S. history, as the U.S. prepared for and started a war that was largely unpopular throughout the world. Clearly, students' national identity would be of immediate concern to them in this context.

However, I argue that the relevance of national identity as a paradigm for understanding the study abroad experience extends beyond this one, perhaps isolated, moment. My previous research (Dolby, 2004) indicates that even before September 11th, students' experiences studying abroad were largely structured through what I have termed an "encounter" with their American self. The students in the current phase of this study did not "encounter" their national identity in the same way that the earlier group did, as they already had heightened awareness of what it meant to be an American in the post September 11th era. Furthermore, my earlier research study with Australian students who studied abroad in the United States (Dolby, 2005) indicates that Australian students do not focus on their national identity while abroad: they are, in contrast, more likely to display the global, or what I term "networked" (Castells, 2000), outlook that American study abroad programs strive to instill.

While global perspectives are certainly a worthy goal of study abroad programs, it appears that at least some American students are more concerned with understanding the role of the United States in the world than attempting to achieve the nebulous and diffuse stage of "global awareness." While global awareness is vague, contested, and perhaps can only be achieved through multiple, extended sojourns abroad, the goal of critical reflection on U.S. national identity is considerably more achievable.[6]

When students return from studying abroad, many are clearly able to articulate aspects of their role in the world as American citizens, something they could not easily identify before. The courses in political science may teach students the theories of empire, yet it was the experience of constantly being questioned and probed about American foreign policy while abroad that had a more lasting impact on students. Students returned with insights that were largely unavailable to them from their vantage point inside the United States (Bourdieu & Wacquant, 1992). Thus, they began to ask critical questions about their relationship to nation, the value and place of patriotism, and the geopolitical realities of the world. In arguing for the continuing relevance of the focus on internationalization in study abroad programs, Lester McCabe highlights the benefits of this approach, in contrast to the more recent emphasis on globalization:

> I believe that internationalization will always be secure in its position as a process that serves as a cornerstone and initial building block that allows people to develop skills and tools that will become necessary for surviving in a globalized world. Such skills might include language proficiency, cross-cultural understanding, and an awareness of one's own ethnocentric tendencies (p. 142).

The research discussed in this essay underscores the continued importance of these skills, which McCabe categorizes as "internationalization" (see also Knight, 2004). Specifically, in the U.S. environment, I argue that it is particularly important that students' American national identity be examined and explored in the context of education abroad. While language proficiency and cross-cultural understanding are both important, an emphasis on only those two aspects of internationalization can easily overlook the geopolitical realities of the world—leaving students with an appreciation for other cultures, but little understanding of how those cultures and nations are related within what Immanuel Wallerstein (2004) refers to as a world-system.

The students who participated in this study abroad research study reflected on and questioned their national identity. However, their exploration would have been richer, and ultimately more beneficial, if structured, academic re-entry programs engaged with the complicated issues of nation, power, and identity that arise for American undergraduates abroad. Such an approach may be a first step toward preparing students for the conflicted terrain that will provide the framework for their lives as national, international, and global citizens.

Endnotes

1. For example, Harvard University now expects that students will spend time abroad. See Polsky (2004).
2. See http://www.northwestern.edu/study abroad and http://www.usg.edu/oie/study_abroad.
3. For current research on study abroad in the United States, see *Frontiers: The Interdisciplinary Journal on Study Abroad* (http://www.frontiersjournal.com).
4. Thirteen focus groups were conducted at three different Big Ten universities in the Midwest. One (two-person) focus group was conducted at a regional, research extensive university.
5. For example, students who traveled abroad in January 2001 attended a mandatory pre-departure orientation in November 2000. As is customary during such pre-departure

orientations, students who are nationals of the destination country (in this case, Australia) attended the orientation in order to give the outgoing Americans a sense of Australian culture. In this case, an Australian woman flatly stated that, "Australians hate Americans." This comment produced a flurry of concern among the outgoing Americans, almost all of whom raised it during the pre-departure interview as something that they were worried about and did not understand. In the second phase of the study in 2003 and 2004, outgoing American students were clearly well-aware of anti-American sentiment in Australia and elsewhere.

6. The concept of "global awareness" is contested. For example, see the contrasting perspectives of Nussbaum (1996), Robbins (1998), and Gutmann (1996).

7. One example of such a course in the United States is "Cultural Difference and Social Change" at the University of Notre Dame. While restricted to students who studied in developing countries, the course provides students with an academic setting in which to explore issues of national and global relations, identities, and power (see also Downey, 2005). In the United States, Duke University, Northwestern University, and Carleton College, among others, offer courses for students who have returned from study abroad.

References

Akande, Y., & Slawson, C. (2000, May/June). *Exploring the long-term impact of study abroad: A case study of 50 years of study abroad alumni.* Paper presented at the annual meeting of NAFSA: Association of International Educators, San Diego, CA.

Allen, H., & Herron, C. (2003). A mixed-methodology investigation of the linguistic and affective outcomes of summer study abroad. *Foreign Languages Annals 36*, 370–385.

American Council on Education (2003). *Mapping internationalization on U.S. campuses.* Washington, DC: Author.

Anderson, B. (1983). *Imagined communities: Reflections on the origins and spread of nationalism.* London: Verso.

Appadurai, A. (1993). Patriotism and its futures. *Public Culture, 5*, 411–429.

Appadurai, A. (1996). Sovereignty without territoriality: Notes for a postnational geography. In P. Yaeger (Ed.), *The geography of identity* (pp. 40–58). Ann Arbor, MI: The University of Michigan Press.

Apple, M. (2002). Patriotism, pedagogy, and freedom: On the educational meanings of September 11. *Teachers College Record 104*, 1760–1772.

Bacon, S. (2002). Learning the rules: Language development and cultural adjustment during study abroad. *Foreign Language Annals 35*(6), 637–646.

Bolen, M. (2001). Consumerism and U.S. study abroad. *Journal of Studies in International Education 5*, 182–200.

Bourdieu, P., & Wacquant, L. (1992). *An invitation to reflexive sociology.* Chicago: University of Chicago Press.

Calhoun, C. (2002). Imagining solidarity: Cosmopolitanism, constitutional patriotism, and the public sphere. *Public Culture 14*, 147–171.

Castells, M. (2000). *The rise of the network society* (2nd ed.). Oxford: Blackwell Publishers.

Commission on the Abraham Lincoln Study Abroad Program. (2004). *The study and future of study abroad in the United States.* Washington, DC: Author. Available: http://www.lincoln-commission.org/lincolnbriefingbook.pdf

Commission on the Abraham Lincoln Study Abroad Program. (2005). *Global competence and national needs: One million Americans studying abroad.* Washington, DC: Author. Available: http://www.lincolncommission.org/LincolnReport.pdf

Denzin, N. (2000). The practices and politics of interpretation. In N. Denzin and Y. Lincoln (Eds.), *Handbook of qualitative research* (2nd ed., pp. 897–922). Thousand Oaks, CA: Sage Publications.

Dolby, N. (2004). Encountering an American self: Study abroad and national identity. *Comparative Education Review, 48,* 150–173.

Dolby, N. (2005). Globalisation, identity, and nation: Australian and American undergraduates abroad. *Australian Educational Researcher, 32*(1), 101–118.

Douglas, C., & Jones-Rikkers, C. (2001). Study abroad programs and American student world-mindedness: An empirical analysis. *Journal of Teaching in International Business, 31,* 55–66.

Downey, G. (2005). From personal reflection to social investigation: Undergraduate research as an antidote to autobiographical cliché. In L. Anderson (Ed.), *Internationalizing undergraduate education: Integrating study abroad into the curriculum* (pp. 117–121). Minneapolis, MN: University of Minnesota Press.

Freed, B. (Ed.). (1995). *Second language acquisition in a study abroad context.* Philadelphia: John Benjamins.

Gramsci, A. (1971). *Selections from the prison notebooks of Antonio Gramsci.* (Q. Hoare, & G. N. Smith, Eds. & Trans.). London: Lawrence and Wishart.

Gutmann, A. (1996). Democratic citizenship. In J. Cohen (Ed.), *For love of country: Debating the limits of patriotism* (pp. 66–71). Boston: Beacon Press.

Hobshawn, E. (1994). The nation as invented tradition. In J. Hutchinson, & A. D. Smith (Eds.), *Oxford readers: Nationalism* (pp. 76–82). Oxford: Oxford University Press.

Institute of International Education (2007). *Open doors 2007.* New York: Author. Retrieved at http://www.iie.org on November 12, 2007.

Jack, I. (2002). What we think of America [Special issue]. *Granta: The Magazine of New Writing, 77.*

Jurasak, R., Lamson, H., & O'Maley, P. (1996). Ethnographic learning while studying abroad. *Frontiers: The Interdisciplinary Journal of Study Abroad, 2,* Article 2. Retrieved February 16, 2003, from http://www.frontiersjournal.com/issues/vol2/vol202_Jurasek.htm

Kamberelis, G., & Dimitriadis, G. (2005). Focus groups: Strategic articulations of pedagogy, politics, and inquiry. In N. Denzin and Y. Lincoln (Eds.), *Handbook of qualitative research* (3rd ed., pp. 887–903). Thousand Oaks, CA: Sage Publications.

Knight, J. (2004). Internationalization remodeled: Definition, approaches, and rationales. *Journal of Studies in International Education, 8,* 5–31.

Lederer, W., & Burdick, E. (1958/1999). *The ugly American.* New York: W.W. Norton and Company.

Levitt, P. (2001). *The transnational villagers.* Berkeley, CA: University of California Press.

Lincoln Fellowship Commission. (2004). *The state and future of study abroad in the United States* (2004). Washington, DC: U.S. Government Printing Office.

McCabe, L. (2001). Globalization and internationalization: The impact on education abroad programs. *Journal of Studies in International Education, 5,* 138–145.

NAFSA: The Association of International Educators. (2003). *Toward an international education policy for the United States: International education in an age of globalism and terrorism.* Washington, DC: Author.

Nussbaum, M. (1996). Patriotism and cosmopolitanism. In J. Cohen (Ed.), *For love of country: Debating the limits of patriotism* (pp. 3–17). Boston: Beacon Press.

Ong, A. (1999). *Flexible citizenship: The culture logics of transnationality.* Durham, NC: Duke University Press.

Polsky, S. (2004, June 10). College will expect time abroad. *The Harvard Crimson*. Retrieved on February 17, 2005, from http://www.thecrimson.com/article.aspx?ref=502863

Robbins, B. (1998). Introduction, part I: Actually existing cosmopolitanism. In P. Cheah, & B. Robbins (Eds.), *Cosmopolitics: Thinking and feeling beyond the nation* (pp. 1–19). Minneapolis, MN: University of Minnesota Press.

Sassen, S. (2001). *The global city: New York, London, Tokyo* (2nd ed.). Princeton, NJ: Princeton University Press.

Shannon, E. (1995). Reflections on the meaning of study abroad. *Frontiers: The Interdisciplinary Journal of Study Abroad, 1*, Article 5. Retrieved February 16, 2003, from http://www.frontiersjournal.com/issues/vol1/vol1-05_Shannon.htm

Strauss, A., & Corbin, J. (1998). *Basics of qualitative research: Techniques and procedures for developing grounded theory* (2nd ed.). Thousands Oaks, CA: Sage Publications.

Van Hoof, H., & Verbeeten, M. (2005). Wine is for drinking, water is for washing: Student opinions about international exchange programs. *Journal of Studies in International Education 9*, 42–61.

Wagner, K., & Magistrale, T. (1995). *Writing across culture: An introduction to study abroad and the writing process*. New York: Peter Lang.

Wallerstein, I. (2004). *World systems analysis: An introduction*. Durham, NC: Duke University Press.

Weis, L., & Fine, M. (2004). *Working method: Research and social justice*. New York: Routledge Falmer.

Whalen, B. (1996). Learning outside the home culture: An anatomy and ecology of memory. *Frontiers: The Interdisciplinary Journal of Study Abroad, 2*, Article 1. Retrieved February 16, 2003, from http://www.frontiersjournal.com/issues/vol2/vol201_Whalen.htm

CHAPTER 6

The Effects of College on African Americans' Volunteer Experiences After Graduation

Lamont A. Flowers

Abstract: Data analyzed from the Baccalaureate and Beyond Longitudinal Study indicated that hours spent engaging in volunteer activities during college had small, yet negative, significant effects on the amount of time that African Americans spent volunteering four years after college. The statistical results also indicated that African Americans who majored in social science and business were more likely to volunteer than African Americans who majored in science and engineering.

Each year, many individuals in the United States volunteer to help other people, community organizations, and schools achieve important goals (Hayghe, 1991; Johnson, Beebe, Mortimer, & Snyder, 1998; United States Department of Labor, 2007). According to Wilson (2000), volunteering refers to "an activity in which time is given freely to benefit another person, group, or organization" (p. 215). Other researchers have described volunteering as an experience in which individuals provide tangible and intangible resources for others without compensation (Hayghe, 1991; Musick, Wilson, & Bynum, 2000; Sergent & Sedlacek, 1990). Studies have also shown that volunteers serve in several ways to assist citizens as well as social and political institutions in pursuing purposeful endeavors (Hayghe, 1991; Jayson, 2004). Moreover, volunteers expend considerable energy to provide services for a variety of people as well as donate their time and resources in some capacity to accomplish particular objectives (Simon & Wang, 2002). Additionally, volunteers contribute financial and other resources for the betterment of society by engaging in specific helping behaviors to achieve special and meaningful aims.

National data suggests that college students and college graduates constitute the largest percentage of volunteers in America (Astin & Sax, 1998; Ingels, Curtin, Kaufman, Alt, & Chen, 2002; Johnson, 2004; Knox, Lindsay, & Kolb, 1993; Sax & Astin, 1997; United States Department of Labor, 2007). Hayghe (1991) analyzed nationally representative data in 1989 and reported that "Education is apparently another important determinant of volunteering. Adults with a college degree are much more likely to do volunteer work than those with fewer years of schooling" (p. 18). In a more recent report by the National Center for Education Statistics (NCES) entitled, *Coming of Age in the 1990s: The Eighth-Grade Class of 1988 12 Years Later* (Ingels et al., 2002), findings showed that individuals who had completed a Bachelor's degree were nearly twice as likely to volunteer in a youth organization than were individuals who did not pursue postsecondary education. Statistical findings from the same NCES study showed that individuals who had completed a Bachelor's degree were more likely to volunteer in civic or community organizations than were individuals who did not pursue a postsecondary education.

Moreover, three other national studies have demonstrated the impact of college attendance on volunteering. Each study was based on data from the Current Population Survey (CPS), a survey of households conducted by the Bureau of Census in conjunction with the Bureau of Labor Statistics (United States Department of Labor, 2007). In each CPS study, a volunteer was defined as an individual who performed work without remuneration for an organization (e.g., schools, youth organizations, non-profit groups). In the first CPS study (United States Department of Labor, 2003), of the more than 63 million people who performed volunteer work at least once during September 2002 to September 2003, data showed that persons who had a Bachelor's degree volunteered 12 more hours a year than persons whose highest level of educational attainment was a high school diploma or equivalent (60 median annual hours and 48 median annual hours, respectively). In the second study, of the nearly 65 million people who volunteered in some way during September 2003 to September 2004, data showed that persons who had a Bachelor's degree volunteered 10 more hours a year than persons whose highest level of educational attainment was a high school diploma or equivalent (United States Department of Labor, 2004). In the third CPS study (United States Department of Labor, 2005), data revealed that college graduates were still more likely to volunteer their time than persons who did not attend college (55 median annual hours and 48 median annual hours, respectively). Another national study also had similar results (United States Department of Labor, 2007).

Research and national data has also informed our understanding of racial differences in volunteering (Musick et al., 2000; Stoll, 2001; United States Department of Labor, 2003, 2004, 2005, 2007). For instance, Hayghe (1991) found that Whites were more likely than African Americans to perform volunteer work. Table 1, highlighting CPS data collected in 2003, 2004, and 2005, shows marked racial differences in volunteering behaviors. As shown in Table 1, African Americans were less likely than Whites to volunteer in 2003, 2004, and 2005. However, among the individuals who volunteered in 2003, Table 1 showed that both African Americans and Whites spent approximately the same amount of time a year volunteering (52 median annual hours). In contrast, in 2004 and 2005, African Americans spent more time volunteering than Whites. Table 2 further highlighted racial differences in volunteering experiences. More specifically, these data indicated that in 2003, 2004, and 2005 Whites were more likely than African Americans to volunteer in two, three, four, and five or more organizations. However, in contrast to the research findings discussed in this section, Stoll (2001), analyzing data from the 1993–1994 Los Angeles Survey of Urban Inequality, found that the African Americans in his study participated in more voluntary associations than did other racial and ethnic minority groups.

Table 1. Volunteers by Selected Characteristics, 2003, 2004, 2005, and 2006

Characteristics	2003			2004			2005			2006		
	Number	% of Pop.	Median Annual Hours	Number	% of Pop.	Median Annual Hours	Number	% of Pop.	Median Annual Hours	Number	% of Pop.	Median Annual Hours
Educational Attainment[a]												
Less than a high school diploma	2,793	9.9	48	2,718	9.6	40	2,837	10.0	48	2,615	9.3	50
High school graduate, no college[b]	12,882	21.7	48	12,709	21.6	50	12,594	21.2	48	11,537	19.2	52
Less than a bachelor's degree[c]	15,966	34.1	52	16,414	34.2	52	16,452	33.7	50	15,196	30.9	52
College graduates	23,481	45.6	60	23,880	45.7	60	24,517	45.8	55	23,808	43.3	55
Race												
African American	5,145	20.0	52	5,435	20.8	56	5,879	22.1	52	5,211	19.2	52
White	55,572	30.6	52	55,892	30.5	52	56,170	30.4	50	52,850	28.3	52

Note. Table adapted from Volunteering in the United States, 2006, published by the Bureau of Labor Statistics in the US Department of Labor. Numbers in thousands.

aData refer to persons 25 years and over.

bIncludes high school diploma or equivalent.

cIncludes the categories "some college, no degree" and "associate degree."

Table 2. Volunteers by Number of Organizations for which Volunteer Activities Were Performed and Selected Characteristics, 2003, 2004, 2005, and 2006

Characteristics	Total Volunteers	One	Two	Three	Four	Five +	Not Reporting No. of Orgs
2003							
Educational Attainment[a]							
Less than a high school diploma	2,793	87.2	9.5	2.1	.5	.5	.3
High school graduate, no college[b]	12,882	78.0	15.4	4.5	1.1	.7	.2
Less than a bachelor's degree[c]	15,966	69.9	19.4	7.2	2.0	1.4	.2
College graduates	23,481	59.5	23.4	10.4	3.7	2.6	.3
Race							
African American	5,145	80.5	13.5	3.4	1.3	1.1	.3
White	55,572	68.0	19.7	7.9	2.5	1.7	.3
2004							
Educational Attainment[a]							
Less than a high school diploma	2,718	88.2	8.1	2.3	.5	.8	0
High school graduate, no college[b]	12,709	78.0	15.6	4.2	1.4	.6	.2
Less than a bachelor's degree[c]	16,414	69.8	19.4	7.1	2.3	1.2	.2
College graduates	23,880	60.1	23.4	10.1	3.7	2.5	.3
Race							
African American	5,435	77.2	15.4	4.0	1.5	1.4	.4
White	55,892	68.4	19.9	7.4	2.6	1.5	.2
2005							
Educational Attainment[a]							
Less than a high school diploma	2,837	88.1	8.6	2.4	.5	.3	.1
High school graduate, no college[b]	12,594	78.3	15.3	4.0	1.3	.8	.2
Less than a bachelor's degree[c]	16,452	70.3	18.8	7.2	2.1	1.4	.3
College graduates	24,517	59.8	23.4	9.9	3.8	2.8	.3
Race							
African American	5,879	77.9	13.9	5.2	1.4	1.2	.4
White	56,170	68.3	19.7	7.3	2.6	1.9	.3
2006							
Educational Attainment[a]							
Less than a high school diploma	2,615	87.2	9.3	2.2	.8	.3	.2
High school graduate, no college[b]	11,537	77.0	16.1	4.3	1.3	1.0	.3
Less than a bachelor's degree[c]	15,196	70.5	19.0	6.8	2.3	1.2	.2
College graduates	23,808	59.3	23.9	10.3	3.5	2.7	.3
Race							
African American	5,211	75.7	14.7	5.3	2.3	1.3	.7
White	52,850	67.3	20.5	7.7	2.5	1.7	.3

Percent Distribution of the Number of Organizations for which Volunteer Activities were Performed

Note. Table adapted from *Volunteering in the United States, 2003, Volunteering in the United States, 2004, Volunteering in the United States, 2005,* and *Volunteering in the United States, 2006* published by the Bureau of Labor Statistics in the United States Department of Labor. Numbers in thousands.
  °Data refer to persons 25 years and over
  ᵇIncludes high school diploma or equivalent
  ᶜIncludes the categories "some college, no degree" and "associate degree"

§

We also know from research that racial differences exist among college student volunteers. Balenger and Sedlacek (1993) found that African American students were more likely than White students to express that they were interested in participating in volunteer activities while in college. Consistent with the Balenger and Sedlacek study, data analyses from the Baccalaureate and Beyond Longitudinal Study showed that African American students who graduated in 1993 were more likely than White students to participate in community service or volunteer activities during their senior year (see Table 3). Of those students who volunteered during their senior year, the data revealed that African American students also spent more time engaging in volunteer activities than White students. Furthermore, based on additional data analyses from the Baccalaureate and Beyond Longitudinal Study, descriptive statistics showed that four years later in 1997, African American college graduates were more likely than White college graduates to report that they had participated in volunteer work. Additionally, as shown in Table 4, African American college graduates spent more time volunteering on average than did White college graduates.

Table 3. Percentage Distribution of 1992–1993 Bachelor's Degree Recipients, by Volunteer Experiences and Race

	Volunteer Experiences		
	Performed Volunteer Work		Average Hours of Volunteer Work
	Yes	No	
Race			
African American	57	43	7
White	45	55	6

Note. U.S. Department of Education, National Center for Education Statistics, 1993/1997 Baccalaureate and Beyond Longitudinal Study, Second Follow-up, (B&B: 1993/1997), Data Analysis System.

§

Table 4. Percentage Distribution of 1992–1993 Bachelor's Degree Recipients, by Volunteer Experiences and Race in 1997

	Volunteer Experiences		
	Performed Volunteer Work		Average Hours of Volunteer Work
Race	Yes	No	
African American	47	53	13
White	43	57	12

Note. U.S. Department of Education, National Center for Education Statistics, 1993/1997 Baccalaureate and Beyond Longitudinal Study, Second Follow-up, (B&B: 1993/1997), Data Analysis System.

§

The extant data and research highlighting racial differences in volunteer experiences clearly showed that while African Americans were less likely than Whites to volunteer among the general population, African American college students and graduates were more likely than White college students and graduates to volunteer. Viewed collectively, these data suggest that college attendance plays a major role in African Americans' volunteer experiences. Accordingly, what remains to be discovered is the extent to which personal factors, institutional variables, and student involvement experiences impact African Americans' volunteer experiences after college. Stated differently, additional research is needed to explore how the impact of institutional control and other important factors such as students' precollege characteristics, institutional type, students' academic experiences, and nonacademic experiences in college influences participation in volunteer activities for African American college graduates.

REVIEW OF RELATED LITERATURE

The literature base that provides the scholarly context for this study can be

1. research examining the reasons why college students volunteer;
2. research that examines the impact of volunteer experiences on student development; and
3. research that explores the effects of college on volunteer experiences.

Research investigating the factors that impact college students' willingness to engage in volunteer work sheds light on the primary rationales that college students employ when deciding to serve as a volunteer or participate in community service (O'Brien, Sedlacek, & Kandell, 1994; Winniford, Carpenter, & Grider, 1997). This line of research suggests that particular demographic characteristics, environmental factors, and student involvement experiences influence college students to volunteer (Astin, Sax, & Avalos, 1999; Balenger & Sedlacek, 1993; Sergent & Sedlacek, 1990; Winniford et al., 1997). Overall, this line of research indicated that students engage in volunteer and community service to satisfy their need to help others, contribute to society, and develop vocational skills. Another important finding of this empirical research, consistent with national data (e.g., CPS, National Education Longitudinal Study of 1988), is that college graduates are more likely to participate in volunteer activities than persons with less educational attainment (Hayghe, 1991; Ingels et al., 2002; Knox et al., 1993).

Regarding the second type of research reviewed for this study, the weight of evidence indicates that college students who participate in volunteer experiences report higher academic and affective outcomes than non-volunteers do (Astin & Sax, 1998; Astin et al., 1999; Sax & Astin, 1997). Surdyk and Diddams (1999), in a study of 185 college graduates, found that volunteer experiences resulted in enhanced occupational status attainment. Overall, this research suggested that volunteer experiences provide college students with a sense of accomplishment and satisfaction that positively contributes to their cognitive and psychosocial development in college. Another line of research has focused on the influence of college on post-college volunteer experiences. This line of research indicated that college attendance positively influences volunteer experiences after graduation (Hayghe, 1991). Data from the National Education Longitudinal Study of 1988 (Ingels et al., 2002) showed that college graduates were twice as likely to participate in volunteer experiences as individuals who did not pursue a postsecondary education (25% and 12%, respectively). Astin et al. (1999), in a longitudinal study, found that participation in volunteer experiences in college had a positive effect on students' post-graduate participation in volunteer experiences. Furthermore, Knox et al. (1993) also found that educational attainment was positively and significantly related to participation in volunteer work after college. Also, findings from Winniford et al.'s study (1997) of college graduates from more than thirty-one institutions in the Appalachian region indicated that participation in volunteer and community organizations on campus positively impacts the degree to which college graduates participate in service-related activities. In contrast to these findings, Vogelgesang and Astin (2005) found, based on a national study of former undergraduates, college graduates become less likely to participate in volunteer activities after graduation.

PURPOSE OF THE STUDY

While the previous research literature on the effects of college on volunteer experiences contributes to our understanding of the influence of college on students' post-college volunteer experiences, the present study seeks to extend the previous research in this area by focusing on the extent to which student characteristics, institutional characteristics, college experiences, and after-college experiences influence African American college graduates to participate in volunteer activities. Toward that end, the purpose of this study was to estimate the direct effects of college attendance on time spent on volunteer experiences after graduation on a nationally representative sample of African American college graduates. Accordingly, data from the 1993/1997 Baccalaureate and Beyond Longitudinal Study (B&B: 1993/1997) were utilized to estimate the direct effects of factors influencing student development and educational outcomes on volunteer experiences for African American college graduates.

THEORETICAL FOUNDATION

For many years, scholars have promulgated and debated views regarding the underlying structures, motivations, and rationales to explain why, how, and to what degree persons participate in volunteer activities (Musick et al., 2000). In an article by Wilson (2000) which discussed scholarly ideas presented over the years to explain why people volunteer, he noted that individuals volunteer for a variety of reasons such as personal attributes, interpersonal resources, and by making rational choices involving tangible and intangible resources. Among the many theories and variables utilized to explain why people devote their time to participate in volunteer activities, Wilson focused heavily on the degree to which an individual's human capital accounts for differences in volunteer experiences.

Human capital refers to physical and conceptual resources (e.g., information, values, skills, etc.) which can be exchanged in a variety of settings and environments for desirable experiences and outcomes (Becker, 1993; Schultz, 1971). Educational attainment (formal and informal) has been viewed as one of the most significant investments an individual can make to accumulate higher levels of human capital (Becker, 1993). A detailed description and thorough discussion of the predictive nature of this theory is abundant in the research literature (Becker, 1993; Knox et al., 1993; Schultz, 1971) and suggests that individuals with a college education are more likely to participate in volunteer activities than those individuals who did not attend college.

Because the present study focused on college graduates, and given a substantial amount of research that seems to support the view that individuals make decisions based on their financial, educational, and other resources, human capital theory is a useful concept to better understand the nature of volunteer activity. Additionally, human capital theory helps to explain why individuals with higher incomes and more education participate in more volunteer activities (Wilson, 2000). Furthermore, the national study of volunteering conducted by the United States Department of Labor (2007) also supports this contention, because these data show that people who are employed full-time are more likely to volunteer and spend more time engaging in volunteer activities than people who work on a part-time basis. The importance of human capital theory in explaining volunteer behavior is also supported by data from Tables 1 and 2, which clearly indicate that educational attainment is associated with the amount of time people spend volunteering. Moreover, Wilson (2000) advanced the view that human capital theory helps to explain racial differences in volunteering.

In light of the fact that the present study is interested in examining the effects of college on the volunteer experiences of African American college graduates, it seems plausible that to ground this investigation solely on the basis of human capital theory would constitute a severe limitation in this research. In contrast, this discussion also considers the role of altruism in explaining why individuals volunteer. In the past twenty years, increased research has addressed the impact of altruism on helping behaviors and volunteering (Rushton & Sorrentino, 1981; Wakefield, 1993; Winniford et al., 1997). According to Wakefield, altruism is demonstrated by helping individuals or groups for the exclusive purpose of benefiting particular individuals or groups. This operational definition of altruism and the research that surrounds this concept suggests that some individuals engage in volunteer activities for the purposes of contributing to the personal and social development of other individuals, organizations, and/or institutions. Given the research on the influence of religion and spirituality for African American students (Constantine, Miville, Warren, Gainor, & Lewis-Coles, 2006; Constantine, Wilton, Gainor, & Lewis, 2002; McEwen, Roper, Byrant, & Langa, 1990; Walker & Dixon, 2002), it is reasonable to infer that perhaps some African American students who volunteer may do so altruistically in an attempt to improve the plight and conditions of others in a manner consistent with their spiritual beliefs. Accordingly, subsequent sections of this manuscript recognize the potential relevance of altruism as an additional explanatory framework to provide the necessary context for this study.

METHOD

Data Source

Student and institutional data for the present study was drawn from the Baccalaureate and Beyond Longitudinal Study (B&B: 1993/1997) (Green, Myers,

Veldman, & Pedlow, 1999). B&B: 1993/1997 is a nationally representative, longitudinal study designed to measure the impact of a wide-array of individual-level factors and institutional-level characteristics on academic achievement, social growth, post-college education experiences and outcomes, and career attainment. The student cohort, who constituted the primary sampling unit in B&B: 1993/1997, was based on the 1993 National Postsecondary Student Aid Study (NPSAS). The NPSAS is a nationally representative database designed to study how college students and their parents or guardians finance the costs of higher education. Using NPSAS 1993 as the base-year cohort, the B&B: 1993/1997 student cohort consisted of a representative sample of approximately 11,162 graduating seniors. The following data were collected from the base-year cohort:

1. precollege characteristics and background information,
2. institutional characteristics,
3. parent data, and
4. student transcript data (Green et al., 1999).

To provide some adjustment for potential sample bias caused by nonresponse and disproportionate probabilities of sample selection in the sample of students and schools selected, sample weights were developed.

First Follow-Up and Second Follow-Up Data Collection of B&B: 1993/1997

Consistent with the base-year sample design, the first follow-up data collection resurveyed base-year students in 1994 (1 year after the base-year data collection) to obtain information pertaining to their post-undergraduate transition experiences. In addition, data were collected on students' marital status and graduate education experiences. Of the approximately 11,000 students who participated in the base-year survey, approximately 10,000 students participated in the first follow-up data collection (Bradburn & Berger, 2002; Green et al., 1999). In 1997 (4 years after the base-year data collection) students were resurveyed to obtain additional information about their post-undergraduate experiences to determine how those experiences influenced important work-related outcomes (Bradburn & Berger, 2002; Green et al., 1999). Of the students who participated in the base-year follow-up data collection, approximately 10,000 students participated in the second follow-up data collection. In the present study, data from 205 African American students were analyzed (154 females and 51 males). This particular sample, employing the weight variable from the B&B: 1993/1997 data, represented approximately 24,000 African American students who graduated from college in 1997.

Methodological Framework

The methodological framework for this study was based on numerous investigations of research on the effects of college on student development, educational outcomes, and labor market outcomes (Astin, 1993; Chickering & Reisser, 1993; Pascarella & Terenzini, 1991, 2005). Overall, this body of research suggests that at least four sources of influence must be considered in attempting to understand the impact of college on student outcomes. These sources of influence were:

1. precollege characteristics,
2. institutional characteristics,
3. students' academic experiences in college, and
4. students' nonacademic experiences in college (Pascarella & Terenzini, 1991, 2005; Terenzini, Pascarella, & Blimling, 1996; Terenzini, Springer, Pascarella, & Nora, 1995).

As such, the methodological framework in this study was based, in part, on the notion that student outcomes were a function of precollege characteristics and background factors, institutional characteristics, academic factors, and nonacademic factors. The methodological framework for this study was used to select appropriate variables to include in the analytical model to estimate the effects of college on time spent volunteering after graduation.

Figure 1. Methodological Framework of the Study

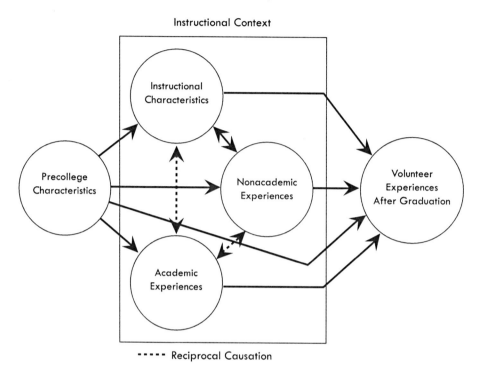

VARIABLES

Dependent Variable

This study sought to assess the impact of college on African American college graduates' volunteer experiences. Thus, the dependent variable was measured by the amount of time African American college graduates spent pursuing volunteer activities. Accordingly, the dependent variable utilized in the study was a continuous variable based on African Americans' self-reports of the number of hours spent volunteering after college ($M = 12$, $SD = 14$).

Independent Variables

Based on the methodological framework and existing research, this study incorporated a number of independent variables. The first set of independent variables consisted of students' precollege characteristics:

1. age,
2. gender,
3. parents' educational attainment, and
4. income.

The second set of variables consisted of characteristics of the institution:

1. institutional control,
2. student enrollment, and
3. college racial composition (i.e., attended a HBCU or a PWI).

Students' academic experiences constituted the third set of independent variables:

1. college major and
2. grade point average.

Students' nonacademic experiences in college constituted the fourth set of independent variables:

1. hours spent working per week in college and
2. hours spent volunteering during the senior year in college.

Precedent for using these independent or predictor variables to estimate the influence of college can be found in other research investigations estimating the impact of college attendance on student outcomes (Astin et al., 1999; Pascarella & Terenzini, 1991, 2005). Operational definitions of the dependent and independent variables are shown in Table 5. Selected descriptive statistics of the dependent and independent variables are reported in Table 6.

Table 5. Operational Definitions of Variables from the B&B: 1993/1997

DEPENDENT VARIABLE

Average Hours Spent Volunteering After College: A continuous variable based on a college graduate's self-report of the number of hours spent volunteering after college.

INDEPENDENT VARIABLES

Precollege Characteristics

Age: A continuous variable based on a self-reported measure of the student's year of birth.

Gender: A categorical variable was coded: 1 = female; 0 = male.

Parent's Educational Attainment: A categorical variable based on the highest educational level attained by either parent was coded: 1 = Less than high school; 2 = High school graduate or equivalent; 3 = Some college; 4 = Associate's degree; 5 = Bachelor's degree; 6 = Master's degree; 7 = Advanced degree (e.g., Doctoral degree, and/or First-Professional degree).

Income: A continuous variable based on a student's total family income._

Institutional Characteristics

Institutional Control: A categorical variable was coded: 1 = Attended a public institution; 0 = Attended a private institution.

Student Enrollment: A continuous variable based on the full-time student enrollment during the 1992–1993 academic year.

College Racial Composition of the Institution: A categorical variable was coded: 1 = Attended a historically Black college and university; 0 = Attended a predominantly White institution.

Academic Experiences

College Major: A categorical variable based on a student's self-report of his or her major in college was coded: 1 = social science and business (e.g., humanities, social/behavioral sciences, education, business/management); 0 = science, engineering, and other (e.g., life sciences, physical sciences, math, computer/information science, engineering, health, vocational/technical, other technical/professional).

Grade Point Average: A continuous variable based on a student's cumulative grade point average. The grade point average was reported by the institution and was based on a 4.0 scale.

Nonacademic Experiences

Hours Per Week Spent Working: A continuous variable based on a student's self-report of the number of hours worked per week in the senior year.

Average Hours Spent Volunteering During College: A continuous variable based on a student's self-report of the number of hours spent volunteering during the senior year.

Analytical Techniques

Employing ordinary least squares regression, the dependent variable was regressed on the entire set of independent variables (Pedhazur, 1997). Because the sampling procedures utilized to construct the B&B: 1993/1997 sample were based on complex sampling procedures (Bradburn & Berger, 2002; Broene & Rust, 2000), *AM Statistical Software* was used to analyze all data using the appropriate weight variable and design effects variables, based on the guidelines outlined in the *Baccalaureate and Beyond Longitudinal Study: 1993/97 Second Follow-Up Methodology Report* (Green et al., 1999). Due to the fact that the small unweighted sample size decreased statistical power and increased the likelihood of making a Type II error, results were reported significant at $p < .10$ (Hays, 1994).

Table 6. Selected Descriptive Statistics for the African American College Graduates in the Sample

Dependent Variables	Mean	Standard Deviation
Average Hours Spent Volunteering After College	12	14
Independent Variables		
Age	25	7
Family Income	$32,148	$29,001
Student Enrollment	10,877	10,258
Grade Point Average	2.78	.55
Hours Spent Working	18	15
Average Hours Spent Volunteering During College	5	8

RESULTS

In this study, I estimated the direct effects of college on the amount of time that African Americans spent volunteering after college. Controlling for an extensive set of independent variables, African Americans' volunteer activities were significantly impacted by the amount of time they spent engaging in volunteer activities during college. More specifically, the study showed that the amount of time African Americans spent pursuing community service and volunteer activities during their senior year in college negatively impacted the amount of time they spent volunteering after college ($B = -.13, p < .10$). Also, the results showed that college major played a role in the number of hours African American college graduates spent volunteering four years after graduation. Students who majored in social science-related disciplines and business spent more time volunteering than their peers who majored in science, engineering, and technical/professional disciplines ($B = 3.23, p < .10$).

The limitations of this research study which may impact the generalizability of the study's findings include the following:

1. the institutional sample did not include all postsecondary institutions;
2. the student sample may not reflect the volunteering experiences of all African American college graduates because only data from graduates of four-year institutions were analyzed in the present study; and
3. some of the data used in this study were based on information reported by the student (Anaya, 1999; Pike, 1995, 1996).

Furthermore, there may have been other precollege characteristics, institutional characteristics, and college experiences that were not included in the regression model that may have also explained additional variance in time spent on volunteering for African American college graduates such as precollege volunteer experiences.

DISCUSSION

The primary aim of this study was to estimate the effects of an array of precollege characteristics, institutional characteristics, college experiences, and post-undergraduate experiences on the amount of time African Americans spent volunteering after college. Accordingly, a variable indicating the extent to which African Americans engaged in volunteer experiences four years after college was regressed on a host of independent variables that have been shown to impact college student outcomes in general and volunteer experiences in particular (Astin et al., 1999; O'Brien et al., 1994; Pascarella & Terenzini, 1991, 2005). The results of this study revealed that volunteer experiences in college significantly influenced time spent volunteering after college for African Americans. Moreover, it was found that participation in community service and volunteer activities during college was negatively related to the amount of time African Americans participated in volunteer activities after college. Descriptive data from this study also revealed, however, that African American college graduates reported that they spent twice as much time participating in volunteer activities after college as they did while in college (12 hours and 5 hours, respectively). Given these findings, it suggests that additional research is needed to probe this issue and examine African American college students' volunteer experiences as well as African American college graduates' volunteer experiences to further investigate the study's findings. It should also be noted that the findings from the present study were somewhat consistent with a national study conducted by researchers at the Higher Education Research Institute at the University of California, Los Angeles (Vogelgesang & Astin, 2005) which showed that, based on data from more than 8,000 persons who completed a survey in 2004 (six years after completing an initial freshman survey), college graduates were less likely to participate in volunteer activities after graduation than while they attended school.

In light of other national studies on the effects of college on volunteer experiences after college, this study's primary finding is noteworthy and requires additional research to further explore this topic. For example, in another national study involving more than 12,000 students, Astin et al. (1999) examined data from the Cooperative Institutional Research Program (CIRP) to determine whether the effects of volunteer experiences during college had persistent and enduring effects after college. Employing multivariate analyses, results from the Astin et al. study indicated that volunteer experiences during college positively influenced the amount of time that students engaged in volunteer experiences after college. More specifically, they reported the following result:

> Although the simple correlation between these two variables is quite modest ($r = .22$), how much a student volunteers during college can clearly have a substantial effect on how much that student volunteers after college. Thus, spending six or more hours per week in volunteer work during the last year of college, as compared to not participating in volunteer work, nearly doubles the student's chances of being engaged in volunteer work in the years after college, and more than doubles his or her chances of spending either one, three, or six plus hours per week in postcollege volunteer/community service work. (p. 195)

Astin et al.'s findings further supports the need to expand service learning opportunities and experiences in higher education as well as increase the number of volunteer programs available to college students. However, despite the significance of the Astin et al. study, data from the present study showed that for African American students, the impact of college volunteer participation was negatively related to after-college volunteer service. This particular finding from the present study suggests that while African Americans still volunteer at high levels after college, perhaps there are factors inherent within or specific to their volunteer experiences and educational outcomes in college that may impact the time spent engaging in volunteer experiences after college. If this is true, student development professionals should begin thinking about how this is likely to occur and what personal, social, and institutional characteristics may be influencing African Americans' post-college volunteering behaviors.

Also, the present study found that college major played a role in African American students' volunteer experiences after college. While the present study included college major (not occupation) in the analyses, this particular finding seems inconsistent with Surdyk and Diddam's (1999) study of 185 college graduates, which found that occupational type did not significantly impact volunteer participation rates. The other major finding of this study is that no other variable utilized in this study significantly impacted volunteer experiences after college for African American students. This particular finding indicated that precollege characteristics (e.g., gender), institutional characteristics (e.g., college racial composition), and academic experiences (e.g., grade point average) did not substantially influence after-college volunteer experiences for African Americans. Given the small sample size in the present study, additional research is needed to confirm and extend these results.

IMPLICATIONS FOR PRACTICE AND FUTURE RESEARCH

In light of the continual need to prepare future leaders, democratic citizens, and volunteers in our diverse and multicultural society, this study is important in that it sought to explore the impact of college attendance on the extent and magnitude of African American college graduates' participation in volunteer experiences. The goals of this research resonate with Boyer's (1987) contention that "[i]n the end, the quality of the undergraduate experience is to be measured by the willingness of graduates to be socially and civically engaged" (pp. 278–279). Also, because prior research has indicated that racial and ethnic minority groups are least likely to volunteer in community organizations (Hayghe, 1991; United States Department of Labor, 2003, 2004, 2005, 2007), this study is extremely important in helping to identify the factors that may influence African American college students to participate in volunteer organizations after graduation.

The findings from this study shed light on the primary indicator of volunteer experiences for African American college graduates. Thus, this study will permit researchers and institutional leaders to begin thinking of ways to facilitate the recruitment and retention of African American volunteers at the local, state, and national levels. One approach to begin this effort might be to connect to and explore the volunteer experiences of African American college students in an attempt to better understand the quality of these experiences. Furthermore, higher education and student affairs researchers as well as student affairs professionals should survey and interview African American students and conduct in-depth analyses that would deeply investigate African American students' perceptions of volunteering in order to examine African American students' plans for long-term volunteer service after college. By employing these approaches, quantitative data as well as qualitative data would exist that could shape interventions and related programs designed to ensure that African American students' volunteer experiences might lead to continued volunteer service after college. Moreover, in light of the study's findings, future research should investigate the effects of college on African American students' civic participation and voting practices during and after college. These future studies will be of interest to higher education and student affairs researchers and may ultimately lead to additional research that will continue to explore how higher education is serving the public good.

References

Anaya, G. (1999). College impact on student learning: Comparing the use of self-reported gains, standardized test scores, and college grades. *Research in Higher Education, 40*, 499–526.

Astin, A. W. (1993). *What matters in college: Four critical years revisited.* San Francisco: Jossey-Bass.

Astin, A. W., & Sax, L. J. (1998). How undergraduates are affected by service participation. *Journal of College Student Development, 39*, 251–263.

Astin, A. W., Sax, L. J., & Avalos, J. (1999). Long-term effects of volunteerism during the undergraduate years. *The Review of Higher Education, 22*, 187–202.

Balenger, V. J., & Sedlacek, W. E. (1993). Black and White student differences in volunteer interests at predominantly White universities. *NASPA Journal, 30*, 203–208.

Becker, G. S. (1993). *Human capital: A theoretical and empirical analysis, with special reference to education.* Chicago: University of Chicago Press.

Boyer, E. L. (1987). *College: The undergraduate experience in America.* New York: Harper & Row.

Bradburn, E. M., & Berger, R. (2002). *Beyond 9 to 5: The diversity of employment among 1992–93 college graduates in 1997* (NCES 2003-152). Washington, DC: U.S. Department of Education.

Broene, P., & Rust, K. (2000). *Strengths and limitations of using SUDAAN, Stata, and WesVar PC for computing variances form NCES data set* (NCES 2000–03). Washington, DC: U.S. Department of Education.

Chickering, A. W., & Reisser, L. (1993). *Education and identity* (2nd ed.). San Francisco: Jossey-Bass.

Constantine, M. G., Miville, M. L., Warren, A. K., Gainor, K. A., & Lewis-Coles, M. E. L. (2006). Religion, spirituality, and career development in African American college students: A qualitative inquiry. *The Career Development Quarterly, 54*, 227–241.

Constantine, M. G., Wilton, L., Gainor, K. A., & Lewis-Coles, E. L. (2006). Religious participation, spirituality, and coping among African American college students. *Journal of College Student Development, 43*, 605–613.

Green, P., Myers, S., Veldman, C., & Pedlow, S. (1999). *Baccalaureate and Beyond longitudinal study: 1993/97 second follow-up methodology report* (NCES 1999-159). Washington, DC: U.S. Department of Education.

Hayghe, H. V. (1991). Volunteers in the U.S.: Who donates the time? *Monthly Labor Review, 114*(2), 17–23.

Hays, W. L. (1994). *Statistics* (5th ed). Fort Worth, TX: Harcourt Brace College.

Ingels, S. J., Curtin, T. R., Kaufman, P., Alt, M. N., & Chen, X. (2002). *Coming of age in the 1990s:*

The eighth-grade class of 1988 12 years later (NCES 2002-321). Washington, DC: U.S. Department of Education.

Jayson, S. (2004, December 9). Building on volunteerism: Young people increasingly are giving of themselves. *USA Today*, p. 10d.

Johnson, D. I. (2004). Relationships between college experiences and alumni participation in the community. *The Review of Higher Education, 27*, 169–185.

Johnson, M. K., Beebe, T., Mortimer, J. T., & Snyder, M. (1998). Volunteerism in adolescence: A process perspective. *Journal of Research on Adolescence, 8*, 309–332.

Knox, W. E., Lindsay, P., & Kolb, M. N. (1993). *Does college make a difference? Long-term changes in activities and attitudes*. Westport, CT: Greenwood Press.

McEwen, M. K., Roper, L. D., Byrant, D. R., & Langa, M. J. (1990). Incorporating the development of African American students into psychosocial theories of student development. *Journal of College Student Development, 31*, 429–436.

Musick, M. A., Wilson, J., & Bynum, W. B. (2000). Race and formal volunteering: The differential effects of class and religion. *Social Forces, 78*, 1539–1571.

O'Brien, K., Sedlacek, W. E., & Kandell, J. J. (1994). Willingness to volunteer among university students. *NASPA Journal, 32*, 67–73.

Pascarella, E. T., & Terenzini, P. T. (1991). *How college affects students: Findings and insights from twenty years of research*. San Francisco: Jossey-Bass.

Pascarella, E. T., & Terenzini, P. T. (2005). *How college affects students (Vol. 2): A third decade of research*. San Francisco: Jossey-Bass.

Pedhazur, E. J. (1997). *Multiple regression in behavioral research: Explanation and prediction* (3rd ed.). Orlando, FL: Harcourt Brace College.

Pike, G. R. (1995). The relationships between self-reports of college experiences and achievement test scores. *Research in Higher Education, 36*, 1–22.

Pike, G. R. (1996). Limitations of using students' self-reports of academic achievement measures. *Research in Higher Education, 37*, 89–114.

Rushton, J. P., & Sorrentino, R. M. (Eds.). (1981). *Altruism and helping behavior: Social, personality, and developmental perspectives*. Hillsdale, NJ: Lawrence Erlbaum Associates.

Sax, L. J., & Astin, A. W. (1997). The benefits of service: Evidence from undergraduates. *Educational Record, 78*, 25–32.

Schultz, T. W. (1971). *Investment in human capital: The role of education and of research*. New York: Macmillan.

Sergent, M. T., & Sedlacek, W. E. (1990). Volunteer motivations across student organizations: A test of person-environment fit theory. *Journal of College Student Development, 31*, 255–261.

Simon, C. A., & Wang, C. (2002). The impact of Americorps service on volunteer participants: Results from a 2-year study in four western states. *Administration & Society, 34*, 522–540.

Stoll, M. A. (2001). Race, neighborhood poverty, and participation in voluntary associations. *Sociological Forum, 16*, 529–558.

Surdyk, L. K., & Diddams, M. A. D. (1999). Doing well by doing good: Career attainment and volunteerism. *Journal of Volunteer Administration, 17*(2), 11–24.

Terenzini, P. T., Pascarella, E. T., & Blimling, G. S. (1996). Students' out-of-class experiences and their influence on learning and cognitive development: A literature review. *Journal of College Student Development, 37*, 149–162.

Terenzini, P. T., Springer, L., Pascarella, E. T., & Nora, A. (1995). Influences affecting the development of students' critical thinking skills. *Research in Higher Education, 36*, 23–39.

United States Department of Labor. (2003). *Volunteering in the United States, 2003*. Retrieved May 9, 2006, from http://www.bls.gov/news.release/archives/volun_12172003.pdf

United States Department of Labor. (2004). *Volunteering in the United States, 2004.* Retrieved May 9, 2006, from http://www.bls.gov/news.release/archives/volun_12162004.pdf

United States Department of Labor. (2005). *Volunteering in the United States, 2005.* Retrieved May 9, 2006, from http://www.nationalservice.gov/pdf/volunteer_study_05.pdf

United States Department of Labor. (2007). *Volunteering in the United States, 2006.* Retrieved November 11, 2007, from http://www.bls.gov/news.release/pdf/volun.pdf

Vogelgesang, L. J., & Astin, A. W. (2005). *Post-college civic engagement among graduates.* Los Angeles: University of California, Los Angeles, Higher Education Research Institute.

Wakefield, J. C. (1993). Is altruism part of human nature? Toward a theoretical foundation for the helping professions. *Social Service Review, 67,* 406–458.

Walker, K. L., & Dixon, V. (2002). Spirituality and academic performance among African American college students. *Journal of Black Psychology, 28,* 107–121.

Wilson, J. (2000). Volunteering. *Annual Review of Sociology, 26,* 215–240.

Winniford, J. C., Carpenter, D. S., & Grider, C. (1997). Motivations of college student volunteers: A review. *NASPA Journal, 34,* 134–146.

CHAPTER 7

"To Share With All:"

VIDA SCUDDER'S EDUCATIONAL
WORK IN THE SETTLEMENTS

Julia Garbus

Abstract: Vida Scudder, a progressive-era professor and activist, created community programs to share her intellectual inheritance. The first, College Extension, teaching "high" culture to immigrants, was ultimately unsuccessful and undoubtedly condescending. However, in the long-lasting, successful Circolo Italo-Americano, Italian immigrants and Americans met for debates, concerts, parties, and lectures. Italian newcomers and long-time Bostonians governed the group together. The Circolo fostered cross-cultural friendship and mutual learning.

In a speech during Smith College's 25th anniversary celebration, alumna Vida Dutton Scudder championed the idea that college-level education or "intellectual privilege" should be available to everyone, uniting society instead of dividing it:

> We can tolerate no fixed class of the intellectually privileged; we demand that our colleges and universities be in the truest sense centers of democracy, and that from them proceed ceaselessly influences seeking to share with all, the gifts which they impart.... Learning itself, alas, acts too often as a dividing rather than a uniting force, adding to all other distinctions that final, most inexorable distinction between the literate and illiterate. (as cited in McManus, 1999, p. 118)

When she made the speech, Scudder had spent two decades trying to make colleges "centers of democracy" and creating programs to "share with all" the gifts her Smith experience had given her. In this article I introduce Vida Dutton Scudder, describe and critique the educational programs she started at her settlement house, and use her experiences to suggest principles that may apply today. I rely on archival materials such as daily records from Denison House and letters Scudder wrote, as well as Scudder's memoirs, novel, and articles. I have also consulted secondary materials from fields such as history and rhetoric.

Radical educator, tireless activist, and accomplished orator, Scudder (1861–1954) was a triple threat to the turn-of-the-century's complacent elite. Scudder wrote of her life, "I was perpetually drawn in three directions at once, and racked in consequence" (Scudder, 1937, p.175). "The calm college world," her first direction, provided her salary (Scudder, 1937, p. 175). Both in her Wellesley classroom and across the college campus, she emphasized social justice themes and taught women to be effective, committed citizens, agents of social change. In articles and speeches, she urged college-educated women to use their academic skills for the good of their communities. Her work linking academic study with settlement work created an historical antecedent for one innovative, currently popular way of connecting academia and community work: service learning.

Scudder's second direction, "the tumultuous world of social reform," claimed her attentions as much as teaching (Scudder, 1937, p. 175). In the first half of her life, she concentrated her energies on settlement houses—comprehensive neighborhood centers in urban ghettoes, mostly staffed by college-educated, upper-middle-class women. She and her friends, calling themselves the College Settlement Association, founded some of the country's first settlements. Scudder's home settlement, Denison House, was in Boston's South End. Although Scudder never lived there, remaining with her widowed mother, she helped run the settlement and many of its programs. Scudder's experience working among the poor inspired her to become "ardently and definitely a socialist" (Scudder, 1937, p. 161). This radicalism eventually alienated her from her settlement colleagues. After leaving settlement work, she spent 42 years concentrating her activism within the Episcopal church, forming social justice organizations and arguing that socialism and Christianity were complementary. Finally, "in time jealously snatched from other matters" (1937, p. 180) Scudder produced a staggering number of books and magazine articles exhorting educated readers to work for an equitable society.

A well-known whirlwind of activity in her lifetime, Scudder now is usually relegated to footnotes. The only settlement worker to whom scholars devote detailed attention is Jane Addams. As for scholarship in education, Gerald Graff (1987) calls Scudder "one of the great neglected figures of English studies" (p. 335), yet only two articles about her in this context has appeared. In the theological arena, being a socialist Anglican woman ensured Scudder's obscurity outside of the Episcopal Church during her life. For instance, the arguments in Scudder's (1912) *Socialism and character* parallel—but extend—those of her still-famous friend Walter Rauschenbusch. Scudder's unique theology, fortunately may now garner some attention because of Elizabeth Hinson-Hasty's 2006 book *Beyond the social maze: The theology of Vida Dutton Scudder* and Gary Dorrien's discussion in his ambitious series *The making of American liberal theology: Idealism, realism, and modernity 1900–1950.*

Each of Scudder's three paths merit study. Scudder and her colleagues created the most radical settlements in the country, publicly aligning themselves with labor and striving to combat public scorn or paternalism about poor immigrants. Her educational innovations include developing the first course about socialist themes in literature; linking classroom work with community work; soliciting student suggestions for topics; and the community ventures I discuss here. Both her theology itself and her strong influence within her denomination during her lifetime warrant the attention they are finally receiving.

Furthermore, Scudder's lifelong struggle to connect academia and activism offer inspiration for college instructors today who want to responsibly combine community work and scholarship. As historian Peter Frederick (1976) writes, "Her story reveals the often painful process of the professor who seeks to balance a professional obligation to the pursuit of learning with a personal commitment to social and political activism" (p. 115). Indeed, Scudder's troubles merging academics and activism parallel the perils facing contemporary academics committed to social change work. Scudder grappled with the challenging issues of the extent and basis of the elite's responsibility to improve society, of colleges' responsibilities to their communities and of relations between server and served. In a 1999 *College English* article, Ellen Cushman pointed out that many conceptualizations of the public intellectual envision a public composed of middle- to upper-middle-class policymakers, administrators, and professionals, not the local community. Citing a growing pressure for intellectuals to contribute to a more just social order, Cushman advocated a different kind of public intellectual: one who combines her research, teaching, and service efforts in order to address social issues important to community members and under-served neighborhoods. One hundred years before Cushman wrote her article, Scudder strove to exemplify Cushman's public intellectual.

Her learning curve was painful, though. As Cushman (1999) notes, public intellectuals "need to first understand that what they count as art and political choices does not necessarily match what community members count as art and political choices" (p. 334). Scudder's first venture, "College Extension," imposed her taste in art upon community members who eventually refused to accept it.

After a painful year of reflection about settlements' purposes and efficacy, Scudder changed course. She then formed the Circolo Italo-Americano (Circolo) with an Italian friend.

"Eradicating a Distinction"?

Settlements had come into being not primarily as sites for food distribution, day care, or emergency services but because of educated people's desires to share their intellectual riches with the poor. Early settlers truly believed that by "eradicating the distinction between the literate and the illiterate," as Scudder put it in her Smith College speech, they could best set immigrants on the path to becoming the kinds of citizens settlers privileged. Stanton Coit patterned his Neighborhood Guild, the first American settlement, partly on Frederick Denison Maurice's Working Men's College in London (Davis, 1967). (Scudder and her mother both revered Maurice, a Christian Socialist clergyman in the 1850s.) Jane Addams and Ellen Starr began teaching and lecturing at Hull House as soon as it opened. Starr organized a group that read George Eliot, Dante, Browning, and Shakespeare; another settler started a Sunday Afternoon Plato Club to discuss philosophical questions (Davis, 1967). The University of Chicago offered college credit for the courses.

One program seen as successful at the time took place a mile away from Denison, in Boston's North End. Mrs. Quincy Agassiz Shaw established the Civic Service House in 1901 to promote civic and educational work among immigrants. Several of the staff had been involved in settlement activities as children, such as Meyer Bloomfield, who had attended classes at New York's University Settlement, and Philip Davis, a Russian immigrant whose love of learning started at Hull House. The men organized clubs and classes, helped immigrants learn English, and encouraged them to join trade unions.

In 1905 Frank Parsons, a Boston University law professor, started the Breadwinner's College at Civic Service House. It offered adult men courses in history, civics, economics, philosophy and psychology in which the works of James, Santayana, and Royce were discussed, taught by their own Harvard students. In addition to Parsons, Bloomfield, and Davis, instructors included Ralph Albertson, an itinerant reformer who had organized a failed Christian Commonwealth in Georgia, and Harvard and Boston University students, including Walter Lippman. Apparently the teachers liked to mix "a little radical social thought" with their explications of Longfellow and Emerson (Davis, 1967, p. 41). Breadwinner's College offered a diploma at the end of two years. Some graduates became government workers: a judge, a Department of Labor official, and an assistant attorney general. Parsons soon realized, however, that Breadwinner's students, no matter how enthusiastic and talented, graduated to face uncertain job prospects with no expert guidance. Therefore, he developed a new field, vocational counseling, and wrote the first book on the topic (Davis, 1967).

"A Rare Opportunity"?

For the first ten years of Denison House's existence, Scudder tried to impart "the joy and freedom of higher learning" through her College Extension program (College Settlements Association, 1896, p. 5) for immigrant "neighbors," as settlement workers ("settlers") called the ghetto residents living near their settlement houses. A woman could attend "to improve herself," to experience "the pleasure of interesting studies," and to find joy in poetry. Scudder offered seemingly practical courses as well (Scudder, 1895, n.p.). Students could take writing to learn to "write letters easily and correctly" and spelling because "bad spelling is a great disadvantage in practical life" (Scudder, 1895, n.p.). Because "American women ought to know something of the story of their land," Scudder offered American history (Scudder, 1895, n.p.). Finally, she showed her political leanings, offering a course in trade unions: "What they have done, what they mean, what they want to do" (Scudder, 1895, n.p.). No homework for the courses was necessary.

Many of Scudder's ambitions matched her goals for her Wellesley students as well as for Denison settlers, for whom she created reading lists and tried to start discussion groups. Scudder sought to expand students' horizons by introducing them (in person or through literature) to members of other classes and races; to foster appreciation for certain authors; and, ultimately and most importantly, to transform everyone inwardly, producing a classless Christian society. During College Extension's existence, she also had goals specific to poor, uneducated neighbors, often Irish: "to share our intellectual inheritance" (Scudder, 1902, p. 817). The word "our" encompassed settlers and other established Anglo-Saxon Americans, and "intellectual inheritance" meant the newly developing literary canon and other European works then seen as masterpieces.

In addition, she saw College Extension programs as a means to "interpret" different classes and nationalities to each other—to create an idealized version of what English professor Mary Louise Pratt (1991) calls "the contact zone," "a social space where disparate cultures meet, clash, and grapple with each other" (pp. 34–40). Immigrant students could interact with settlers and "meet" literary texts. Scudder herself tried to be the interpreter; she wrote articles in newspapers and the *Atlantic Monthly* detailing her experiences with immigrants.

In her autobiography and her settlement house novel, Scudder referred to immigrant women by their nationalities: a Russian Jewish woman, an Irish laundry worker (Scudder, 1937, p. 225). In her announcements for the programs, she assimilated them instantly by calling them American women. The difference suggests that although she wanted the women to see themselves as Americans, she actually thought of them as representatives of their respective countries (Scudder, 1937).

Throughout the 1890s, College Extension offered similar courses yearly. Scudder taught some courses, introducing immigrant women to her beloved poets; settlers taught other classes, and undergraduates taught a few. Men could take courses, too, although Scudder's students seem to have been women only. Scudder reminisced in her autobiography that the future president of Smith College, William Allen Neilson, taught a Shakespeare course for men while a Harvard graduate student (Scudder, 1937). Another course, among whose students was labor leader Jack O'Sullivan (Carrell, 1981), was made up of, in Scudder's words, "labor men who wanted to understand what poetry had done for the labor movements and who hope to find in Burns and Shelley some refreshment from their hard practical work" (Scudder, 1895, n.p.). O'Sullivan's wife, labor activist Mary Kenney O'Sullivan, took a course on Dante (Scudder, 1895, n.p.). Another settler taught the proto-feminist "Women Worth Knowing" course, featuring, among others, Deborah, Cleopatra, Mary Stuart and Elizabeth Barrett Browning (College Settlements Association, 1906, p. 35). Teachers and students met occasionally for evenings of talk, music, and readings (College Settlements Association, 1896, n.p.).

Theatre at Denison provided another way for settlers to teach immigrants about English masterworks. Men's dramatics clubs at Denison put on abridged versions of Shakespeare plays, with men playing the female parts. "Portia, by Jack Cronan, was a beautiful piece of work. The disguise was complete, and the lines were rendered with much expression and good judgment," one newspaper article reported (Converse, n.d. [b], n.p.). Hull House had similar programs. The Henry Street Settlement in New York, too, offered courses in art, music, and theatrical performance, often slated to promote social change. Its Neighborhood Playhouse Theatre put on innovative performances including an anti-lynching drama by the grandniece of the abolitionist Grimke sisters (Sharer, 2001).

Unfortunately, the only glimpse of what went on in classes comes from Scudder, not from students or even other teachers. The way Scudder and the other College Extension teachers described their students makes one wonder whether students found them respectful, patronizing, or an odd mix of the two. In her autobiography, Scudder never *overtly* condescended. "I grew to care in a special way for some of the working girls in my little classes. I shared my beloved poets with them in a manner quite different from those possible in college classes" she wrote, leaving one wondering what was different about her presentation and the students' responses at Denison (1937, p. 146). She also discussed immigrant students in different terms than she used for college women. The word "little" pops up often; the working girls in her "little classes" (Scudder, 1937, p. 146) read "a little Shelley, and a little Wordsworth, and a little Tennyson, and a little Browning" and copied poems into a "little book" (College Settlements Association, 1896, p. 19).

When Scudder reported her adult students' accomplishments she almost gloated, as if displaying diamonds in the rough that she and the other College Extension teachers had discovered:

> The class in Poetry "couldn't see why people think Browning hard." The teacher of the class, having surreptitiously noted all the questions asked by a grave professor in a college graduate seminary [sic], put them to her working-girls, and triumphantly reported that they answered much better than the graduates. Indeed, the instinctive sense for poetry of these girls is remarkable (College Settlement Association, 1896, p. 19).

Here Scudder spoke in terms of her working students' instincts, whereas when she discussed Wellesley students, she emphasized the students' hard work, and her own. The distinction evokes a Romantic idea of the child as *tabula rasa*, keenly and intuitively perceptive. Interestingly, although here she focuses on the immigrant students and not her own pedagogy, when she discusses college teaching in her autobiography she made "avaunt" [boasted] of her own effectiveness and popularity (1937, p. 114). In the draft manuscript of the autobiography in the Smith College Archives, someone—perhaps Scudder herself, perhaps her companion, Florence Converse—has written on the margin of the teaching chapter, "Insert some humility—Balance—don't purr!"

Scudder also used words like "unspoiled" when she spoke of immigrants, as if she thought them purer and closer to God because of their lack of education, like the Romantic concept of children: "The lack of training is compensated for to a certain degree by unspoiled intuitions, and a poetic sensitiveness in artistic and literary lines rare in more highly trained students. If you cannot turn out scholars, you can make happier women" (College Settlements Association, 1897, p. 20). Scudder loathed paternalism and condescension, but she never escaped it herself.

Yet Scudder's own "[u]nconscious snobbism," as Mina Carson put it, pales next to the lack of respect and the stereotyping of other settlers (1990, p. 104). A Wellesley alumna living at the settlement, Caroline Williamson (1895), wrote, "It was interesting to find that they had intelligent ideas on theme-writing and Shakespeare" (p. 237). Williamson expressed surprise that some of her students "showed a keenness of insight in literary interpretation and criticism which many a college student might envy" (p. 238). Williamson also felt guilty: "A bachelor of arts felt that she had not improved her opportunities, when she saw the avidity with which the girls who worked ten hours a day could seize a chance to study Ruskin, Shakespeare, Wordsworth, or Homer" (p. 238). Master stereotyper Florence Converse, running a dramatics club for young men, reported that although she did not know whether "the Russian Jew, or the Italian, or the German, or the Syrian," would thrive on dramatics, for "the Irish boy" Shakespeare was "the best text book," teaching "English, and History, and Patriotism, and Courtesy" (Converse, n.d. [a], n.p.).

Whether College Extension was successful depends on how one defines success. Scudder barely mentioned the program in her memoirs, and never discussed why she stopped participating in it after 1901. The number of students taking classes, however, increased throughout the 1890s. In October 1894, College Extension offered a Shakespeare reading class on Wednesday evenings, two literature classes on Fridays, and lectures by Scudder on Saturday nights; by 1901, there were 10 classes and 109 students. In the 1895–1896 CSA Annual Report, Scudder wrote that the classes "were a great pleasure alike to teachers and scholars" (College Settlements Association, 1896, p. 15).

The next year, though, her report sounded disappointed. She even, atypically, disparaged her students: "You cannot make scholars out of people whose chief nerve force is given to manual work all day long. You must take them as they are, ignorant and immature" (College Settlements Association, 1897, p. 20). By the late 1890s, in fact, the College Extension program incurred criticism from within and without. Some other settlers thought it unrealistic to teach literature and art to people with such difficult lives, and neighbors themselves began requesting more skill-oriented classes (McManus, 1999). In Scudder's 1903 novel *A Listener in Babel*, a caustic settler expressed Scudder's own doubts about College Extension's value to exploited workers:

> The topics will be chosen with a view to the popular mind...I think the most valuable course will be on the History of Art. The class will be exposed alternately to photographs from the most dislocated of the old masters and to glaring chromos. Differences will be explained and tests of appreciation applied. Any expression of wandering thoughts will be severely reprimanded. Most of the class will be in a state of uncertainty concerning their food or shelter for tomorrow; some of them will have left hungry families at home. It will be a rare opportunity for them to practice concentration of mind and detachment from material things (Scudder, 1903, pp. 127–128).

In early 1901, Scudder collapsed from exhaustion and spent a year recuperating in Italy. While there, she wrote a series of articles for the *Atlantic Monthly* recounting her experiences fostering cross-class fellowship. They are a record of thoughts as she mulled over the failures and successes of her settlement work in light of her goals, exhorted her upper-class readers to value immigrants, and tried half-heartedly to justify her former approach while searching for new ideas and approaches. In "Democracy and Education" (1902) she reflected on College Extension. It is disappointing, she wrote, that popular movements to bring "what education may be" to busy workers have not been totally successful. It is hard to get through to exhausted laborers, she continued. Lecturing is difficult because working people are tired out, and "all arts of delivery" are needed to "carry across the invisible leagues that separate the speaker and the hearers" (p. 818). Such talks, then, should only last an hour and be clear-cut, well-put, and interesting; the speaker must steer between "the Scylla of obscurity" and "the Charybdis of childishness" (p. 818). She should be vivid, pictorial, and emotional. "Be brief; be clear; be coherent. Be dignified; be pictorial; be impassioned," Scudder exhorted. Even an excellent lecturer, though, will "reach two or three listeners" only (p. 819).

The lack of common ground posed one problem. "On what grounds shall we try to meet? It is painfully evident that uneducated people do not naturally like the same things as the children of privilege" (1902, p. 820). But while Scudder realized that people's tastes depend on their class and education level, she still believed there were "wholesome, universal and enduring" works of art that all classes could enjoy (p. 820). For example, she reported that boys enjoyed Homer's *Odyssey* and everyone liked Shakespeare. Of course, her own privileged class was the one making these determinations of universality—a point Scudder never acknowledged. She insisted that the uneducated, without guidance, liked "nothing good," favoring "cheap music, vulgar chromos, and so on" (pp. 820–821).

Informal contact in settlements offered better chances for intellectual fellowship than lectures, Scudder concluded. When people spend time together, she wrote, there develops a "natural unity of consciousness" so that "intellectual fellowship between people of different traditions will probably crystallize" (1902, p. 820). Real change occurs not through improved educational systems or formal personal contact, but through "a genuine living of the common life" (p. 822). Then, "small groups, rarely numbering more than a dozen, will gather around some lover of art, history, literature, to share his delights" (p. 820). The "probably" and "will gather" hint that these hoped-for outcomes had not materialized at Denison by 1902; in fact, Scudder confessed, "we see as yet only faint beginnings of what we desire" (p. 820). Of course, that Scudder was writing to a distinctly non-radical audience, *Atlantic Monthly* readers. Rhetorically astute, she chose not to reveal her conviction that only through socialism would everyone would live the common life; she simply implied that under current conditions, truly educating immigrants was impossible.

When Scudder returned to the United States in 1902, longtime Denison resident Bertha Scripture had taken over College Extension. The Irish who lived near the settlement in its early years had moved to the suburbs, replaced by

Italians, Syrians, and Chinese (Corcoran, 1973). In 1903 an Educational Center had opened in South Boston that offered industrial classes. Consequently, College Extension attendance declined, though Scudder continued to offer literature courses (McManus, 1999). In 1904, she turned her attention to Boston's Italians.

Scudder's goals for College Extension sound unrealistically rosy. Yet community colleges, which educate 44 percent of the nation's postsecondary school adults, were originally founded in part on the principles that inspired Scudder to offer her program. The first community college opened in 1901—the same year that Scudder stepped down as head of Denison House's College Extension. The men who presided over the early community college movement saw their task as bringing "the blessings of expanded occupational opportunity to the people" (Brint & Karabel, 1989, p. 10). Humanities instruction, they felt, was vital. Before 1970, most community college students agreed. They shunned vocational education, preferring liberal arts courses that might earn them admission to four-year colleges (Brint & Karabel, 1989).

Community colleges, however, began to offer vocational training as well as liberal arts education soon after their founding. The leaders of the movement baldly stated a rationale that would have horrified Scudder though not surprised her. Despite its language to the contrary, these founders said the United States was actually class-stratified, a situation these leaders saw no reason to challenge. Offering community college students hope of a four-year degree when many would not make the grade would give students falsely high hopes, perhaps causing mass discontent. Vocational training, on the other hand, would not only give them marketable skills but also placate them. As James Russell, Dean of Teachers College, Columbia University, put it in 1908, "If the chief purpose of schooling be to promote social order and civic responsibility, how can we justify our practice of schooling the masses in precisely the same manner as we do those who are to be our leaders?" (as cited in Brint & Karabel, 1989, p. 11). The conflict between the different tasks of the community college continues: on the one hand to provide students with a common cultural heritage and educate them to be thoughtful citizens, as Scudder hoped College Extension would do; on the other, to promote economic efficiency, keep the masses in their place, and respond to the demands of employers.

The Clemente Course, a present-day college-level course in the humanities for people living in poverty, is an even more direct analogue to College Extension, though much less prominent than community colleges. Earl Shorris, Clemente's founder, based it on Robert Maynard Hutchins' Great Books courses, which Shorris took at the University of Chicago. The Course teaches moral philosophy, literature, history, art, and writing—which the founders added when they realized that Clemente students panicked about writing. Clemente's Western cultural canon-oriented curriculum makes it vulnerable to charges of cultural imperialism. Yet, Shorris developed and taught a Clemente course in Mexico's Yucatan Peninsula using Mayan cultural works, and one in Alaska has been given using Eskimo texts and in an Eskimo language. In its first eight years Clemente enrolled 1,480 students. Approximately 900 completed the full course of study, 780 earned college credit, and 670 went to four-year colleges and universities (Bard College, 2004).

Shorris's argument for humanities' value to the poor focuses on systemic change as well as individual transformation. Substandard schooling cheats the poor because it gives the humanities short shrift, he argued. Students who study high culture intensively develop reflective thinking capacities; "the humanities teach us to think reflectively, to begin, to deal with the new as it occurs to us, to dare" (cited in O'Connell, 2000, p. 2). He acknowledged that reflective thinking and appreciation for high culture will not automatically transform a poor person's material circumstances: "How can a museum push poverty away? Who can dress in statues or eat the past? The answer was politics, not 'the moral life of downtown.' Only politics could overcome the tutelage of force. But to enter the public world, to practice the political life, the poor had first to learn to reflect" (Shorris, 1997, p. 336).

Shorris hopes that Clemente graduates will go on to challenge societal priorities that relegate poor people to substandard schooling and limited opportunities. However, I have found no information on what Clemente graduates have done post-course or post-college. Are they practicing the political life? We do not have that information—though we could get it, unlike our situation with Scudder's students.

CRITIQUES OF HUMANITIES
TEACHING TO THE POOR

Sinclair Lewis parodied the educational fare in a fictional settlement as "lectures delivered gratis by earnest advocates of the single tax, trout fishing, exploring Tibet, pacifism, sea shell collecting, the eating of bran, and the geography of Charlemagne's Empire" (cited in Davis, 1967, p. 41). His parody exemplifies the most common argument against College Extension type courses: that they were impractical. Historian Allen Davis (1967) noted "an element of the unreal and esoteric about the early settlement workers' attempts to dispense the culture of the universities to workingmen" (p. 41). He concluded that most neighbors were uninterested in extension classes, instead wanting to learn "something useful, concrete, and related to their daily lives, such as manual training, homemaking, the English language, or basic American government and history" (p. 43). Jane Addams herself eventually declared, "[t]he number of those who like to read has been greatly over-estimated" (as cited in Davis, 1967, p. 49).

Even at the Breadwinner's College, with eager students who became successful, "the founders realized that many of their students had problems, such as unemployment or bad jobs, that no course in philosophy or ancient history could solve" (Davis, 1967, p. 53). Davis (1967) implied that Frank Parson's vocational counseling was more useful than his Breadwinner's College teaching. In an award-winning dissertation, Wendy Sharer (2001) repeated the non-practicality critique, writing that the early Hull House classes initially captured the interest of the local neighbors but could not sustain interest because they lacked direct connection to the lives of the immigrant workers.

Some College Extension courses, such as the one where Scudder dictated poetry to the students so they could work on their manual writing skills as they learned about literature, taught practical skills alongside mainstream cultural appreciation. Furthermore, Scudder's (1903) *Babel* parody shows she was aware of the critique. Still, she continued to believe, first, that if she picked the right authors, neighbors would derive the same aesthetic and spiritual benefits from literature that she did; and second, that high aesthetic pleasures were more important than material comforts. Both beliefs are hard to justify, especially since neighbors enjoyed entertainments of their own without the guidance of College Extension. As Ellen Cushman (1999) writes:

> If public intellectuals hope to find and generate overlaps between aesthetics and politics, they need to first understand that what they count as art and political choices does not necessarily match what community members count as art and political choices. Because community members tend to esteem their own brand of knowledge more than popular forms of knowledge, they deepen the schism between universities and communities (p. 334).

Another argument against College Extension is that immigrants did not learn enough, or the right way, by just listening to lectures: "The need for beautiful things could be better satisfied by letting the people themselves create things rather than having them merely look and listen," Allen Davis argues (1967, pp. 48–49). When Scudder headed Denison's Italian Department, however, she created chances for immigrants to make and sell traditional Italian crafts. While Shorris' Clemente students do not create artwork, they do more than look and listen; they are required to study outside of class, write papers, and invest much time and energy on projects.

This commitment of energy, however, brings up another major difficulty of teaching humanities to poor adults. Scudder emphasized the exhaustion her students suffered, even concluding that their harsh living conditions made it impossible for her students to become "scholars" (College Settlements Association,

1896, p. 20). Articles about scholars in the Clemente Course highlight the many different pressures they face: long work hours, sick family members, lack of facility in English, AIDS. Some community college students face such pressures, some do not. It is interesting that other settlement education programs, such as those at Hull House, the University Settlement in New York City, and the Breadwinner's College, did produce some scholars, such as Philip Davis and Meyer Bloomfield (Davis, 1967).

A similar critique is that College Extension required, and Clemente requires, a level of sophistication even at the outset that many would-be participants do not have. As Davis (1967) wrote with stunning condescension, College Extension courses provided "intellectual stimulation for the 'transfigured few' in the neighborhood capable of abstract thought" (p. 43). Community colleges, on the other hand, seem to meet students at the students' own levels, offering basic humanities courses as well as more advanced ones.

In the second decade of Scudder's settlement involvement, she developed another program that she found more rewarding. The Italian-American Circle or the Circolo Italo-Americano, as she preferred calling it, was limited to a hundred chosen Italian and American members with intellectual interests. It held lectures, concerts, debates, and parties. Scudder and the group's Italian co-founder, Francesco Malgeri, aimed to educate Italians and Americans about the gifts the other nationality offered as well as to teach Italian immigrants their civic responsibilities in their new country. Scudder emphasized that she especially wanted Americans to appreciate the new immigrants' contributions. Scudder and Malgeri wrote newspaper articles about Circolo events for those who could not share in the experience.

In 1903 Scudder took Italian lessons from Francesco Malgeri, a recent immigrant. Pointing to her fascination to "a dead Italian," St. Catherine of Siena, Malgeri asked Scudder to turn her attention to live Italians in Boston, "neglected and sadly in need of fellowship" (Scudder, 1937, p. 253). Scudder agreed. She went on to spend ten years working with Boston's Italian immigrants, both as "La Bossa" (her term) of a group of hand-picked, educated Italian and Americans, the Circolo Italo-Americano, and as head of the Denison House Italian Department.

The Italian Department worked with poorer immigrants, providing sewing classes, women's and boys' clubs, relief assistance and visiting, and a circulating library. It ran both English classes for adults and Italian classes for children, so that they would not "lose the tongue of their own country as they acquire that of the new" (College Settlement Association, 1904, p. 33). As a newspaper article of the time noted, "Settlement workers have tried to repossess the young Americanized Italians of their Italian language, and to wake in them a pride in the literature and history of Italy" (Bouve, 1912, n.p.). Like the Labor Museum at Hull-House, the

Italian Department also encouraged immigrants' art and artisan work, organizing a Folk Handicraft Association. The settlement held a large exhibition of Italian painting and sculpture and helped skilled silversmiths and lace makers sell their work (Scudder, 1937).

In her autobiography, though, Scudder focused on the Circolo rather than the Italian Department, calling her Circolo experience "the most exciting, quickening, and fruitful social adventuring I have known" (1937, p. 254). She wrote, "I feel [the Circolo] enriched lives more than any other social activity in which I was ever engaged" (1937, p. 268). In a 1911 *Boston Transcript* (1911) article, she described one major benefit of Circolo activities: increased appreciation for diversity. "Americans scattered through the audience enjoy a unique opportunity to learn what new citizens are really thinking about our bewildering civilization" (1911, n.p.).

Run by both Scudder and Malgeri, the Circolo consisted of about a hundred members, mostly Italians, all either professionals or persons would have had professional careers in Italy but had been "forced here into the industrial world" (Scudder, 1937, p. 257). The group planned "equal interchange of ideas and gifts" between the two cultures, although Scudder wanted to emphasize those of the Italians (Scudder, 1937, p. 257). The club language was Italian; Scudder (1937) poked fun at her own attempts to lead meetings despite an Italian friend's observation that she spoke Latin instead of Italian. In her memoirs she always referred to the group as the Circolo Italo-Americano, not "the Italian-American Circle." The "circle" image evokes unity and equality, and having the club's name in Italian and placing "Italian" before "American" in the name shows the group's emphasis on the immigrants' culture.

The Circolo held lectures, receptions uptown in American homes, spring and summer fests in the suburbs, "musicales," and many Columbus Day celebrations (Scudder, 1937, pp. 259–260). Scudder and the Circolo, at the request of the Italian Consul, even entertained the sailors on an Italian naval ship stationed in Boston Harbor (Denison House Daybook, n.d., n.p.). Sunday afternoon lecture concerts, open to the public, were particularly popular. Scudder (1937) explained, "[T]he hall was usually jammed. We planned for about half an hour of speaking, followed by music. Usually our speakers were Italian; we had no trouble in securing competent persons, who could talk on anything from hygiene to art" (pp. 260–261). Subjects included cultural highlights of Italy—the Coliseum and "Arte Immortale: Pompei"; late Victorian American icons such as Emerson, Lincoln, and Longfellow; criminal anthropology; and standard settlement house assimilationist topics such as "The American Concept of Home" and "Infectious Diseases" (Scudder, 1937, pp. 261–262).

According to Malgeri, inducing immigrants to assimilate required attention to their particular ethnic characteristics. For example, Malgeri stated that Italians like lectures—although Scudder had found them unsuccessful when she tried them during College Extension:

> Until you shall study your immigrants and adopt methods adapted to their status, their mentality, their ethical characteristics, do not ever hope to realize your dream of assimilation. The Italian for instance must be influenced through lectures, music, diversions. Our lecture-concerts have done more good than a thousand set scholastic classes and ten thousand missionary sermons (cited in Scudder, 1937, p. 262).

Another Circolo member, Dr. Luigi Verde, explained his view of the Circolo's *raison d'etre*. An Italian immigrant, he wrote, arrives in the country ignorant of American languages, habits, and customs, without knowing anyone, and either falls in with "bad people" or remains isolated. But when he meets Americans through the Circolo, he begins to understand that he needs to know English, begins to feel affection for America, and becomes more inclined to obey the law—"and so prepares himself to become a worthy citizen" (as cited in Scudder, 1911, n.p.).

Scudder's own version of becoming a worthy citizen differed from others' versions. To some Italian immigrants, she noted, becoming Americanized was undesirable; it meant becoming "impertinent, and headstrong—and vulgar" (Scudder, 1937, p. 254). Meanwhile, as a scholar noted about New York City schools, industrial schools in tenement areas required immigrant students to recite a pledge evoking scary images of plant-like assimilated children: "We turn to our flags as a sunflower turns to the sun. Then we give our heads! And our hearts! To our country! One country, one language, one flag!" (Hendrickson, 2001, p. 102).

Scudder, in contrast, tried to Americanize immigrants according to her own vision of an ideal America, "an Apocalyptic vision" of "what the emergent people might become, when the glory and honor of many diverse nations should have entered through its gates and created its citizenship" (Scudder, 1937, p. 254). Although she used patriotic language when addressing certain audiences, America's actual condition saddened her. In 1904 she wrote a friend, "I…believe our society to be…permeated with injustice and selfishness. Our claim to offer equal opportunity to all is a lie. Our claim to be a Christian civilization is a lie. Our claim to be a land of liberty is a lie. The sooner we know it the better" (cited in Carrell, 1981, p. 333).

Scudder's ideal society transcended nationality; it combined "the best" of the values immigrants brought to the country with Scudder's own progressive, socialist values. She conceptualized assimilation as a two-way process, with "giving and taking on both sides" and a moral tinge: America should encompass a "right and wholesome fusion of the races" (Bouve, 1912, n.p.).

Free speech was an important component of her ideal America. Scudder and Malgeri tried to model democracy through Circolo discussions. She solicited questions for group discussion, as she did in her Wellesley classrooms. Scudder (1937) sought "genuine democratic contacts" (p. 256). To accomplish that, she explained, "I wanted our lecture platform...to welcome speakers of opposing views" (p. 262). In 1937, however, twenty-five years after she nearly had been dismissed from Wellesley because of her speech at the incendiary Lawrence Textile Strike, she wrote dryly that she no longer had illusions about "the free intellectual atmosphere which, as those days I fondly believed, existed in the U.S.A." (p. 262).

Scudder (1937), without success, "tried to press on those people my own synthesis of a socialist and a Christian creed" (p. 264), and encouraged "a free field and no favor" (p. 265) during discussions. In fact, the Circolo Italo-Americano *was* a "contact zone," in Pratt's (1991) words, complete with clashing and grappling. When Italian immigrants arrived in Boston, they often identified most strongly with their own regions or towns, not as simply as "Italians." They also held strong and divided political viewpoints about the Catholic Church and its clerics, socialism, anarchism. Circolo members came from different parts of Italy and different neighborhoods in Boston. As for politics, one particularly heated debate between socialists and anarchists ended when the police arrived with teargas.

Finally, during a Circolo debate between socialist and anarchist groups on "The Social Ideal of the Future," angered anarchists stormed the speakers' platform and plainclothes police resorted to tear gas. After that, Scudder (1937) recalled, the group avoided controversial topics (p. 266). Writing in 1937, scanning her experiences as she tried to understand Mussolini's appeal, Scudder stereotyped Italians as fundamentally unable to handle unfettered expression: "We Americans... tried to encourage free speech. And it couldn't be done—any more than it can be done in Italy today" (p. 265).

Besides lecture-concerts and debates, Scudder and Malgeri sought to educate through printing. Their monthly *Bollettino*, much of which Scudder wrote, included uplifting quotations, reports of meetings, plans for dramatic events, quotations from Ruskin's *Sesame and Lilies*, extracts from Mazzini, instructions to Italians about their civic duties, a "Decalogo" summarizing them, a translation of the "Declaration of Independence," and a convenient digest of laws affecting immigrants (Scudder, 1937, p. 260).

Such Circolo pamphlets as "My Rights in the City of Boston" and "What America Can Give to the Italians" (McManus, 1999, p. 125) emphasized immigrants' entitlements as well as their responsibilities. The leaflets led to the preparation of *a Civic Reader or Handbook for New Americans* used for night courses in Boston. Scudder wrote a chapter called "Our Country" (Corcoran, 1973, p. 149).

One year, Scudder and Malgeri asked Circolo members what they wanted to discuss. She reported many, though perhaps not all, of the responses, ranging from "Deportation: How to Handle It" to "Why in America are Fearfully Multiplied Drunken Men and Women, Churches, and Prisons?" The questions she enjoyed most, in keeping with her own socialist orientation, included "Are American Trusts Preparing the Way for Collectivism?" and "Dogma the Enemy of Freedom" (Scudder, 1937, pp. 263–264). This attempt to involve all group members seems less autocratic than other group activities run by Scudder and Malgeri.

As with her College Extension students, Scudder essentialized her "good Italian friends" in print. She seems to have realized this; at the beginning of the autobiography chapter about the Circolo, she observes, "You could neither idealize the Italians, nor generalize about them" (Scudder, 1937, p. 255). Yet the rest of the chapter continues typecasting them: they had indefinable qualities, perhaps such as can be possessed only by an ancient race," including courtesy and loyalty (p. 256). To be charitable, perhaps one reasons she stereotyped Italians was to convince xenophobic Yankees that they were good to have around. In newspaper and magazine articles, Scudder explained that Italians can be worthy new citizens, with "great gift[s]" to bring 'to our race': their background gives them imagination and enthusiasm, they have natural social gifts, and they are natural orators and artists" (Bouve, 1912, n.p.). The most egregious example of stereotyping boosterism is an anonymous call for settlement volunteers the *Smith College Settlement News* in 1910: "Seeking volunteer worker/resident at Denison to work with Italians—the eager, impetuous, intelligent, responsive Latins from the Sunny South."

Partially aware of her typecasting by 1937, Scudder strove to portray the Circolo as nonhierarchical, involving "equal interchange of ideas and gifts" between Italians and Americans" (p. 259). Yet even in this autobiography she listed a set of unique characteristics she thought Italians possessed—mostly good ones. She also makes it clear she relished her own role as "Presidentessa," or her "pet name, 'La Bossa,'" of the Circolo and proudly cited—in untranslated Italian—a poem written for her (p. 253).

CRITIQUES OF THE CIRCOLO ITALO-AMERICANO

Scholars have interpreted Scudder's experiences with both College Extension and the Circolo according to the scholars' own historical circumstances and historiographical frameworks. For example, in 1967, Allen Davis charged that Scudder "quickly gave up the idea of reaching the Italian peasant" when she organized the Circolo (p. 89). But Davis' book was focused on settlers' efforts to curb urban poverty; he showed less interest in other aspects of settlement work, such as settlers and "neighbors" engagement in mutually beneficial activities such as parties. Writing from a postcolonialist perspective in 1989, Rivka Shpak-Lissak argued that Jane Addams sought to "disarm workers of their class-consciousness and hostility through personal contact, social services, and cultural indoctrination" (pp. 22–23). Pacification accomplished, Addams could "inculcate them with the proper ideas, sentiments, and norms of behavior that the settlement workers considered indispensable for the unification of the social organism and the restoration of social harmony" (p. 37).

Some scholars, such as Shpak-Lissak, see settlements less as beneficent ventures than as attempts to control a huge influx of immigrants through rapid acculturation with upper-middle-class norms at the expense of immigrants' own culture, ethic identity, and language. None of these "social control" scholars have examined the Circolo—or, indeed, any Denison House programs. If they did, they might view the Circolo as a more mutually beneficial, less paternalistic venture than College Extension. Yet Scudder and Malgeri's emphases on influence and assimilation would surely perturb them. In addition, although some Circolo activities, such as debates, involved audience participation, some did not. Instead of a group of people of different nationalities creating knowledge together, "experts"—whether Italian or American—dispensed knowledge to listeners. Also, as mentioned above, despite her self-confessed poor command of Italian at the beginning of the enterprise, Scudder ran the show; she even proudly recalled that her Circolo title was " Presidentessa," or her "pet name, 'La Bossa'" (1937, p. 253).

Why was the Circolo a success when College Extension was ultimately, not? I suggest several reasons. First, paradoxically, it is easier for people to learn when they already have some education. Circolo participants were professionals in the United States or had been in Italy. Community colleges offer many developmental courses to prepare students for "college-level" work, and many educationally prepared students attend two-year colleges to save money, then transfer to four-year schools. College Extension students, on the other hand, had no educational base from which to work.

Scudder discovered that poor immigrant students' extreme poverty posed a formidable barrier to their learning. As a character in Scudder's (1903) settlement novel reflects, "[i]t isn't easy to care much about beauty and all, when you're hungry" (p. 231). Most community college students are probably not living in extreme poverty, though many work full-time while they attend school. Although Clemente students are impoverished, the program differs from College Extension in several important ways: the students make an intensive, multi-year commitment, and they have an incentive: the opportunity to obtain a free degree from a prestigious college when they finish Clemente.

Incentives are important. Scudder's experiences with both programs highlight the fact that people need tangible reasons to expend the time and effort to learn difficult new things. For Scudder's College Extension students, studying the humanities had little point. Scudder claimed that classes in spelling and writing did yield practical advantages, but she never offered examples of such advantages, either in her announcements to prospective students or in her memoirs.

The Circolo, on the other hand, *did* aid its members tangibly. The companionship made members feel more at home in their new country; practicing English and making new friends among American professionals helped this handpicked group of the Italian intelligentsia; lectures and pamphlets educated them in concrete subjects, such as the benefits and responsibilities of being new citizens, that directly affected their lives.

The disparities between Scudder's relative failure with College Extension and success with Circolo shows that the best learning and most enjoyable experiences come when everyone learns from each other, not when one side does the teaching and the other the learning. In College Extension, Scudder taught and the students learned. In her discussion of the Circolo, in contrast, the language of "teacher" and "student" never appears—yet everyone learned.

During the United States' current obsessive conversations about immigration, few have mentioned benefits that immigrants can offer besides cheap labor. Are the culture and customs of citizens of Mexico and Central America, for example, worthless? Scudder would insist that these new immigrants have much to give and that together citizens and newcomers can create new knowledge.

One basic tenet of current-day service-learning is that such reciprocity makes for the best service-learning experiences. In fact, the term "service" in "service-learning" has drawn criticism for the inequality it implies between server and served—a criticism Scudder (1937) anticipated when she wrote, "Sharing' is a noble and democratic word, when it does not degenerate into cant. Between that and 'serving' there was a line...for the term 'Service' carries a possibly implied condescension" (p. 138). In its mutuality, the Circolo approached Scudder's ideal of a post-revolution world when classes would disappear and ethnicity, and gender no longer divide.

A NECESSARY WRECK?

Scudder's own conclusion based on her settlement work was that settlements' effectiveness was minimal; the country needed (her) new paradigm, not earnest social workers:

> the inadequacy of settlements was becoming clearer and clearer...
> social services...were, as they are yet, a magnificent and paradoxical
> spectacle of compunction, compassion, wisdom, trying valiantly to

retrieve the wrecks of civilization, while often not pausing to demand whether such wreck had been necessary (Scudder, 1937, p. 164).

In other words, Scudder realized that the entire settlement enterprise, including its various educational programs, could "amount to precious little" in a country dependent on social stratification, (p. 160). Nor has much changed in one hundred years. We value immigrants for their cheap labor and show little interest in welcoming them, much less learning from them. Immigrants and other members of the "masses" often attend execrable schools and then are ridiculed for failing to learn. Whether or not we come to Scudder's conclusion that socialism is the answer, Scudder's experiences suggest that scattered programs such as the Circolo or Clemente, however enriching they may be for their participants, can do little to lessen the overwhelming inequities in American education.

References

Bard College. (2004). Clemente course in the humanities. *Academics-additional study opportunities*. Retrieved December 18, 2003, from http://www.bard.edu/academics/additional/additional_pop.php?id=204042

Bouve, P. C. (1912, March 10). My good Italian friends. *The Boston Globe,* n.p. Wellesley, Massachusetts: Wellesley College Archives.

Brint, S., & Karabel, J. (1989). *The diverted dream: Community colleges and the promise of educational opportunity in America, 1900–1985.* New York: Oxford University Press.

Carrell, E. P. H. (1981). *Reflections in a mirror: The progressive woman and the settlement experience.* Unpublished doctoral dissertation. Austin, TX: University of Texas Press.

Carson, M. (1990). *Settlement folk: Social thought and the American settlement movement, 1885–1930.* Chicago: University of Chicago Press.

College Settlements Association. (1896). *Excerpts from annual reports.* Cambridge, MA: Radcliffe College, Schlesinger Library.

College Settlements Association. (1897). *Excerpts from annual reports.* Cambridge, MA: Radcliffe College, Schlesinger Library.

College Settlements Association. (1904). *Excerpts from annual reports.* Cambridge, MA: Radcliffe College, Schlesinger Library.

College Settlements Association. (1906). *Excerpts from annual reports.* Cambridge, MA: Radcliffe College, Schlesinger Library.

Converse, F. (n.d. [a]). The Denison Dramatic Club. *Denison House Papers.* Cambridge, MA: Radcliffe College, Schlesinger Library.

Converse, F. (n.d. [b]). The Merchant of Venice. *Denison House Papers.* Cambridge, MA: Radcliffe College, Schlesinger Library.

Corcoran, C.T. (1973). *Vida Dutton Scudder: The progressive years.* Unpublished dissertation, Georgetown University.

Cushman, E. (1999). The public intellectual, service learning, and activist research. *College English,* 61, 328–337.

Davis, A. (1967). *Spearheads for reform: The social settlements and the Progressive movement*

1890–1914. New York: Oxford University Press.

Denison House Daybook. (1890). Boston, MA: Radcliffe College, Schlesinger Library.

Dorrien, Gary. (2006). *The making of American liberal theology: Idealism, realism, and modernity 1900–1950.* Louisville: Westminster John Knox Press.

Frederick, P. (1976). *Knights of the golden rule: The intellectual as Christian social reformer in the 1890s.* Lexington, KY: University of Kentucky Press.

Graff, G. (1987). *Professing literature.* Chicago: University of Chicago Press.

Hendrickson, M. R. (2001). *Role of the New York City settlement houses in the education of immigrant women.* Unpublished thesis, St. John's University.

Hinson-Hasty, E. (2006). *Beyond the social maze: The theology of Vida Dutton Scudder.*

McManus, M. M. (1999). *"From deep wells of religious faith": An interpretation of Vida Scudder's social activism, 1887–1912.* Unpublished dissertation, Graduate Theological Union.

O'Connell, Kristin. (2000). Social transformation in the humanities: an interview with Earl Shorris. *Massachusetts Foundation for the Humanities.* Retrieved December 18, 2003, from http://www.mfh.org/newsandevents/newsletter/MassHumanities/Spring2000/shorris.html

Pratt, M. L. (1991). Arts of the contact zone. *Profession. 91.* 33–40.

Scudder, V. D. (1895*).* A rare educational opportunity. Cambridge, MA: Radcliffe College, Schlesinger Library.

Scudder, V. D. (1896). *College settlements.* Paper presented at the meeting of the Eastern Kindergarten Association, Boston, MA. Northampton, MA: Smith College Archives.

Scudder, V. D. (1902). Democracy and education. *Atlantic Monthly. 89.* 816–822.

Scudder, V. D. (1903). *A Listener in Babel.* Boston: Houghton.

Scudder, V. D. (1911, January 28). Socializing democracy. *Boston Transcript,* n.p. Wellesley, MA: Wellesley College Archives.Scudder, V. D. (1937). *On journey.* London: Dent.

Scudder, V.D. (1912). *Socialism and Character.* Boston: Houghton.

Sharer, W. B. (2001). *Rhetoric, reform, and political activism in United States: Women's Organizations, 1920–1930.* Unpublished dissertation, Pennsylvania State University.

Shorris, E. (1997). *New American blues: The private life of the poor.* New York: Norton.

Shpak-Lissak, R. (1989). *Pluralism and Progressives: Hull House and the New Immigrants, 1890–1919.* Chicago: University of Chicago Press. 1989. 251.

Williamson, C. (1895). Six months at Denison House. *Wellesley Magazine.* 5: 233–239.

CHAPTER 8

College Graduates' Perspectives on the Effect of Capstone Service-Learning Courses

Seanna M. Kerrigan

Abstract: Service-learning has been promoted as a pedagogy in higher education that deepens students' learning by connecting theory to practice, teaching students skills of citizenship, and empowering them through engagement in projects for the common good. Yet little research has taken place to understand the impact that this pedagogy has on college graduates. The purpose of this study was to document college graduates' perspectives on the effect Capstone service-learning courses had on them three years after graduation. Graduates reported enhanced communication and leadership skills, increased community involvement, deeper appreciation of diversity, and furthered career development. The study also includes challenges faced by participants and suggestions for practitioners in the field of service-learning.

With urgent calls in recent years for colleges and universities to take up the role of educating citizens and to re-connect to their mission to serve the public good, service-learning has emerged as a pedagogy with the possibilities of addressing these important issues. This pedagogy is often carried out in academic programs that engage students with community entities to address pressing societal issues. Although educators understand how to design service-learning programs, it has become increasingly important to also study the long-term outcomes associated with participation in these courses.

One of the largest service-learning programs in the nation is the Senior Capstone at Portland State University (PSU). Each year this program requires approximately 3,000 students to participate in a six-credit service-learning course. At PSU, Capstone courses operate in accordance with the definition of service-learning provided by Driscoll et al. (1998), as they are designed to "combine community service activities with explicit learning objectives, preparation, and reflection" (p. 1). Through the reflection process, students make meaning out of the relationship between theory and practical community experiences. In addition, all Capstone courses are designed to address the four learning goals of the general education program at PSU. Specifically, the courses are designed to improve students':

1. critical thinking skills,
2. communication skills,
3. appreciation of diversity, and
4. understanding of social responsibility (including political engagement).

Despite this intentional programmatic design of Capstone courses, there has been no comprehensive research detailing how students experienced the various service-learning dimensions or whether these courses contributed to any specific outcomes after graduation.

The Grantmaker Forum on Community and National Service (GPCNS, 2000) confirmed that this topic of the effect of service-learning courses is of national significance. The group further questioned what we really know "about service as a result of the research that has been done since 1990" (p. i). After conducting an investigation, GPCNS found insufficient data to support conclusions on the question of impact. This is one indication that there is a gap in the literature on service-learning.

REVIEW OF THE LITERATURE

Previous research confirms that the learning objectives for Capstone courses at PSU are reasonable expectations of service-learning experiences. Numerous studies have shown that as a result of service-learning experiences, participants reported enhanced communication skills (Astin & Sax, 1998; Astin, Vogelgesang, Ikeda, & Yee, 2000; Battistoni, 1997; Driscoll, Holland, Gelmon, & Kerrigan, 1996; Jordan, 1994), a greater sense of social responsibility (Astin & Sax 1998; Astin, Sax, & Avalos, 1999; Astin et al., 2000; Battistoni, 1997; Buchanan, 1997; Driscoll et al., 1996; Eyler, Giles, & Braxton, 1997; Gilbert, Holdt, & Christopherson, 1998; Giles

& Eyler, 1994; Ikeda, 1999; Kendrick, 1996; Marcus, Howard, & King, 1993; Sax & Astin, 1996, 1997), a greater appreciation of diversity (Astin et al., 1999; Astin et al., 2000; Battistoni, 1997; Driscoll et al., 1996; Giles & Eyler, 1994; Hesser, 1995; Jordan, 1994; Kendrick, 1996; Marcus et al., 1993; Myers-Lipton, 1996), and enhanced critical thinking skills (Astin et al., 2000; Batchelder & Root, 1999; Battistoni, 1997; Berson, 1998; Gilbert et al., 1998; Hesser, 1995; Kendrick, 1996; Marcus et al., 1993; Wechsler & Fogel, 1995).

However, almost all of the cited studies assessed short-term outcomes (i.e., outcomes measured while the students were still in college). The majority of studies with longitudinal data were connected to the national student databases owned by the University of California at Los Angeles (Astin & Sax, 1998; Astin et al., 1999; Sax & Astin, 1996, 1997). In these studies authors were able to look at student data during the four years of college and compare changes from freshman to senior year. But few studied post-graduation effects. Only the Astin et al. (1999) study included data from students five years after graduation. Once again, this lack of longitudinal data indicates a gap in the research relative to the impact service-learning courses have on graduates after they leave the college environment.

METHODOLOGY

In order to answer the question of how college graduates perceive the impact of Capstone service-learning experiences three years after graduation, a sample population was identified. Twenty PSU graduates who had completed a Capstone course in 1998–99 were chosen to closely mirror the statistics of the PSU student body. The sample included ten women and four "non-traditional" students (i.e., students who were 30 years or older while participating in the Capstone course). Recruitment of men proved to be more difficult than recruitment of women, and three-fourths of the non-traditional students were women. One shortfall of the study was a failure to recruit non-white participants.

Graduates in this sample accurately reflected the programs of study (i.e., majors) at PSU and completed a wide range of Capstone courses. Some courses served inmates, immigrants, or youth. Others addressed women's issues, technology (video production and geographic information systems), engineering design, and regional history. Of the 20 participants, seven took Capstone courses that provided direct service to clients; 11 focused primarily on indirect service to the community (e.g., through the creation of final products that addressed community issues); and the remaining two took courses that were balanced between direct and indirect service.

One-on-one interviews were conducted with each of the 20 participants following guidelines of Creswell (1994), Patton (1990) and Kvale (1996). Questions intended to elicit a deeper understanding of graduates' perceptions of their Capstone experiences. An interview protocol was utilized to ensure consistency across interviews. The protocol began with a concrete question asking students to describe their Capstone and the service work they may have performed in the context of the course. The interview then moved progressively to more personal questions about their community involvement, voting habits, profession, and changes they would have made to their Capstone experience. Participants were also asked to identify any challenges they faced during their Capstone experience. The final question in the protocol allowed participants to discuss any pressing issues that were not specifically asked in the interview.

The researcher and an additional reader participated in separate but identical protocols for interview data analysis set forth by Tesch (1990) and Creswell (1994). Transcribed interviews were read to elicit core topics and cluster them into topical themes. Topical themes were tested against the data and reorganized as necessary. The researcher and reader then compared their thematic findings and confirmed the results.

After the interview data was analyzed and preliminary conclusions reached, a focus group was employed to verify and clarify initial findings (Guba & Lincoln, 1981). Topical themes were shared to confirm for accuracy or expand as warranted. Six of the 20 original participants participated in a follow-up focus group that took place nine months later. This group consisted of three men and three women representing both direct service (tutoring) and indirect service (engineering and history projects). Two of the six were non-traditional students.

Results

A comparison of themes identified by the researcher/reader and focus group participants are presented in Table 1.

Table 1. Themes Identified by Researcher/Reader and Focus Group Participants

Researcher/Reader	Focus Group Participants
Communication	Communication in teams and with clients
Leadership/project management	Leadership • ownership of project • setting goals and deadlines • independent thinking
"Border crossing"/diversity	Working with diverse populations
Career development/ real-world experience	Career development • "real-time learning" • working with clients • working with teams • accountability • ideas for jobs
Involvement in the community (future volunteerism)	Community connection • connection with people, organizations, parts of town • "one person can make a difference" • desire to volunteer • the different "publics" in a community
Suggestions for the future (including criticism/challenges with service-learning) • time • group process • organizational issues	Challenges • time commitment • more choices of courses • dealing with "slackers" • faculty not prepared to facilitate group process/ project management/reflection • learn more about clients before entering service • make sure there is reflection time in class to process orally • no place on Capstone course evaluation to evaluate faculty's ability to facilitate
Lack of political connection	Confirmed political connection for some and not for others

The graduates' descriptions utilized language almost identical to that of the researcher/reader. However, they frequently gave greater detail in predicting the outcomes. The respondents also confirmed the most common challenges present in their service-learning experiences. Focus-group participants' predictions of the outcomes and challenges mirrored the data found in the individual interviews; participants named every one of the outcomes found in the interviews. They also confirmed and further expanded upon the challenges experienced in Capstones.

Topical Themes

Communication. The most common theme found across the interviews was that Capstone service-learning courses furthered college graduates' ability to communicate and listen effectively in collaborative contexts. Sixteen participants remarked that they gained valuable lessons in multiple forms of communication (i.e., interpersonal connections with others, oral presentations, written communication, and visual expression). Graduates who worked in direct-service Capstone courses mentioned refining interpersonal skills more frequently, while graduates working on indirect service projects discussed the enhancement of writing and presentation skills. Participants also articulated gaining specific skills in facilitating meetings, listening, communicating in groups, and conducting public presentations. In addition, they enhanced their abilities to communicate with various populations (e.g., youth, prisoners, professionals in the community, peers). Finally, participants reported learning the value of interactions across disciplinary divisions and negotiating organizational territories in the community. Repeatedly, participants described enhancing their communication skills through working with their peers, sharing information in their groups, and collaborating with community organizations. One graduate shared:

> I learned that I have a really hard time working with other people and sharing information, which was a good experience, because I had always thought I would ...work well in groups. I was challenged...By the end we had learned how to communicate pretty well...and I was never the best writer in the world, [but] my writing skills and research skills just completely bloomed when I did that project. I felt by the end really confident...like I could go back and do that again. Phenomenal skills.

Furthermore, respondents' communication skills were enhanced by the professional context of their Capstones, in which they were challenged to write public documents, utilize technology, and make public presentations.

Leadership. A second and related theme that emerged from the data was that 15 of the 20 participants enhanced their leadership skills. These graduates consistently spoke of gaining confidence in promoting new ideas, leading peer groups, managing project teams, and serving as advocates for others. Graduates repeatedly commented about how Capstone service-learning experiences prepared them to initiate, organize, and complete collaborative projects in their professional lives. Respondents appreciated the opportunity to coordinate professional-level projects that mirrored the "real-world" tasks required of them after graduation. They emphasized how the Capstone taught them to take on leadership roles, rather than study leadership from a theoretical perspective. Many indicated that it was the first time they had been given the opportunity to engage as a leader in their educational process. A software engineer remarked:

> I left [the Capstone] thinking, if a person wanted to go into business, that would be a great class to let somebody [to develop] the skills that they need to be able to consult themselves out in a professional way to run their own business...I mean, it was really comprehensive from start to finish. Especially [as] I went on in my career, it really helped me to be mature in the way of project management.

Community Involvement/Volunteering. The third theme that emerged from the data was a positive attitude toward involvement in their community (reported by 13 of the 20 participants). Men and women equally reported the value of volunteering in their communities. This theme was reflected in clear statements from the graduates about engaging in the community during Capstone courses, continuing volunteering after college, and contributing to the community through professional service. One participant stated:

> I think that a lot of people, a lot of students or young people really want to volunteer but they never really know how to go about it. And so this provided me an opportunity and an excuse to get involved in a volunteer project that was interesting to me, and it was amazing. I've heard people talk about volunteering before and how much it changes your life, but...I didn't realize how much it did until I was doing it and it gave me access to this population that I'd never been involved with but it also really made me feel as if I was important in the world, and in the scheme of things, and that I had a place.

Participants who continued their community involvement after college stated that the primary way they remained involved in the community was through pro bono professional service. When these graduates were first asked if they were involved in the community, their most common answer was "no"—at least not as traditional volunteers. However, over half of the graduates cited their work or professional service activities as contributions that they were proud to offer to the community. Many respondents saw their contribution to the community as an extension of their profession by offering pro bono work. One multi-media specialist noted:

> We do an awful lot of [pro bono work] in my company. Here we do a lot of giving away of the work that we do and our time and effort. We've chosen to do that...we've done some things for the American Red Cross local chapter, done a lot of work with them free of charge. We helped them build an organization website just to get them started because it's a skill that we have and it was something that we just wanted them to be able to do.

Appreciation of Diversity/Border Crossing. The fourth theme that emerged from the data was students' exposure to and deeper understandings of new populations. Eleven participants described this process as a journey of interacting with populations from which they had traditionally been segregated. Participants also became aware of how borders prohibit various individuals from interacting with one another. Therefore, I chose to call this theme *border crossing.* Graduates described some of their most profound learning with regards to this theme.

As participants crossed borders into new domains, they became more aware of the intricacies of social issues, including the challenges facing immigrants, youth, and survivors of domestic violence. Instead of simply learning a broad-stroke theory pertaining to these social issues, respondents experienced the complexities embedded in providing services to various populations. Participants became aware of how borders exist that prohibit people from interacting with one another. Further, participants were not merely polishing existing skills, but rather developing new ways of thinking about diverse populations, the lives of others, the various contexts and constraints impacting others, and their relationships with one another. As one respondent in the focus group stated, she became more aware of "the many publics that constituted the community."

A professional and graduate student in the field of Administration of Justice (AJ) described her Capstone as a powerful catalyst for border crossing as she learned about the youth who live in a lockdown facility. She described:

> In AJ classes or soc. or psych., they just throw numbers at you, they don't really give you individual cases. Whereas when you're working with these kids, these are the numbers and it makes you realize that each child, I mean each of those numbers is affected differently...I mean, you can sit and take months of different classes but until you actually interact with these children you have no idea what you're dealing with, each child's different, and just like the lockdown, like being in it, like when that door clicks, you're stuck there....They can warn you the first time you go...but until you hear that click...you don't really know what you're in for.

She crossed a border that few people cross and found that she:

> had a lot of preconceived ideas about anyone in lockdown. It's a lot easier to write off those numbers…as "oh well, they deserve it.".… Going there and hearing the kids' backgrounds and everything, it kind of forces you to realize that these kids might have choices… but how much did they have?…[I]n a way going there was bad… because when you're listening to the news or something you can't write it off as "they deserve it.".…Then when you look back on whatever kid stuck out in your mind… that did that same crime it's like well maybe their parents were doing this, you know, why are we locking them down, when we should maybe be treating them, 'cause a lot of the kids had drug convictions. It caused you more to think of them as humans, not numbers.

Career Development. The fifth theme that emerged was the impact that Capstone courses had on participants' career development. Although not usually found in service-learning literature, it was one of the most prominent themes to emerge from the data. When talking about the development of their leadership and project management skills, 16 of the 20 graduates reinforced that the Capstone enhanced skills needed to be successful in their chosen fields. In addition, respondents frequently stated that Capstone courses helped clarify their career aspirations and earn recommendations to acquire future jobs. Regarding a recommendation letter from a partnering community organization, one business student stated:

> I was very blown away with how well it was written and it just knocked me out. I showed it to some professionals, including some people in the college, [and they said] "You must have really done an exceptional job.…This is a very good recommendation letter." It was incredible.…What I learned in the Capstone class that really helped me in success for business was [that] you can do a lot more than jobs tell you…just by presenting a decision, presenting plans, presenting information, doing all the research.… You can get promoted pretty quick with your own business plan.

Throughout the interviews and focus group, the graduates credited the Capstone experience with helping them gain skills and confidence to work successfully in their careers. They viewed the Capstone as an important endeavor because it made them responsible and accountable to work with and produce for a customer or client, which was a new experience for a large majority of the students. Many talked about how the Capstone informed the way they supervise others in a professional context.

Lack of Connection between Social and Political Issues. The sixth theme that emerged from the data was a disconnect between the social issues addressed in the Capstone course and their relationship to larger political issues. Interestingly, 17 out of the 20 participants reported voting on a regular basis. Each of the 17 reported voting both before and after participating in the Capstone. Often, respondents cited family expectations as a common reason for voting in such high numbers: "I grew up in [a nearby community], and if I don't go and vote, my parents can see if I'm marked off, if I voted or not....[So], I'm forced to vote, 'cause if I don't I hear it from my dad the next day."

Despite this high degree of self-reported voting, when asked if there was a connection between the community work performed in their Capstone and political issues involved in various campaigns, only seven out of the 20 participants answered affirmatively. Only one-third of these graduates made conceptual connections between the social issues they engaged with in their courses and the political sphere; the other two-thirds did not.

One woman who went on to pursue a master's degree in Administration of Justice made the connection between a local ballot measure and her service site:

> Measure 11 [a mandatory minimum-sentencing law passed by Oregon voters in a ballot measure] is a huge one, with locking kids down that are 16 into the penitentiary....[Youth are] more protected [in the juvenile detention center than] if you put a 15-, 16-, 17-year-old in Oregon State Penitentiary... for a mandatory sentence of seven-and-a-half years....[It] doesn't make any sense to me that you think you're gonna get a productive citizen afterwards....I don't think when they voted that in that people understood that their kids getting in a fight at a party could end up in the penitentiary for seven-and-a-half years....And I'm not a very big political person and I don't understand a whole lot of the realm of voting, I mean I vote, but I don't...understand [how] the whole works, but that one has caught my attention because of working with those kids.

Many participants were surprised that there was even a question related to voting in the interview. One participant said, "I like the environment and I try and vote for people who are gonna protect it, but I don't really see the connection [between the Capstone and political issues]." Another respondent who participated in a Capstone partnered with the Portland school system (which has experienced a ten-year-old funding shortfall due to failures of various ballot measures) stated:

No, [no connection] at all. For us [politics] just wasn't an issue, I don't think....If I remember correctly, there were a couple of women who were involved in politics on their own...they were involved in it before the...class, but the class itself was completely separate from politics.

Findings Related to Gender

In this study both men and women reported the outcomes discussed as enhancing their communication skills, leadership skills, community involvement, understanding of diversity and career development. Interestingly, men and women equally reported the value of volunteering in their community even though women are frequently perceived as the service providers or volunteers for community causes in the United States. However, male and female participants described their most important learning in distinctly different terms. Out of the 10 men interviewed, eight described their most important learning in terms of transferable professional skills they could take with them into the work world such as leadership development, project management, professionalism, group process skills, and self-efficacy. Men also reported learning valuable insights about how to work in teams, motivate others, create timelines, and get things done in professional contexts. One male participant stated that his primary learning was "definitely finding out where I stand and what my skills are with managing people." A mid-level manager expressed that his most important learning was that:

[you] can have a lot more influence than jobs tell you...[by] presenting a decision, presenting plans, presenting information, doing all the research so you actually propose a plan.... You can get promoted pretty quickly with your own plan....[I learned about] leadership....I took a proactive role....I got the ball rolling. Definitely leadership. Definitely proactive role.

In comparison, women described a wider range of outcomes resulting from their Capstone experiences. Women's important reflections were more likely to be related to their engagement with the population they were working with rather than project management and leadership skills. Out of the 10 women interviewed, five said that their most important learning related to insights about diverse populations. Other responses included learning to conduct complex research projects, more about specific social issues, more about the city of Portland, and teaching techniques in a public school classroom. One woman stated:

I certainly became much more culturally aware than I was before....I'm able to advise students better based on my experiences with certain cultures at IRCO

[Immigrant and Refugee Community of Oregon]....I became much more aware of political problems in the world...what the refugee populations [are] and why and when and how, so that helps me also with the background of students that I work with....I also learned more about immigration law....My most important learning was how well I interacted with people of all cultures.

One contributing factor to the differences between males' and females' most important learning may lie in the types of Capstone courses that each chose to complete. Women had selected courses with more direct contact with a wider variety of community members, whereas men had more exposure to community research projects. The contrast in service experiences may account for at least one reason why men and women report different "most important learnings" from their Capstone experiences.

Challenges Reported by Respondents

Participants in the study described six challenges faced in their Capstone experiences at PSU. First, although the process of working in groups contributed significantly to student learning outcomes, it was also the area in which participants voiced their most common concern. Graduates remembered struggling with the interdisciplinary nature of the groups, the varied levels of responsibility taken on by group members (e.g., what to do with "the slacker"), and the challenge of coordinating their schedules with peers.

Second, respondents stated that they wished they had greater time to focus on the project rather than juggling so many demands (including family, jobs, and other courses).

Third, there were relatively few Capstone courses from which to choose in 1997. In any given term, there may have been only 10–15 Capstones offered. As a result, some participants ended up in projects that did not seem to fit into their areas of study or personal interest.

Fourth, there was lack of organization in a few of the Capstone courses. Participants from three different Capstone courses described feeling like "guinea pigs" as instructors juggled course and community partner logistics (including on-site orientations and trainings). Respondents also recommended greater communication with the community partner, as community organizations were not always as involved in providing feedback to the participants as they had wished.

Fifth, students disliked the structure of journal writing in these courses. Frequently, the graduates referred to the journals as logs recording "time on task" rather than as reflective assignments to help make meaning from their experience.

Finally, focus group participants suggested better faculty training in facilitating student groups. Several respondents reported feeling thrown into the group setting with virtually no support, especially when there was a communication breakdown between group members.

Discussion

Limitations and Suggestions for Future Studies

The primary limitation of this study is the size of the sample. While 20 subjects was ideal for a qualitative study examining the lived experiences of graduates, the size limits the author's ability to make broad generalizations about most college graduates' engagement in service-learning courses. One significant flaw within the small sample size was the absence of ethnic minorities in the study. No ethnic minorities responded to the invitation to participate in the study. PSU is a predominantly Caucasian campus (only 18% of the population identify as an ethnic minority), but more effort needs to take place in the future to recruit non-white respondents. Since there has not been sufficient research on how various ethnic groups have experienced service-learning experiences, there is no hypothesis on how the lack of minorities impacted the outcomes of this research. This is an area ripe for future exploration.

Moreover, future studies are needed to deepen our understanding of the impact that service-learning has on graduates' civic and political engagement. Missing in this study was a question asking students to define "political" or "civic" engagement and how they believe they could demonstrate their political beliefs in the world. Researchers need to better understand college students' perceptions of their responsibility to serve the "public" and their relationship to this notion of public good. For example, studies on graduates' civic engagement could include assessments of beliefs beyond voting, such as the value placed on contributing to the public good, community organizing, participation in public dialogues, conflict resolution, understanding of political processes, analysis of public policies, "boycotting" and "buycotting" products based on their means of production, and other types of civic actions. These measures could help the field of higher education assess whether graduates take political action in their communities, the various ways they do engage, and how they understand the concepts such as political engagement and contributing to the public good.

Throughout the literature on service-learning, authors traditionally report the outcomes associated with participation in service-learning courses, but rarely do researchers examine the data for the different ways these experiences may impact men and women. This study offers preliminary evidence that gender differences may, in fact, play a role in the long-term outcomes of service-learning experiences.

Finally, this study discovered that graduates who were involved in Capstone service-learning courses tended to donate their time to their community by contributing high-level pro bono professional skills (e.g., engineering, high-tech, multi-media design, teaching, coordination of international community events) to local non-profit and governmental agencies. Literature in the field has not focused on the topic of *how* college graduates contribute to the community. These initial findings may serve as a guide to examine whether there is a national trend for service-learning participants to serve their communities in high-skilled pro bono work to their community. Exploration on alumni surveys and in national databases on college graduates are two possibilities to further this research. Thousands of alumni could confirm whether participation in service-learning courses resulted in increased contribution of volunteer services to the community and further describe what skills they offer in their communities. In fact, this recommendation has been implemented by the Higher Education Research Institute (HERI) in the modification of its 2004 post-graduate survey. HERI will include a question on the pro bono contributions made by college graduates, which will be administered to 300,000 graduates. The intent is to study the impact of various college experiences (including service-learning courses) on graduates who have been out of college for ten years.

Recommendations for Practitioners

Several recommendations emerge from this work to improve faculty teaching and deepen student learning in service-learning Capstone courses. The first recommendation is to intentionally enhance the quality of the reflective practices facilitated in service-learning courses. Too frequently, participants reported the use of journals as logs of activities rather than tools to make deep cognitive connections between their service experiences, course concepts, and social and political issues. Reflection should encourage students to make connections between their service work and the political/civic implications of that work. Without this explicit connection, students working on issues such as education and the environment may only see these as social issues to address in a volunteer capacity rather than complex systemic issues deeply impacted by public policies and political agendas.

In order to assist faculty in exploring the notion of making connections between the social issues in their courses and larger systemic political issues, this author co-sponsored faculty development seminars in which faculty explored these connections. As a result of this professional development, faculty documented their plans to make civic and political links more explicit in their courses. Course evaluations have shown that the students enrolled in Capstone courses where faculty have redesigned their assignments to make more explicit the connection between local service work and broader civic implications reported greater agreement that their Capstone courses enhanced their understanding of social and political issues. Furthermore, students have reported a higher level of responsibility to meet the needs of their community (Cress, Kerrigan, & Reitenauer, 2003).

Further, this research revealed that reflection activities must continuously challenge all students to explore issues of diversity. In this study, women were more likely to report new understandings of diverse populations than men. In order to begin addressing this discrepancy, faculty must encourage all students to reflect upon concepts such as race, class, gender, sexual orientation, ability, and other social identity categories as appropriate within the course context.

Finally, graduates in this study suggested that faculty need to gain greater skill in communicating effectively with community partners and facilitating group processes. This includes:

1. educating faculty on the stages of group development,
2. giving faculty tools to assist students in assessing their strengths and weaknesses in groups, and
3. providing information to faculty on how to teach students to facilitate effective meetings as well as how to handle conflict in groups.

Since the mission of institutions of higher education is in part to create effective citizens, then leaders must take responsibility to help prepare faculty to engage in civic education for students.

CONCLUSION

Upon observing the list of national conferences in higher education in 2004, I recognized that there was an overwhelming cry for institutions of higher education to take seriously the task of developing effective citizens for participation in the public good. The Association of American Colleges and Universities (AAC&U, 2004) articulated that higher education is responsible for educating graduates capable of making judgments in the context of evolving geopolitics, fluctuating global economies, diminishing natural resources, and continuing racial/ethnic and cultural differences both domestically and internationally. We owe it to our students to help them develop the competencies to link diverse areas of knowledge in practical unscripted, complex problems.

Service-learning is highlighted throughout these conferences as a powerful pedagogy, capable of engaging students with the community for the good of the public and creating graduates fully able to solve interdisciplinary societal problems. These hopes for service-learning make it imperative to continuously improve the quality of these courses and to further assess the impact that they have on college graduates.

References

Association of American Colleges and Universities. (2004). *General education and assessment: Generating commitment, value, and evidence* [Brochure]. Washington, DC: Author.

Astin, A., & Sax, L. (1998). How undergraduates are affected by service participation. *Journal of College Student Development, 39*, 251–262.

Astin, A. W., Sax, L. J., & Avalos, J. (1999). Long-term effects of volunteerism during the undergraduate years. *The Review of Higher Education, 22*, 187–202.

Astin, A., Vogelgesang, L., Ikeda, E., & Yee, J. (2000). *How service-learning affects students.* Los Angeles: Higher Education Research Institute.

Batchelder, T., & Root, S. (1999). Effects of an undergraduate program to integrate academic learning and service: Cognitive, prosocial cognitive, and identity outcomes. In M. C. Sullivan, R. A. Myers, C. D. Bradfield, & D. L. Street (Eds.), *Service-learning: Educating students for life* (pp. 41–57). Harrisonburg, VA: James Madison University.

Battistoni, R. M. (1997). Service-learning as civic learning: Lessons we can learn from our students. In G. Reeher & J. Cammarano (Eds.), *Education for citizenship* (pp. 31–49). Lanham, MD: Rowman and Littlefield Publishers.

Berson, J. (1998, November). *Doing well by doing good: A study of the effects of a service-learning experience on student success.* Paper presented at the annual meeting of the Association for the Study of Higher Education, Miami, FL.

Buchanan, R. (1997). *Service-learning survey results.* Unpublished manuscript, University of Utah, Bennion Community Service Center, Salt Lake City.

Cress, C. M., Kerrigan, S., & Reitenauer, V. (2003). Making community-based learning meaningful: Faculty efforts to increase student civic engagement skills. *Transformations: The Journal of Inclusive Scholarship and Pedagogy, 14*(2), 87–100.

Creswell, J. W. (1994). *Research design: Qualitative and quantitative approaches.* Thousand Oaks, CA: Sage Publications.

Driscoll, A., Gelmon, S., Holland, B., Kerrigan, S., Spring, A., Grosvold, K., et al. (1998). *Assessing the impact of service-learning: A workbook of strategies and methods* (2nd ed.). Portland, OR: Portland State University.

Driscoll, A., Holland, B., Gelmon, S., & Kerrigan, S. (1996). An assessment model: Comprehensive case studies of impact on faculty, student, community, and institution. *Michigan Journal of Community Service Learning, 3*, 66–71.

Eyler, J., & Giles, D. E. (1999). *Where's the learning in service-learning?* San Francisco: Jossey-Bass.

Eyler, J., Giles, D. E., & Braxton, J. (1997). The impact of service-learning on college students. *Michigan Journal of Community Service Learning, 4*, 5–15.

Gilbert, M. K., Holdt, C., & Christopherson, K. (1998). Letting feminist knowledge serve the city. In M. Mayberry & E. Rose (Eds.), *Meeting the challenge: Innovative feminist pedagogies in action* (pp. 319–339). Newbury Park, CA: Sage.

Giles, D. E., & Eyler, J. (1994). The impact of a college community service laboratory on students' personal, social, and cognitive outcomes. *Journal of Adolescence, 17*, 327–339.

Grantmaker Forum on Community & National Service. (2000). *The state of service-learning related research: Opportunities to build a future.* Berkeley, CA: Author.

Hesser, G. (1995). Faculty assessment of service-learning: Outcomes attributed to service-learning and evidence of change in faculty attitudes about experiential education. *Michigan Journal of Community Service Learning, 2*, 33–42.

Ikeda, E. K. (1999). *How does service enhance learning? Toward an understanding of the process.*

Unpublished doctoral dissertation, University of California, Los Angeles.

Jordan, K. L. (1994). *The relationship of service learning and college student development*. Unpublished doctoral dissertation, Virginia Polytechnic Institute and State University, Blacksburg, VA.

Kendrick, J. R. (1996). Outcomes of service-learning in an introductory to sociology course. *Michigan Journal of Community Service Learning, 2,* 72–81.

Markus, G. B., Howard, J. P., & King, D. C. (1993). Integrating community service and classroom instruction enhances learning: Results from an experiment. *Education Evaluation and Policy Analysis, 15,* 410–419.

Myers-Lipton, S. J. (1996). Effect of a comprehensive service-learning program on college students' level of modern racism. *Michigan Journal of Community Service Learning, 3,* 44–54.

Sax, L., & Astin, A. (1996, May). *The impact of college on post college involvement in volunteerism and community service.* Paper presented at the annual meeting of the Association for Institutional Research, Albuquerque, NM.

Sax, L.J., & Astin, A.W. (1997). The benefits of service: Evidence from undergraduates. *Educational Record, 78,* 25–32.

Tesch, R. (1990). *Qualitative research: Analysis types and software tools.* New York: Falmer.

Wechsler, A., & Fogel, J. (1995). The outcomes of a service-learning program. National Society for Experiential Education Quarterly, 21(4), 6–7, 25–26.

CHAPTER 9

Contested Moral Ideals
and Affirmative Action:
THE IMPORTANCE OF PUBLIC DELIBERATION

Michele S. Moses

Abstract: This paper concerns an issue that often remains implicit within the public debate over affirmative action and related race-conscious education policies: What role do contested moral ideals play in the disagreement over affirmative action? I outline what a moral disagreement is and then examine the roots of the disagreement over affirmative action. Using philosophical inquiry, I make a case for the importance of illuminating and understanding the moral disagreement over affirmative action in order to inform the public deliberation over race-conscious education policies, especially given that affirmative action and related policies continue to be challenged in the public political arena. I hope to help raise awareness about how differing political commitments drive important policy decisions and serve either to constrain or expand educational opportunity as a result. When meaningful higher education opportunities are expanded, universities achieve a crucial part of their missions by serving not only individual students, but also the public good.

For proponents of the importance of diversity in fostering a rich and meaningful educational experience, the United States Supreme Court's decisions in the University of Michigan cases, *Grutter v. Bollinger* (2003) and *Gratz v. Bollinger* (2003), came as a relief. Finally the Court ruled on the question of whether colleges and universities could legally consider race and ethnicity in their admissions processes.

Any relief, however, was short-lived. Consider the following political developments affecting race-conscious education policies that have occurred in the time since the Supreme Court decisions.

- Just one month after the Supreme Court rulings were announced, Ward Connerly, Chair of the American Civil Rights Coalition, announced that he would propose an amendment to Michigan's state constitution that would eliminate affirmative action in state universities and government. The proposed amendment was passed by voters in November 2006. The amendment, known as the Michigan Civil Rights Initiative, prohibits the state's universities and all other state entities from "discriminating or granting preferential treatment based on race, sex, color, ethnicity, or national origin" (Michigan Civil Rights Initiative, 2004).

- The Center for Individual Rights, the group that sponsored the plaintiffs in *Hopwood* (1996), *Gratz*, and *Grutter*, has pledged to monitor how U.S. institutions of higher education respond to the decisions in the University of Michigan cases. They have promised to bring legal action against any campuses whose affirmative action policies do not follow the rulings to the letter (Schemo, 2003).

- Under pressure from the Center for Equal Opportunity, an advocacy organization that supported the plaintiffs against the University of Michigan, Yale University has disbanded a number of programs aimed at minority students, including a 34-year-old orientation program for students of color. The Cultural Connections program allowed approximately 125 incoming first-year undergraduate students annually to visit the campus and begin acclimating before classes start in the fall.

- Indeed, the Center for Equal Opportunity sent letters to some 100 institutions of higher education warning them that the race-sensitive programs they have in place may be suspect in light of *Gratz* and *Grutter*. In addition to Yale, Harvard University, the Massachusetts Institute of Technology, Princeton University, and the University of Virginia have all discontinued some programs aimed at students of color (Schmidt, 2004b).

Since the Supreme Court rulings, opponents of race-conscious education policies seem to feel a renewed urgency to prohibit the consideration of race and ethnicity in higher education admissions and related programs. The debates over race-conscious education policy have moved from the Supreme Court to the court of public opinion. Education theorists concerned with diversity and equality of educational opportunity are now thrust into the role of messengers of public information. Education policy research centered on race-conscious policies is needed not only to increase understanding and inform policy making, but also to contribute thoughtfully to the public debate and deliberation about the connections between race and education.

Given the recent political developments surrounding race-conscious education policies, I argue that if there is to be a future for race-conscious policy at all, education policy researchers and theorists need to focus on examining and illuminating the roots of the moral and political disagreement over such policies. Such examinations contribute to deeper understandings about, and better-informed public deliberation over, contested race-conscious policies. The central aim of this paper is to take some first steps toward that type of contribution.

In what follows, I first describe what makes a particular disagreement a moral one. This discussion provides the context necessary to understand the most prominent moral and political ideals at issue in the debate over affirmative action. Differing political theories of justice, such as liberal egalitarian theory and libertarian theory (to be explained in detail later), each seem to agree on the importance of the moral ideal of basic equality, and yet vehemently disagree about whether affirmative action is a defensible policy to help bring about basic equality. The final section centers on the importance of education research on race-conscious policies that informs public deliberation.

DEFINING MORAL DISAGREEMENT

What is moral disagreement? How is it important for examining affirmative action policy?

Fittingly for a discussion on disagreement itself, there is no easy agreement among theorists as to what exactly constitutes a *moral* disagreement. There is even little agreement on what such disagreements ought to be called; the terms "radical moral disagreement," "partial moral disagreement," "moral conflict," "intractable controversy," "internal moral disagreement," "irreconcilable moral disagreement," "reasonable disagreement," and so on are all present within the scholarly literature.

So, what makes a particular disagreement a moral one? Moral disagreements concern enduring, contested public issues involving values, relationships, and ideals, as opposed to individual, personal disputes (Gutmann & Thompson, 1996). There can certainly be personal disputes embedded in larger moral disagreements, but disagreements become moral ones when they center on public issues with broad social consequences. The affirmative action debate is an example of a moral disagreement, one that arouses profound conflict over fundamental moral ideals such as equality and liberty. Moral disagreements are qualitatively different from disagreements based on factual issues or differences of opinion, taste, or style. Two people may disagree over whose car reached the stop sign first after a fender-bender, or they may disagree about whether to root for the Mets or the Yankees. These are not moral disagreements. But if two people disagree or two political perspectives conflict about the state's role in providing public aid for people living in poverty, this is likely a *moral* disagreement. For at root, this is a disagreement over what priority should be given to the fundamental moral ideals of equality and liberty in a democratic society such as that of the United States. Moral disagreements are based largely on the conceptual schemes and theories of justice that underlie peoples' views.

Moral disagreements endure despite significant agreement about factual and even moral considerations. Disputants may agree about factual claims and (some) moral values, but disagree in their moral evaluations, i.e., about what to *do* about the disagreement. So, in the case of race-conscious education policies like affirmative action, there exists a persistent moral disagreement despite ostensible *agreement* about the importance of basic moral ideals such as freedom and equality. Of course, the opposing sides do not agree on all moral ideals. Agreement about moral basics does not mean that there will be the same moral beliefs about certain kinds of cases. For example, those who hold libertarian political theory to be tenable can value equality, but believe that affirmative action is not the means to that end, whereas those with a liberal egalitarian perspective may believe that affirmative action serves to foster equality. But is there an irreconcilable disagreement (i.e., a moral deadlock)? There is a difference of moral opinion to be sure, and different moral priorities. Moral deadlock, Ronald Milo (1986) allowed, can be the end result of this type of moral disagreement. It can stem from bad reasoning or conflicting interpretations of shared moral ideals. For instance, both liberal egalitarian and libertarian theories of justice, which underlie the main opposing positions in the public moral disagreement over affirmative action, may claim to value the basic moral ideals of liberty and equality. But how each ideal is interpreted and prioritized within these theories of justice differs substantially. In addition, the motives behind the claims can be questioned. Thus there is born a persistent moral disagreement despite seemingly shared central moral and political ideals.

Accordingly, Amy Gutmann and Dennis Thompson (1996) called moral disagreement the most formidable challenge to democracy today; they lamented that we have no adequate way to cope with fundamental value conflicts. Their answer was to conceive of a democracy that has a central place for moral discussion in political and public life—what they and others call deliberative democracy. Part of good deliberation is gaining a more nuanced understanding of the nature of the disagreement, the moral ideals involved, and the political commitments invoked.

Serious debate occurs over policy, but generally scant attention is paid to the moral principles and political commitments that underlie it. Too often this results in an unreflective acceptance of ideas and policies that claim to uphold such principles as if they are uncontroversial. In American society, it is difficult to argue against broad and often vague concepts such as justice, equality of opportunity, liberty, etc. Milo (1986) maintained that productive moral disagreement is only possible if there is substantial agreement between opposing sides on what the relevant issues and principles are within the debate. Otherwise there is absolutely no basis for even a conversation, much less any resolution. From what I have discussed so far, the debate over affirmative action policy constitutes a moral disagreement, one in which there is agreement by both sides about the relevance of the moral and political ideals of equality and liberty. There is, at the very least, basis for a conversation, one that may lead to better understanding.

THE ROOTS OF THE DISAGREEMENT OVER AFFIRMATIVE ACTION

I argue that illuminating the moral and political roots of the disagreement over affirmative action is important for gaining a more profound understanding of how to best inform public discussion of such race-conscious policies. That said, the long-standing disagreement over affirmative action has its roots in other factors as well, not the least of which is racism (Feagin, 2002). While those social roots have received attention in the scholarly literature (e.g., Feagin, 2002; Feinberg, 1998; West, 1993; Williams, 1991), the political theories of justice that underlie the disagreement have not. These roots concern the moral ideals of equality and liberty, which often have been viewed as fundamentally in opposition to each other.

Specific conceptions and political uses of the moral ideals of equality and liberty characterize the political commitments central to libertarian and liberal egalitarian theories of justice. With the firm acknowledgement that there is substantial complexity and overlap within and among prominent theories of justice along the political spectrum, I have purposefully chosen to focus this examination on the opposing commitments of liberal egalitarian political theory and libertarian political theory. Either explicitly or implicitly, these two theories underlie much practical policy debate in the United States.[1] Whereas liberal egalitarian political theory tends to underlie many "liberal"—as popularly understood—policy positions, libertarian political theory underlies a good portion (though certainly not all) of "conservative"—again, as popularly understood—policy positions. In this section, I endeavor to clarify what the prominent ideals mean within libertarian and liberal egalitarian theory and how those meanings inform policy views. How are important ideals like equality and liberty defined and interpreted?

Equality and Liberal Egalitarian Theory

A discussion of equality at a high level of abstraction may be unproblematic regardless of one's underlying theory of justice. All persons are purportedly equal under the law. It is at a more practical level that differences arise more readily, especially in interpretation (Rosenfeld, 1991). Two prominent strands of liberal egalitarian theory emphasize different ideas central to the concept of equality. One emphasizes equality itself, while the other emphasizes equality of opportunity. However, the two strands of liberal egalitarianism are each characterized by a concern for *social* justice, as compared with the libertarian concern for individual justice. Whereas social justice is inextricably bound up with equality, individual justice is intertwined with personal autonomy and liberty.

The first strand of liberal egalitarian theory has held that equality is *the* fundamental moral ideal (Dworkin, 2000; Kymlicka, 1992). Ronald Dworkin (2000) articulates this perspective well: "Equal concern," he wrote, "is the sovereign virtue of political community—without it government is only tyranny—and when a nation's wealth is very unequally distributed, as the wealth of even very prosperous nations now is, then its equal concern is suspect" (p. 1). In order for people to be treated with equal concern, they need to have equality of resources. By resources, Dworkin means something akin to opportunities and possibilities for flourishing. For a theory of justice to be taken seriously, Dworkin concluded, each person has to matter equally, to be treated as equal. Of significant note here is that *treatment as equals* does not necessarily imply getting the *same* treatment. For example, the Supreme Court's ruling in *Lau v. Nichols* (1974), held that for limited English proficient students to be treated as equals within the public education system, they needed to be treated differently from students whose primary language is English; that is, they needed to receive instruction in their native languages. In this case, receiving the same treatment resulted in vast inequality of educational opportunity for limited English proficient students.

The second strand of liberal egalitarianism follows more closely the work of Rawls (1971, 1993, 2001) by emphasizing equality of opportunity and "justice as fairness." Consequently, treatment as equals requires equality of opportunity. As such, each person has a right to equal basic liberties; positions and offices are open to all under the principle of fair equality of opportunity; and inequality is permissible so long as any inequalities result in maximizing the position of the worst off, that is, those with the fewest primary goods. For Rawls (1971), persons' talents, abilities, and initial life circumstances are morally arbitrary and, as such, are an unfair basis from which to delineate their life chances. From this perspective, affirmative action policies are permissible in order to ensure that students of color are granted equal basic liberties and fair equality of opportunity.

The concepts of equality and equality of opportunity can be interpreted to mean a variety of quite different and often conflicting things. Consider the following examples of two policy organizations that both champion the ideal of equality (in fact, their names explicitly invoke the ideal); the first is concerned with Dworkin's ideal of treating people as equals and Rawls's idea of justice as fairness, and the second is not. The "Center for Equality," which is concerned with conducting research that fosters economic equality (i.e., the redistribution of wealth and resources) operates from within a liberal egalitarian political perspective. By contrast, libertarian (rather than liberal egalitarian) political theory underlies the views of the aforementioned "Center for Equal Opportunity," led by Reagan-era appointee Linda Chavez, which opposes bilingual education and affirmative action policies intended to remedy educational inequalities. Even though there appears to be a consensus about the importance of equality as a fundamental value, the consensus can be misleading. Indeed, concepts may be used for political reasons, with little to no regard for their more complex meanings or what they require of social policy.

Nevertheless, there is often agreement between political theories about the principle of basic equality—that persons should be treated as equals and that the state ought to treat persons with equal concern and respect (Dworkin, 1977). This nominal agreement is positive, yet a conflict still occurs in defining what *treatment as equals* means. For libertarians, treatment as equals means that we respect a person's property ownership—her or his self as well as her or his material goods. The fact that such a primary principle may result in vast socioeconomic inequality is unproblematic within libertarian political theory, so long as property rights and procedures for the acquisition and transfer of property are fair.

Liberty and Libertarian Theory

Libertarians characterize the moral and political ideal of liberty as "requiring that each person should have the greatest amount of liberty commensurate with the same liberty for all" (Sterba, 1992, p. 5). The role of the state is to protect human rights that are centered on liberty. John Hospers (1974) names three human rights as central to a libertarian theory of justice: the right to life (to protect people from force and coercion, unjust killing), the right to liberty (to protect freedom of speech, press, assembly, ideas), and the right to property (to protect material and intellectual property from theft, fraud, slander, etc.). This understanding of liberty excludes certain rights from the right to life category, such as the right to receive public aid. Similarly, the right to property is considered a right to acquire goods and resources by fair means, rather than a right to receive goods from others who are better off in order to promote one's own welfare.[2]

Often cited as a source for libertarian political theory, Friedrich von Hayek (1960) argued that the libertarian ideal of liberty is characterized by two primary tenets:

1. "equality before the law" as "the only kind of equality conducive to liberty and the only equality which we can secure without destroying liberty" rather than "substantial equality" and
2. "reward according to perceived value" rather than "reward according to merit" (p. 85).

As a result, inequalities caused by birth circumstances and talent are perceived as just. Justice is seen as an individual principle that ought to take place between individual persons, rather than a social one.

Nozick (1974), long held as the representative of libertarian political philosophy,[3] put forward a libertarian theory of "justice as entitlement." This view is characterized by respect for rights of ownership of self and property, which allows persons the freedom to choose how they want to live their lives without the intrusion of the state. Why should any goods acquired within the free market be redistributed when one's talents, abilities, work ethic, and possessions are one's own? Libertarianism holds that vast structural inequalities could be just, that is, could come about in a just manner. There might be bad luck involved in people's starting places in life—even unfairness—but not injustice. If people's property rights are respected and the state fosters liberty and is not coercive, then the distribution of goods that results can be considered just. As a result, a formalist notion of opportunity that calls for equal access (i.e., no official barriers) to education is considered just (Howe, 1997).

The libertarian interpretation of liberty does not mean that libertarians do not care whether less advantaged people have their basic needs met; instead, it means that libertarians believe that the state has no duty to provide for those needs. Social welfare is therefore the requirement of charity, not of justice. One contemporary example of this idea in practice was the Bush Administration's call for faith-based charities and organizations to lead in the provision of social services for needy people. This call is justified through the belief that under a free market system and a minimal state, the least advantaged will have access to adequate opportunities and resources to make sure that their basic needs are met.

Are the Conflicting Emphases on Equality and Liberty Irreconcilable?

Given the long-standing theoretical dispute over which of these two ideals ought to take priority in a democratic society, is the conflict impossible to resolve in the case of the moral disagreement over affirmative action?

This is a very sobering question, especially because there seem to be myriad examples of impossible moral conflicts. Consider the debates on abortion and euthanasia, the conflict between creationism and evolution, competing claims about the state's responsibility to poor people or undocumented workers; the list could go on. So, what good does it do to try to understand the basic moral ideals at issues in the affirmative action debate if there is no hope for resolution on the horizon? Should we, then, make no final judgments? Where would that take us?

There are two related possible conclusions: moral relativism and irreconcilable worldviews. A moral relativism argument goes like this: When faced with a moral disagreement that seems irreconcilable, theoretical and practical considerations will lead to moral relativism. That is, if disputing parties cannot reach a mutually acceptable resolution, then they must accept (without judgment) that one particular answer may be correct for one side, whereas a different answer may be correct for the other side.

Believing it to be an inevitable response to a society rife with difficult moral disagreements, David Wong (1991) characterized relativism as a "common response to the deepest conflict we face in our ethical lives" (p. 442). The opposing sides in such conflicts each may be right, or perhaps their views are not as inconsistent as first they appeared. On the other side, Nicholas Sturgeon (1994) argued that although moral relativism is a possible response to moral disagreement, it does not make sense. According to the antirelativist position, opposing views can be understandable and even right about subsidiary points, but both cannot be morally *right* on the whole.

I do not aim to solve the issue of objective versus subjective truth herein. Nevertheless, the discussion about relativism is instructive. Does the existence of difficult—even intractable—moral disagreement necessarily point us toward relativism? I am swayed by the antirelativist position here. Robert George (1999) made a cogent point: "To say that a moral question is difficult...is in no way to suggest that it admits of no right answer" (p. 186). An illuminating example in support of this conclusion is the U.S. Supreme Court's separate but equal doctrine that held that racial segregation in the U.S. was legally permissible. The moral disagreement surrounding the issue of legal racial segregation adjudicated in *Brown v. Board of Education* (1954) seemed irreconcilable, with each side certain of the moral rectitude of its position. In hindsight, I believe there was *one* morally correct answer: Racial segregation because one race is deemed inferior to another is morally wrong, regardless of whether or not the separate facilities are equal. This is not to say that widespread social agreement about the moral wrongness of racial segregation in theory has resulted in integrated schools and communities in practice. Indeed, there remain those who champion racial segregation. But that view holds significantly less weight in the 21st century, and American society is working to catch up to the ideal of integration highlighted in *Brown* and the ideal of diversity put forward in *Grutter*. As George (1999) went on to say: "Even reasonable disagreement does not indicate an absence of objective truth" (p. 186).

The argument for the impossibility of resolving serious moral disagreements based on irreconcilable worldviews is put forth by George Lakoff (2002), who suggested that impossible conflicts underscore that the major political division within everyday political discourse in the U.S. is at bottom a moral one, based on core personal and family values. He posited that the main ideals are strictness (on the Right) and nurturance (on the Left), that these values are fundamentally opposed, and that all social and political debates reflect that one major, deep difference. An important consequence is that many moral differences between the two groups may be irreconcilable.

Lakoff (2002) (dis)missed the basic commonalities between, and values shared by, those on the Left and those on the Right. Through discourse analysis, he highlighted the similarity of the metaphors used for moral issues, but he did not consider that those similar metaphors might have their roots in certain shared moral ideals. As such, Lakoff is too quick to point out only the moral differences that lead to divergent worldviews and irresolvable policy disputes.

Moral disagreements may get reconciled in different ways:

1. moral argumentation (deliberative argument and discussion akin to Gutmann and Thompson's ideas),
2. empirical discoveries (e.g., scientific discoveries about fetuses or second language acquisition); and
3. educational, cultural, and/or experiential influences (e.g., when a student leaves home believing that affirmative action is wrong, but then in college is exposed to diversity, etc., and changes her view) (Silver, 1994).

The existence of difficult, intractable moral disagreements need not imply that disputants have divergent worldviews that *cannot* be overcome.

Basic Equality as a Shared Ideal

Even though a liberal egalitarian theory of justice considers equality of income or resources to be a prerequisite for treating people as equals and a libertarian theory of justice deems the right to one's own work, effort, and property as a requirement for treating people as equals, both theories invoke the ideal of basic equality. Competing political theories may not agree on how to define and interpret concepts like equality, yet they are still invoking the concept positively (e.g., Linda Chavez's Center for Equal Opportunity); at the very least, such a positive reliance on the concept holds promise for finding some basic agreement from which to move forward in better understanding each others' positions. Will Kymlicka (1992) pointed out that, traditionally, theorists have believed that there is a continuum of political theories of justice from the left to the right, and that each of these appeals to a different ultimate foundational value. The theories, therefore, have been seen as incompatible, their differences as incapable of resolution. However, he followed Dworkin in saying that a regard for *basic equality* (characterized not by an equal distribution of income and wealth, but by the more abstract idea of treating people as equals) is what should be viewed as the *ultimate* foundational value held by political theories from the left to the right. Kymlicka's (1992) point is this: "A theory is egalitarian in this sense if it accepts that the interests of each member of the community matter, and matter equally....This more basic notion of equality is found in Nozick's libertarianism as much as Marx's communism" (p. 4).

This is a key point. The ideal of basic equality holds an important place in both liberal egalitarian and libertarian political theory. Some citizens, educators, researchers, and other policy actors may feel clear about how they interpret and prioritize the moral and political ideals that guide their policy positions. Nevertheless, the ideals and their place in the conceptual schemes that drive positions are often implicit, which makes it difficult to make informed choices about policy prescriptions. In order to make the most knowledgeable, coherent, and consistent choices, citizens and policy actors need to be clear about their moral ideals and the moral ideals within opposing views. There is, of course, no guarantee that a more profound understanding of one's own views as well as the views of one's opponents will lead one to change her or his positions on policy issues. Many factors other than rational deliberation and argument make up conceptual schemes and influence policy views. What is important to take away from the preceding discussion is that, regardless of the motivations, there is at least some agreement over basic ideals. The moral disagreements over policy stem from a combination of contrasting prioritization, interpretation, and application of the salient principles. Within libertarianism, basic equality is perceived as necessary for enhancing liberty. As a result of the different ideas of what liberty and equality involve, justice for libertarians may require laws and policies that conflict with what justice requires for liberal egalitarians. But there is hope to be found. Because there are important similarities in basic moral ideals, deeper understanding of the ideals and how they affect policy controversies may serve to enhance the public's ability to deliberate about the complex moral disagreement over affirmative action.

INFORMING PUBLIC DELIBERATION

The most recent political test faced by affirmative action policy in the form of the Michigan Civil Rights Initiative has lent a sense of immediacy to new scholarship concerning race-conscious policies. Connerly's American Civil Rights Coalition has announced campaigns for similar ballot initiatives in several more states for the election of 2008. Education research on race-conscious policy will need to emphasize providing information and rationales that are most likely to inform public deliberation and understanding.

Lessons from Gratz and Grutter

In these cases, the Supreme Court upheld Justice Powell's opinion in *Bakke* (1978) that student diversity is a compelling state interest. Therefore, admissions policies that satisfy the strict scrutiny standard can be considered constitutional. That is, they do not necessarily violate the 14th Amendment's Equal Protection clause, so long as they serve a compelling interest either to remedy past discrimination or foster racial and ethnic diversity among the student body, and are narrowly tailored to further the compelling interest. By upholding the University of Michigan Law School admissions policy, the Court endorsed policies that follow its guidelines in letter and spirit. In the majority opinion of *Grutter*, Justice O'Connor (2003) wrote, "The hallmark of that policy is its focus on academic ability coupled with a flexible assessment of applicants' talents, experiences, and potential 'to contribute to the learning of those around them.' The policy requires admissions officials to evaluate each applicant based on all the information available in the file" (*Grutter* Opinion, section IA). In order to comply with the high court's rulings, colleges and universities need to do the following:

1. seriously (though not necessarily exhaustively) consider race-neutral alternatives before settling on race-conscious admissions policies;
2. consider race and ethnicity as one qualification among many—a plus-factor, not a deciding factor;
3. develop an admissions plan that is narrowly tailored to further the compelling governmental interests of remedying the present effects

of past discrimination or adding to the racial and ethnic diversity of the student body without unreasonably constraining the rights of non-minority applicants;

4. review student applications individually (i.e., holistically) taking into account quantitative as well as qualitative measures of student academic, social, and personal merit; and

5. set up a process to periodically review the policy or a sunset provision for the policy.

Opponents of race-conscious policies will remain on the lookout for any missteps by institutions of higher education when crafting and justifying their admissions policies. In fact, in his dissent in *Grutter*, Justice Scalia (2003) went so far as to outline the next steps in the legal battle against affirmative action. He cautioned that future lawsuits would likely center on whether institutions are indeed conducting sufficiently individualistic reviews of applicants or on whether any educational benefits can be shown to flow from student diversity on campus.

As Justice Scalia's dissent itself shows, the high court's rulings did not put an end to the moral disagreement over affirmative action. As a result, prominent opponents of affirmative action and the diversity rationale will take the issue to the ballot, first in Michigan, and later in other states that allow public referenda. Such ballot initiatives create intense political campaigns, with each opposing side struggling to get their core message to the voting public. Educational researchers have a valuable opportunity to bring their scholarship to bear on the public political debate over affirmative action and related race-conscious education policies.

A Promising Rationale for Race-Conscious Education Policy

There are several important lines of research that can inform the larger conversation about race and education policy (e.g., Chang, 1999, 2001; Gurin, 1999; Gurin et al., 2002; Hurtado, 2001; Marin, 2000; Moses, 2001, 2002; Yun & Moreno, 2006). Here I want to consider an additional line of inquiry into how educational research and theory on race-conscious education policy might serve to influence the public moral and political debates over affirmative action. With the legal battle won for now, the next battle concerns public (mis)information and (mis)understanding.

There is a need for cogent information that can be used to educate the general public about what *Gratz* and *Grutter*, affirmative action-related ballot initiatives, and the diversity rationale mean for the relationship between race and education in the U.S. Consider that both the University of Michigan and Ohio State University received substantially fewer applications from black students in the wake of the

Supreme Court rulings (Schmidt, 2004a). It would be helpful for applicants and their families to understand how the rulings are affecting college admissions processes, as well as how race is considered and diversity is valued on campus. The University of Michigan's National Forum on Higher Education for the Public Good has begun substantive efforts at informing the public discussion about these important issues through its Access to Democracy project (http://www.thenationalforum.org). The key is to provide outreach and information that is well grounded in theory and research from the humanities and the social sciences.

Providing credible information that helps advance public deliberation and debate over controversial issues is the responsibility of academic theorists and researchers. When it comes to the issues discussed herein, involving race-consciousness and education policy, well-informed public deliberation is all the more important. As Glenn Loury (1999) has pointed out, we live in a "divided society" (p. 1). Public deliberation over critical issues can function to clarify contested values, increase public understanding, foster people's willingness to reconsider their own views, and increase communication between opposing sides on a given issue (National Issues Forums Institute, 2001). For example, scholars can help members of the public question unexamined assumptions and structures that serve to exacerbate inequalities (e.g., the reliance on quantifiable measures of merit in admissions processes).

Gutmann and Thompson (1996) have developed a conception of democracy that emphasizes public deliberation. Regarding education policy disputes, "deliberative democracy can contribute, for example, in clarifying and, perhaps, reconciling conflicting research findings or conflicting values" (Moses & Gair, 2004). Because they believe moral disagreement to be a significant challenge to democracy, Gutmann and Thompson envision a democratic society that emphasizes moral discussion in political life in an effort to cope with fundamental values conflicts. They identify three conditions that structure the deliberative *process* of politics:

1. reciprocity, by which reason-giving and justification for mutually-binding policies are seen as a mutual endeavor;
2. publicity, which stipulates that policy makers, researchers, officials, and members of the public in general should have to justify their decisions and actions in public; and
3. accountability, which requires those who make policy decisions to answer to those who are bound by those policies.

Along with these three conditions, Gutmann and Thompson describe three principles that govern the *content* of deliberations:

1. basic liberty, which controls what government and society can demand of people and what people can demand of one another;
2. basic opportunity, which involves the distribution of goods necessary for pursuing a good life (e.g., basic income); and
3. fair opportunity, which has to do with the distribution of goods to people based on their qualifications.

Public discussions of race-conscious education policies in general, and the political challenges to affirmative action in higher education admissions in particular, can serve to clarify and demystify the rationales both for and against such policies. Such discussions occur through various media including print newsletters, newspapers, and journals; electronic sources; televised debates and events; workshops; public lectures; and community meetings. Education policy scholars would be able to contribute in meaningful ways to public information and deliberation over controversial policies. For example, the preceding analysis of the affirmative action debate, which framed this issue as a moral disagreement founded on contested moral ideals from libertarian and liberal egalitarian political theory, can add a missing dimension to the overall conversation about the nature of the dispute between affirmative action supporters and their opponents.

One substantive criticism against the significance of public deliberation is the idea that policy processes are much more political than rational (Stone, 2002). The policy making process can be understood as a political spectacle that is less about democracy and moral ideals and more about gaining political advantage and power (Edelman, 1988; Smith et al., 2003). The general idea here is that moral disagreements over education policy and the concepts and ideals involved can never be taken at face value, especially when race and class are at issue. Powerful forces strategically invoke certain moral ideals in order to further their political agendas, with little regard for issues of justice or for the least advantaged persons. For example, the Michigan Civil Rights Initiative (MCRI) used the language of civil rights in its ballot language. However, the ballot initiative's sponsoring group argues against race-conscious education policies, the very policies developed during the Civil Rights Movement to further civil rights, diversity, and equality. It invokes the concept of "discrimination" using a simplistic perspective that ignores the idea that equal treatment does not necessarily entail identical treatment. In doing so, MCRI's backers are following the successful strategy of other, similar ballot initiatives, including California's Proposition 209 that eliminated affirmative action in college admissions and hiring practices in state colleges, universities, and government positions.

Issues of power certainly lurk beneath the surface of moral-political debates, and it is fascinating to examine how power and politics affect the language and concepts used by policy actors. Nonetheless, it would be unproductive to respond by merely "throwing up one's hands" and saying that the ideal of equality is sometimes invoked for purely strategic political purposes rather than for any real concern for equality. It would be far more constructive to try to understand how each side conceptualizes the ideal of basic equality and capitalize on what common ground there is. People may support whatever moral ideals they believe will keep them in power or give them political advantage, but the fact remains that once a moral ideal like equality is used, careful analysis may illuminate the political theories underlying political positions as well as help uncover deeper reasons for its use within particular political theories of justice. Consider that the Bush Administration's *Amicus Curiae* brief to the Supreme Court in *Grutter* cited diversity as a desirable characteristic of a strong democratic state, yet urged the Court to strike down affirmative action in higher education admissions. We could attribute this support of diversity to disingenuous use of the concept of diversity in order to seem sympathetic to voters of color, which is certainly one viable interpretation. However, I argue that it is important to go further to endeavor to understand the seeming agreement between the Right and the Left about diversity in this case, in order to make sense of the subsequent disagreement over affirmative action policy. At the very least, clarity of meaning and interpretation can serve to highlight the importance of moral ideals like equality and diversity, and delineate what they require of public policy. When communities actually engage in deliberative democratic processes, the results are promising. Studies of public deliberation in communities in Oregon, Colorado, and California have shown that deliberative dialogues can foster greater understanding of contested issues and willingness to break moral and political deadlocks (Weeks, 2000).

It is often difficult to ascertain what morality and justice require in persistent political controversies. This is especially true about controversial issues of education policy having to do with race and ethnicity. How do we make sense of competing views on policy issues that carry vast significance for students? Is it possible that the conflicting sides can each be right? What does that mean for education policy decisions? Typically, there will be some fallout for making morally controversial decisions. Regardless of this, moral disagreement can serve to move people—and society—forward. One need only think of the Supreme Court decision in *Brown* to understand how moral disagreements can serve as catalysts for positive social change. This is exciting. Moral disagreement can be positive, so long as we are willing to work to understand reasonable opposing views with mutual respect.

Justice O'Connor (2003) pointed out that the Supreme Court has "repeatedly acknowledged the overriding importance of preparing students for work and citizenship, describing education as pivotal to 'sustaining our political and cultural heritage' (*Plyler v. Doe,* 1982) with a fundamental role in maintaining the fabric of society" (*Grutter* Opinion, Section III A). This underscores the role of higher education in informing public deliberation over contested issues and fostering equality of educational opportunity in order to cultivate the public good. Michael Eric Dyson (2004) puts it well: "knowledge must be turned to social benefit if we are to justify the faith placed in us" (p. B12). In the arena of race-conscious education policy, education theorists and policy researchers have a significant responsibility to contribute theoretical and empirical grounding for the information that the public receives as they attempt to understand and negotiate their way through some of the most contentious moral disagreements faced by society.

ACKNOWLEDGMENT

I gratefully acknowledge Lirio Patton and Nick Bowman's thoughtful feedback on this paper, the completion of which was made possible by funding from the Spencer Foundation, as well as an award from the National Forum on Higher Education for the Public Good. All views expressed herein are, of course, mine alone.

Endnotes

1. In addition to affirmative action, another salient current example is the debate over social welfare reform. The arguments for social welfare programs and public aid for the needy have a marked egalitarian cast (see Holyfield, 2002). By contrast, the arguments against social welfare programs have a significant libertarian flavor (see Murray, 1984).
2. These are circumscribed by Nozick's (1974) three principles guiding initial acquisition, voluntary transfer, and rectification.
3. Nozick is widely cited as such, despite the complexity of his ideas to be found in *Philosophical Explanations* (1976), for example.

References

Brown v. Board of Education of the City of Topeka, 347 U.S. 483 (1954).

Dworkin, R. (1977). *Taking rights seriously.* Cambridge, MA: Harvard University Press.

Dworkin, R. (2000). *Sovereign virtue: The theory and practice of equality.* Cambridge, MA: Harvard University Press.

Dyson, M. E. (2003, December 5). The public obligations of intellectuals. *The Chronicle of Higher Education,* pp. B11–B12.

Edelman, M. (1988). *Constructing the political spectacle.* Chicago: The University of Chicago Press.

Feagin, J. R. (2002). *The continuing significance of racism: U.S. colleges and universities.* Washington, DC: American Council on Education.

Feinberg, W. (1998). *On higher ground: Education and the case for affirmative action.* New York: Teachers College Press.

George, R. P. (1999). Law, democracy, and moral disagreement. In S. Macedo (Ed.), *Deliberative politics* (pp. 184–197). New York: Oxford University Press.

Gratz v. Bollinger, 123 S.Ct. 2411 (2003).

Grutter v. Bollinger, 123 S.Ct. 2325 (2003).

Gurin, P. (1999). Selections from the compelling need for diversity in higher education: Expert report of Patricia Gurin. *Equity & Excellence in Education, 32*(2), 36–62.

Gurin, P., Dey, E. L., Hurtado, S., & Gurin, G. (2002). Diversity and higher education: Theory and impact on educational outcomes. *Harvard Educational Review, 72,* 330–366.

Gutmann, A., & Thompson, D. (1996). *Democracy and disagreement: Why moral conflict cannot be avoided in politics, and what should be done about it.* Cambridge, MA: The Belknap Press.

Hayek, F. A. (1960). *The constitution of liberty.* Chicago: University of Chicago Press.

Holyfield, L. (2002). *Moving up and out: Poverty, education, and the single parent family.* Philadelphia, PA: Temple University Press.

Hopwood v. Texas, 78 f. 3d 932 (5th cir. 1996); cert. Denied, 518 U.S. 1033 (1996).

Horn, C. L., & Flores, S. M. (2003). *Percent plans in college admissions: A comparative analysis of three states' experiences.* Cambridge, MA: The Civil Rights Project at Harvard University.

Hospers, J. (1974). What libertarianism is. In T. Machan (Ed.), *The libertarian alternative* (pp. 3–20). New York: Nelson-Hall Inc.

Howe, K. R. (1997). *Understanding equal educational opportunity: Social justice, democracy, and schooling.* New York: Teachers College Press.

Hurtado, S. (2001). Linking diversity and educational purpose: How diversity affects the classroom environment and student development. In G. Orfield (Ed.), *Diversity challenged: Evidence on the impact of affirmative action* (pp. 187–203). Cambridge, MA: Harvard Education Publishing Group and The Civil Rights Project at Harvard University.

Kymlicka, W. (1992). *Contemporary political philosophy.* Oxford: Clarendon Press.

Lakoff, G. (2002). *Moral politics: What conservatives know that liberals don't* (2nd ed.). Chicago: University of Chicago Press.

Lau v. Nichols, 414 US 563, (1974).

Loury, G. C. (1999). *The divided society.* Vienna: IWM Working Paper No. 8.

Marin, P. (2000). The educational possibility of multi-racial/multi-ethnic college classrooms. In American Council on Education (Ed.), *Does diversity make a difference: Three research studies on diversity in college classrooms* (pp. 61–83). Washington, DC: Editor and American Association of University Professors.

Marin, P., & Lee, E. K. (2003). *Appearance and reality in the sunshine state: The talented 20 program in Florida.* Cambridge, MA: The Civil Rights Project at Harvard University.

Michigan Civil Rights Initiative. (2004). Retrieved December 1, 2004, from http://www.michigan-civilrights.org

Milo, R. D. (1986). Moral deadlock. *The Journal of the Royal Institute of Philosophy, 61,* 453–471.

Moses, M. S. (2001). Affirmative action and the creation of more favorable contexts of choice. *American Educational Research Journal, 38*(1), 3–36.

Moses, M. S. (2002). *Embracing race: Why we need race-conscious education policy.* New York: Teachers College Press.

Moses, M. S., & Gair, M. (2004). Toward a critical deliberative strategy for addressing ideology in educational policy processes. *Educational Studies, 36,* 217–244.

Murray, C. (1984). *Losing ground: American social policy, 1950–1980.* New York: Basic Books.

National Issues Forums Institute. (2001). *Organizing for public deliberation and moderating a forum/study circle*. Washington, DC: Author.

Nozick, R. (1974). *Anarchy, the state, and utopia*. New York: Basic Books.

Nozick, R. (1976). *Philosophical explanations*. Cambridge, MA: Belknap.

O'Connor, S. D. *Opinion for Grutter v. Bollinger*, 123 S.Ct. 2325 (2003).

Orfield, G., with Kurlaender, M. (Eds.). (2001). *Diversity challenged: Evidence on the impact of affirmative action*. Cambridge, MA: The Civil Rights Project at Harvard University, and Harvard Education Publishing Group.

Plyler v. Doe, 457 U.S. 202, 221 (1982).

Rawls, J. (1971). *A theory of justice*. Cambridge, MA: Harvard University Press.

Rawls, J. (1993). *Political liberalism*. New York: Columbia University Press.

Rawls, J. (2001). *Justice as fairness: A restatement*. Cambridge, MA: The Belknap Press.

Regents of the University of California v. Bakke, 438 U.S. 265 (1978).

Rosenfeld, M. (1991). *Affirmative action and justice: A philosophical and constitutional inquiry*. New Haven, CT: Yale University Press.

Scalia, A. (2003). *Dissent, Grutter v. Bollinger*, 123 S.Ct. 2325 (2003).

Schemo, D. J. (2003, June 25). Group vows to monitor academia's responses. *The New York Times*, p. A22.

Schmidt, P. (2004a, February 23). Fewer black students are applying to Ohio State and Michigan since Supreme Court rulings. *The Chronicle of Higher Education*.

Schmidt, P. (2004b, February 25). Yale U. opens an orientation program, formerly for minority students only, to all freshmen. *The Chronicle of Higher Education*.

Silver, M. (1994). Irreconcilable moral disagreement. In L. Foster, & P. Herzog (Eds.), *Defending diversity: Contemporary philosophical perspectives on pluralism and multiculturalism* (pp. 39–58). Amherst, MA: University of Massachusetts.

Smith, M. L., Jarvis, P. F., Heinecke, W., Miller-Kahn, L., & Noble, A. J. (2003). *Political spectacle and the fate of American schools*. New York: Routledge.

Sterba, J. P. (1992). *Justice: Alternative political perspectives* (2nd ed.). Belmont, CA: Wadsworth.

Stone, D. (2002). *Policy paradox: The art of political decision making*. New York: W. W. Norton.

Sturgeon, N. L. (1994). Moral disagreement and moral relativism. *Social Philosophy and Policy*, *11*(1), 80–115.

Weeks, E. C. (2000). The practice of deliberative democracy: Results from four large-scale trials. *Public Administration Review*, *60*, 360–372.

West, C. (1993). *Race matters*. Boston: Beacon Press.

Williams, P. J. (1991). *The alchemy of race and rights*. Cambridge, MA: Harvard University Press.

Wong, D. (1991). Relativism. In P. Singer (Ed.), *A companion to ethics*. Oxford: Basil Blackwell.

Yun, J., & Moreno, J. F. (2006). College access, K–12 concentrated disadvantage, and the next 25 years of educational research. *Educational Researcher*, *35*(1), 12–19.

CHAPTER 10

21st Century Self-Sufficiency:

A COMMUNITY-UNIVERSITY PARTNERSHIP EXPLORES INFORMATION TECHNOLOGY'S POTENTIAL FOR EMPOWERING LOW-INCOME INDIVIDUALS AND FAMILIES

Richard L. O'Bryant

Abstract: This paper uses data collected from a two-year community-university partnership and longitudinal study, called the Camfield Estates-MIT Creating Community Connections Project, in order to address the following questions: Can personal computing and high-speed Internet access support community building efforts? Can this access to technology empower low-income community residents to do more for themselves? The study revealed that residents who have a personal computer and Internet access in their homes feel a sense of community, experience an increase in their social contact with others, and strengthen their social ties. This research also explores whether outcomes achieved through in-home computing can promote an increased sense of empowerment and the capacity to access independently relevant information related to a resident's needs, wants or purposes.

Two Ph.D. candidate researchers from the Massachusetts Institute of Technology (MIT) worked resident the resident leadership of Camfield Estates in Boston, Massachusetts and MassHousing, a local housing authority, to form a unique community based research Camfield Estates-MIT Creating Community Connections Project.

Through this distinct community-university initiative thirty-seven participating households received a free computer and training with 20 participants completing the project requirements. The majority of participating households were single-parent, African American and Hispanic female-headed households with related children under 18 years of age. Results indicated regular computer and Internet use and some positive correlation between in-home computing/internet use and a sense of connection to family, friends and their local community. There was no evidence that in-home computer use led to family and/or social isolation.

§

Progressives who are concerned about the current social conditions of the have-nots and the future generation of have-nots not only have to fight against the current public policy strategies; they are morally obligated to offer alternative strategies designed to alleviate, not exacerbate, the plight of the poor, the jobless, and other disadvantaged citizens of America.

—William Julius Wilson, 1996

Today, more than ever, policy makers are struggling with the challenges that new technology presents and how to best ensure access to the Internet by all. One way is to consider how a technology like the Internet can be used to address the persistent problem of how to connect low-income individuals and families with relevant information and resources. Can in-home access to personal computing and the Internet, as a linkage institution,[1] be an efficient and resourceful method for moving low-income communities, families, and individuals toward empowerment and self-sufficiency? This is a question for the discussion of policy makers at all levels. The communities that many federal programs have targeted and sought to move toward becoming more self-sufficient are low-income inner-city neighborhoods that are considered the most at risk of struggling against society's challenges (Wilson, 1996). According to census statistics for Boston, the female-headed household poverty rate dropped by 2.1% from 1990 (31.1%) to 2000 (29.0%). However, in 2000, 37% of female-headed families, regardless of race, in Boston that have related children under the age of 18 were below the poverty level. This would suggest that policy makers should continue to target services toward making the most at-risk population—single African American and Hispanic female-headed households with children—more self-sufficient.[2]

This chapter presents one community-university partnership's effort, the Camfield Estates-MIT Creating Community Connections Project,[3] to connect electronically a low-income community's residents with resources, services and one another. Beginning in the fall of 2000, in two years the Creating Community Connections Project enabled 37 families at Camfield Estates—more than 50% of the community at that time—to gain basic personal computing skills, connect to the Internet, and communicate with family members, friends and other Camfield residents. This chapter attempts to expand and extend the discussion of what modern-day strategies are necessary to help low-income community residents do more for themselves in the 21st century. I begin with the importance of refocusing efforts to make low-income residents more self-sufficient, and of using a community technology framework and strategy (community content, community networks, and community technology centers) (Beamish, 1999) to link residents to information-based resources. I follow this with a description of the mixed method approach used and findings from the Camfield Estates-MIT Creating Community Connections Project, and I close with a discussion of the potential role that the Internet can play in empowering low-income families toward becoming more self-sufficient.

SELF-SUFFICIENCY AND COMMUNITY TECHNOLOGY

The federal government, in particular the Department of Housing and Urban Development, initially narrowly defined self-sufficiency as having enough income to cover your expenses from month to month without the assistance of a subsidy. The Miller and Din (1996) model captures self-sufficiency as having some semblance of control over the basic functions and fundamentals of an individual and/or a family's life. The basic functions of self-sufficiency include stability of income, education and life skills, housing stability, adequate food, safety, the availability and accessibility of needed services, relationships (social networks), and strong personal attributes (motivation, desire, etc.) (Miller & Din, 1996).

A greater sense of freedom and greater control of one's life is gained from being self-sufficient. As technology aims to make life easier, it also becomes important that a level of technological proficiency is present. This means that in today's information-based society access to information about what affects one's life can become a basic component in fulfilling the basic needs mentioned earlier. Self-sufficiency is a way of life that reduces dependency on external support in order to thrive. This is by no means an easy feat since it requires considerable self-discipline, motivation and determination, especially in today's society where some have grown accustomed to depending upon others to provide necessary resources for their basic needs.

Using information technology to move toward self-sufficiency is of critical concern because of the vast array of resources that are made available electronically on the Internet. It is not that traditional methods of getting information are not feasible. However, when having to do a mundane task such as searching for job opportunities the Internet provides a vehicle that is considerably faster than visiting a local agency and looking through thick binders of employment listings. Moreover, for entry-level jobs, an Internet search may in fact be more suitable. With the paper-intensive, centralized method there are three obstacles to overcome:

1. getting to a local or central office,
2. conducting a job search with many other people doing the same tasks and the limitations in viewing the same information at the same time, and
3. the fact that not all agencies have the infrastructure to keep employment listings current.

Through technology, a central location of listings is no longer a requirement; it is much easier and faster for employers to keep their listings relatively current. Moreover, many services allow you to post your resume, so the job search becomes a two-way proposition and connection: the individual searching for employers and employers searching for individuals with particular skills, background and experience. Being able to search for essential information at one's convenience also makes the proposition of an Internet job search more time-efficient. Although this new method for job searching is convenient, it is also complex and should not become a substitute for face-to-face interactions.

The Digital Divide and the Role of Community Technology

The digital divide, as it is commonly called, is defined as the disparity in computer and Internet access and use between various social, economic, and racial groups within the United States. The National Telecommunications and Information Administration (NTIA) concluded that the divide has been getting progressively wider (1995, 1998, 1999). In their latest report (2000), analysts from NTIA concluded that the divide was showing a slight decrease; however, a significant divide still remains. As a result of the concerns provoked by the digital divide, many community initiatives were established by providing access to computers and related technology at schools, community centers, libraries and churches, etc. (Beamish, 1999; Morino, 1994; Pinkett, 2001), and by creating community-specific applications and software. The increasing demands for access and the nature of the different types of access have come-up against the limited capacity of community technology centers (CTCs). Consequently, efforts are now underway to augment traditional community computing efforts by bringing computers and communication technologies into the homes of low-income residents (Bishop, Tidline, Shoemaker, & Salela, 1999).

Community technology centers have played a significant role to date in helping to build capacities of low-income communities. Moreover, CTCs have established themselves as necessary institutions in low-income communities. Indications from a study conducted by the Community Technology Center Network (CTCNet) titled *Community Technology Centers: Impact on Individual Participants and their Communities* (see Mark, Cornebise, & Wahl, 1997), and research conducted by others involved with community technology initiatives call for the continued development of the technological capacity of low-income communities. This suggests that the availability of technology in the home in addition to technology centers is a critical factor. In 1998, one of the concerns raised in the CTCNet report on community technology centers was the ability of CTCs to sustain staff, resources and programming. Although technology in the home can be looked at as an alternative to the technology diffusion approach of CTCs, it really should be considered as the next step along the continuum of technology capacity building. Additionally, CTCs can serve as support and a location for future training for home-based technology use.

Based on existing literature and this current study it is believed that the use of community technology, personal computing and Internet access is an efficient and resourceful method for linking low-income communities, families, and individuals to relevant information necessary for making an informed decision about what can affect their lives.

An Approach to Low-Income Communities, Self-Sufficiency and Information Technology

In attempting to understand information technology's potential with low-income community efforts of self-sufficiency, it is important to understand what ingredients bind self-sufficiency, low-income communities, and information technology together. By understanding this, it becomes possible to develop a theoretical approach. To merge the self-sufficiency discussion, it is critical to have access to relevant information to make an informed decision about what is of interest to the individual.

A Community Technology Center's primary function is to build human capital by assisting its users in their efforts to establish and/or nurture a certain standard of technological proficiency. Moreover, CTCs assist users in developing a level of comfort such that their newly developed technological ability enables them to explore new ways to use technology. Community content can be viewed as the fuel to sustaining interest in, and the perceived utility of, technology. Without relevant timely content, it is virtually impossible for technology to play a role in a low-income community's efforts toward self-sufficiency. Community networks build social capital by enabling users of technology to share relevant ideas for change and relevant information for individual and community decision-making, and to build and nurture social connections. Social capital refers here to features of social organization, such as trust, norms and networks, which can improve the efficiency of society, facilitating and coordinating actions (Putnam, 1993).

Finally, for all these components to come together it is important for the individual to believe that achieving these levels of understanding and technological use is in fact possible. It is important that the individual have a sense of inspiration and motivation to achieve a sense of empowerment.

Partnering with Camfield Estates
and Implementation Objectives

Camfield Estates, originally Camfield Gardens, was built in 1971. By the late '70s and well into the '80s Camfield experienced many of the troubles that plagued low-income communities generally—deteriorating properties, absentee landlords, problem tenants and an increase in drug-related crimes. These troubles contributed to the deterioration of not only Camfield's physical environment, but also Camfield's cherished community relations. After organizing themselves in the late '80s and early '90s, Camfield residents chose to participate in HUD/MassHousing's Demonstration Disposition[4] or "DemoDispo" Program to have their property rebuilt. While the Camfield property was being rebuilt, residents were all relocated throughout the greater Boston area for nearly two years. The relocation forced the previous form of resident-to-resident communication to become more centralized. The main form of communication between relocated residents was funneled through the Camfield Tenant Association and circulated via newsletters, phone calls and regular meetings.

Camfield residents began returning to their newly developed town homes in the spring of 2000. Residents soon found that the community relations they had remembered had gone through a dramatic change. Because of the relocation, interpersonal relations and connections had dramatically declined. At the time we introduced the Creating Community Connections Project, the residents were faced with the challenge of how they would rebuild their old sense of community and a sense of control of their environment. Personal computing, Internet use and an on-line community would become methods by which some Camfield residents would be able to address this challenge. After identifying Camfield Estates as the research site, a detailed plan was developed for accomplishing seven implementation objectives:

1. offer new computers as opposed to old or refurbished computers,
2. have the computer put into residents' homes,
3. provide high-speed Internet connectivity,
4. provide Internet access supported by a dedicated web portal and online community,
5. engage participants in the design and implementation,
6. provide training and support to increase participant fluency in the use of technology, and
7. raise the necessary funds for the project.

The Creating Community Connections System (C3) and Participant Training

The on-line community and web portal was named the Creating Community Connections (C3) System.[5] The C3 system is a password-protected system designed to support specifically asset- and information-based community building, empowerment and self-sufficiency. Camfield Estates residents, through the C3 system and Internet access, would have the capacity to extend and amplify their community networks electronically. The Camfield estates website has the capacity to provide resident profiles, e-mail list-serves, discussion groups, calendar utility, chat and file storage. The dedicated on-line community had capabilities that were geared for Camfield residents to be able to communicate, discuss issues and share files. Moreover, users were able to post important dates and events. This functionality was intended to support personal connections to other residents and to support exchange of important information (for a more comprehensive discussion of this system and rationale for particular functionalities, see Pinkett, 2001).

The C3 system was accessible by Camfield users through both Microsoft Internet Explorer and Netscape web browsers and an Internet connection. The C3 system contains several functional modules that support Internet communications. The modules included links to state and local police departments, links to publicly-elected officials including the President of the United States, links to news sources (newspaper, television, radio), news and announcements, organization and business databases, geographic information system (GIS) maps, job and volunteer opportunity postings, surveys and polls, on-line resumes, personalized web portals, and site-wide search capabilities.

In addition to the physical infrastructure (the computer and physical Internet connection), the project offered an intellectual infrastructure through a mandatory eight-week basic computer training course and several non-mandatory, but targeted workshops. Participants who could demonstrate some degree of basic technological proficiency were allowed to test-out of the required eight-week training course.[6]

Participants also received mandatory training on the Creating Community Connections (C3) System which included how to use the Camfield website and how to explore its functionality and specific components. The C3 System is based on the principles of sociocultural constructionism[7] (Pinkett, 2001). It is a database-backed web system designed to establish and strengthen relationships among community residents, local businesses, and neighborhood organizations and institutions (e.g., libraries, schools, etc.). Monthly non-mandatory workshops were also conducted, related to educational, financial, government, and housing services. These workshops were specifically designed to address and provide the necessary skills to participants who wanted to learn how to search for specific information on the Internet.

The Camfield Estates Neighborhood Technology Center (CENTC) has a unique support structure. MassHousing, as the primary funding agency, developed a community-based process to decide what happens with the center. The Camfield Tenants Association (CTA), in existence more than 20 years, has played a significant role in decisions made in relation to the CENTC. The technology contractor and consultant, Williams Consulting, works very closely with both MassHousing and the CTA to ensure resident involvement in structuring and maintaining the NTC programs and curriculum. All of the partners meet regularly, both formally and informally to communicate about the CENTC and its delivery of technology.

After completing the eight-week training course and/or having successfully completed the test-out requirement, participants were given a personal computer to place in their home and were set up with two years of high-speed Internet access.

METHODS

A mixed-methods approach was used, which allowed various competing research methods to be triangulated, thus increasing the validity and credibility of results (Gaber & Gaber, 1997). This approach allowed the capture of not only the breadth of the study through the quantitative results, but also the depth of the study through qualitative results. The primary source of data for this manuscript is from the longitudinal survey research designed study of the Camfield Estates-MIT Creating Community Connections Project. The qualitative data was gathered through face-to-face survey interviews conducted both before and after the project by the co-researchers and trained research assistants over a 12- to 14-month period. The survey instrument included closed- and open-ended questions, which took approximately two hours to complete. The survey instrument covered a number of areas; for the purpose of this study, items on the pre- and post-surveys captured data on community, empowerment, self-sufficiency and participant demographics. The pre-survey instrument contained questions regarding computer experience and exposure to computers (i.e., skill level), which was collected only at time one. The post-survey data was collected in follow-up interviews in the fall of 2001. The interviews were relatively informal and usually conducted in the participant's home. Web logs of participant Internet access activities were analyzed, including statistics gathered regarding hits to the Camfield Estates website. In addition to individual interviews, qualitative data included field observations of community meetings and other resident gatherings. Additional targeted qualitative information was gathered on family uses and the mentor relationship that developed between a participant and the co-researchers.

Findings and Analysis

There were 37 participating Camfield households, which constituted 54% of 69 eligible households. Twenty of the 37 participating households were classified as full participants. Full participants were those individuals who completed the required training and follow-up interviews, and received uninterrupted Internet connectivity. Individuals that did not meet all three of the full participant requirements were not classified as full participants.[8] The average project participant was a single (including widowed or divorced), African American female, between the ages of 40 and 69, and at least one child under 18 in the household. The average household income was under $30,000 and many of the project participants had some formal education ranging from high school to no more than two years of college.

Sixty-two percent of participants considered themselves beginners at the start of the project, 27% reported intermediate experience with computers, and 11% considered their skills advanced. Pre-survey data revealed that among the 37 participants 46% reported that they owned a computer and 54% did not. Beginners were least likely to own a computer while intermediate and advanced were more likely to own a computer. Out of the 37 participants that considered themselves beginners, 35% were single African American and/or Hispanic female with related children under 18 years of age.

In April of 2001, the most common websites visited by participants were community/cultural, E-Commerce and entertainment. One of the e-commerce sites, vstore.com, focused specifically on starting an online business. Unfortunately, in May of 2001, the Internet service provider discontinued operation of the transparent-proxy server that was collecting web traffic information.

Respondents that completed the post-survey reported using their computers an average of 3.8 hours per day. Fifty-five percent and 35% of post-survey respondents reported using their computer with the Internet everyday and almost everyday, respectively. The twelve most frequently performed Internet tasks from most frequent to least frequent were browsing; sending/receiving email; work/school related tasks; games; researching a topic, hobby or interest; accessing educational resources for children; communicating with family/friends; continuing education; using Microsoft Office applications; using instant messaging programs; career or job exploration; and business or entrepreneurial activity.

Sense of Connectedness and Social Contact

Research suggests that the Internet decreases social contact and causes isolation (see Kraut et al., 1998; Nie & Erbring, 2000; Stoll, 1995). As discussed earlier, relationships and social networks are an important aspect of self-sufficiency because self-sufficiency does not mean total isolation. In fact, from a socio-economic perspective, total isolation can make one less self-sufficient. Therefore, it was important through this study to understand whether the presence of Internet access in the homes of low-income residents increased or decreased social isolation. In this study it was found that, after having computers and Internet access for more than a year, full participants overwhelmingly felt equally (32%) or more connected (37%) to other Camfield residents than they did before receiving Internet access (see Table 1). This feeling of connectedness was enhanced by the ease of information access from Internet and e-mail use. As one participant stated, "It's easy to get a message to the residents and I can do it from home." Another participant said, "It's especially good for those residents that are not able to get out as often, so they are able to stay connected with what is going on at Camfield." Additionally, it was found that participants felt equally (37%) or more connected (21%) to the Camfield Tenant Association (CTA) board. "To obtain information regarding Camfield, I usually go to our site," acknowledged one participant. Finally, residents felt equally (32%) or more (53%) connected locally, and equally (26%) or more (53%) connected beyond their local area to family members. This was confirmed by one participant who stated, "I am able to share information about hereditary family health conditions with family members here at Camfield and in other parts of the country."

Table 1: Full participants' feeling of connectedness* since receiving a computer and Internet access, and Internet and e-mail use

	Responses			Correlation	Coefficients
Question [a]	More Connected	Equally Connected	Less Connected	E-mail Use	Internet Use
Family/friends in your local area?	53%	32%	5%	.615 [d]	–
Family/friends not in your local area?	53%	26%	11%	.500 [c]	–
Residents at Camfield?	37%	32%	5%	–	–
Camfield Tenants Association Board?	21%	37%	16%	–	.438 [b]
People inside your local community?	32%	26%	16%	–	.332 [b]
People outside your local community?	42%	26%	11%	.461 [c]	–

a n=20
b Correlation is significant at the 0.10 level for small sample size (2-tailed)
c Correlation is significant at the 0.05 level (2-tailed)
d Correlation is significant at the 0.01 level (2-tailed)
*This measure is coded as 1 = not sure, 2 = less connected, 3 = equally connected, 4 = more connected

The apparent relationship between e-mail use and participants' sense of connectedness to family, friends and people outside of their local community is interesting. It suggests that e-mail has a role in supporting interpersonal connections with people over distances. Also interesting is the possible relationship between Internet use and connectedness locally with the Camfield board and with people inside their local community. This suggests that other on-line functionality besides e-mail use may encourage local connectivity. Feeling connected to the Camfield board was most likely influenced by on-line CTA information and communication to residents.

It was also found that social contact increased not only between participant families but also between participants and other Camfield residents. For example, participants' average visits to one another's homes and average times talking to one another on the phone increased over the 10- to 12-month period in which this study took place. The increase was proportionally similar for full participants and other Camfield residents. Contrary to public perception and the findings of some researchers such as Nie and Erbring (2000) that Internet and e-mail use would decrease human contact, participants in this study actually reported greater levels of connectedness and social contact.

Empowerment and Self-sufficiency

Empowerment can be looked at as the enabling ingredient in the self-sufficiency model. The empowering process includes learning decision-making skills, managing resources, and working with others, while empowerment as an outcome involves a sense of control, critical awareness and participatory behavior (Zimmerman, 2000). In this study, empowerment meant that individuals have beliefs that certain goals are possible and believe that they have the means available to accomplish those goals. Participants' remarks during post-survey interviews reveal the impact and complexity of the role of a personal computer. Qualitatively, the revelations are full of supportive ideas, expressions, emotions, states of being and understanding that directly signify feelings of empowerment and self-sufficiency. Individual responses from full participants showed what they have learned as a result of the Creating Community Connections Project and that the project has inspired continued computer use.

Many respondent comments are related to the influence of the intellectual infrastructure (human capital) that their participation provided and the development of their technological skill sets. One participant expressed pride and a sense of independence obtained through the project, stating "it [computer training] has changed my life a lot just because it has enhanced my knowledge of computers. I know a lot more how computers work and how to go online and use e-mail."

Further this quote denotes how technology nurtures feelings of independence, and the impact of this recognition of the power associated with in-home access. In addition to the impact of recognizing the relevance and the role of a personal computer, the following remark captures the potential role of technology in another respondent's broader life and future outlook: "I don't have to go to a library. I can't go out of my house. How am I going to a library? The computer is a library. I have it in my home....I mean, this is something that connects you throughout the world. And I found it incredible."

Knowledge gained about technology and the desire (goal) to learn was evident in the following respondent's remarks. Learning as a goal is generally a reasonable pursuit. The possession of understanding and motivation to pursue this goal corresponds with the notion of empowerment. Specifically one respondent commented:

> [The project] has changed my life in more ways than one. A good example of this is that I found enough courage to teach myself HTML. Had I not had this opportunity, I might still be looking to muster up the courage. I know that technology is key to the

future and I know that I could personally do anything with it that I put my mind to.

Full participants' awareness of "associations and organizations that serve the community" increased over the 12-month period from 25 to 55 percent. Awareness of "volunteer opportunities in the community" and awareness of "social services and programs provided for the community" both increased 40 percentage points from the pre-survey (time1) to post-survey (time2). Awareness of "institutions located in the community (e.g., libraries and schools)" and awareness of "products and services sold by local businesses" both stayed about the same from time1 (75%, 35%) to time2 (85%, 35%) respectively. Awareness of "community projects, activities, and events" showed the largest increase of 50 percentage points from time1 to time2. Finally, awareness of "employment opportunities in the community" increased from 5% to 35% from time1 to time2. Awareness of internal resources, "skills and abilities of other residents at Camfield Estates," as shown in Table 2, rose 20% from time 1 to time 2.

Table 2: Awareness of community resources*

Responded[a] very well or well informed			
	Time 1	Time 2	Diff
Skills and abilities of other residents at Camfield Estates.	10%	30%	20%[b]
Associations and organizations that serve the community.	25%	55%	30%[b]
Volunteer opportunities in the community.	5%	45%	40%[d]
Institutions located in the community (for example, libraries and schools).	75%	85%	10%
Social services and programs provided for the community.	25%	65%	40%[d]
Community projects, activities, and events.	10%	60%	50%[d]
Businesses located in the community.	55%	65%	10%
Products and services sold by local businesses.	35%	35%	0%
Employment opportunities in the community.	5%	35%	30%[c]

a n=20
b Difference is significant at the 0.10 level for small sample size (2-tailed)
c Difference is significant at the 0.05 level (2-tailed)
d Difference is significant at the 0.01 level (2-tailed)
* This measure is coded as 0 = not informed, 1 = somewhat informed, 2 = well informed, 3 = very well informed

Full participants responded that computer access was instrumental in their becoming more aware of available resources in their neighborhood and surrounding community. As discussed earlier, access to relevant information is an important component in the self-sufficiency model. This access is critical to an individual's ability to make informed decisions about how to deal with what affects his or her life and the lives of one's family. Key factors according to several respondents, in addition to Internet access, were their ownership of and motivation to get information and use the information:

> I think it was important for [residents] to go out and find that information ourselves [via the Internet] because that, in itself, was an exercise in community building. We are the ones that live here and this is going to benefit us and these are things that we should know.

The responses of full participants showed awareness of resources outside of the Camfield community. Specific to ownership and use of information, a respondent remarked about electronic communication as having an advantage over flyers that sometimes get lost:

> We are communicating more without a doubt. They [Camfield Tenants Association] send out e-mails to keep us updated. I think we are finding out more because they are sending it out. People had a problem finding out what was going on because they would say, 'I didn't get this or that' like the flyers or something that the kids would send out, then if they didn't get it they didn't know.

Technology's role in bolstering communication efforts and awareness is evidenced in the data and observed in participant remarks. The remarks include references to their sense of control, improved ability to communicate, ownership of online contents, taking responsibility for and sharing information and an overall sense of independence that translated into feelings of empowerment and self-sufficiency.

DISCUSSION AND CONCLUSION

Universities are continually grappling with ways to positively contribute to society. A community-university partnership is one approach. Moreover, through community based research, community-university partnerships develop data that can inform public policy debate. Given this study's demographic population, which is characteristic of many low-income communities, it is important that more IT initiatives are undertaken in efforts to address the digital divide and inform the public policy process. This study revealed that once participants recognized the relevance of IT to their daily lives, including the ability to access as well as connect to family and friends, their computer use increased. Perhaps the cost of IT, and not a lack of relevancy, is a more likely inhibitor for IT use. Households with only one wage earner usually have much less dispensable income, as compared to two-income households (Wilson, 1987, 1996). The average cost of a new computer is roughly $1,000 dollars; in addition, the cost of high-speed Internet access can be as high as $40 to $50 per month (or ~ $600 per year). The prospect of even a one-time expense of a thousand dollars (or more), not to mention the steep learning curve associated with setting up a computer and installing and using software (if one has never done it before) means that information technology may ultimately lose out to more pressing economic and time-related family matters. This initiative was able to remove many of the economic barriers to IT use by providing free computers and access along with comprehensive computer training.

As discussed earlier, full participants reported using their computers and the Internet every day or almost every day for several hours per day. In addition to browsing the Internet and using e-mail frequently, many full participants also reported frequently doing work- or school-related tasks, researching a topic, hobby or interest, accessing education resources for their children, and communicating with family and friends. Reported usage gives important insight into the regularity with which the computer and Internet were used as a resource. Moreover, these findings also seem to refute some of the other studies that suggest Internet use and email contribute to social isolation. As the community and technology debate plays out over the next several years, I suspect concerns about Internet use causing isolation will take a different form and will have little effect on the continuing rapid growth of home computer and Internet use. That is not to suggest concern over Internet and isolation is not legitimate, but rather, the focus should be on the nature of on-line community connections and whether or not those on-line connections translate into something meaningful for the user.

The empowerment and self-sufficiency findings suggest that a personal computer and Internet access can play a role in empowering low-income individuals in becoming more self-sufficient. Moreover, Internet access plays a role in one's sense of control because of access to information, which can influence behaviors and encourage the opportunity to do more for oneself. Low-income communities and their residents have relied historically on third-party organizations to assist them in finding jobs, housing, services and other information. A personal computer and

Internet access, along with comprehensive training, can help low-income residents to do more of these types of tasks on their own.

Empowerment and self-sufficiency are topics that are difficult to quantify because the definition of each can have different meanings for different people. The qualitative findings, such as self-reported feelings of empowerment and observations of self-sufficiency, provided a framework for allowing a certain degree of quantification. These findings can lead one to believe that Internet use is the sole cause of the increased sense of community, increased awareness and participatory behavior reported by participants. However, this cannot be said definitively. At the very least it can be said that Internet use did not take away from a participant's sense of community, empowerment or self-sufficiency as others have suggested.

In closing, empowerment, self-sufficiency, and community are not concepts that are unfamiliar to Camfield residents, nor are these elements completely absent in this community. Residents desire all of the positive effects that result from achieving these ideals. The challenge is *how* one goes about being empowered or self-sufficient. Camfield residents, as do residents in many other low-income communities, want to be more self-sufficient and empowered and to live in safe, supportive and involved communities. This special community-university partnership, Camfield Estates-MIT Creating Community Connections Project, supports the residents of Camfield Estates' efforts toward identifying solutions to longstanding socio-economic challenges for them and other low-income communities. Public policy has not been completely successful in its approach to promoting self-reliance. Rather, finger pointing continues to be directed at the individual and not at institutional barriers (Wilson, 1996). It is hoped that similar studies will continue to shed light on technology's role in sharing information and resources that could potentially empower an individual to become more self-sufficient.

Endnotes

1. Linkage institution is defined in this instance as an entity that plays the role of connecting individuals and communities with information and resources (i.e., job opportunities, housing opportunities, economic opportunities, health care information, educational resources, etc.) which traditionally requires intervention by an outside agency or organization.
2. Self-sufficiency for this paper is defined as a way of life that reduces or minimizes external support in order to survive and thrive.
3. www.camfieldestates.net
4. The Housing and Urban Development (HUD)/MassHousing Demonstration Disposition Project is a $200 million pilot project targeted at rehabilitating or rebuilding physically deteriorating HUD owned, low-income housing developments. Once renovated, development ownership would be transferred to residents in the form of homeownership opportunities.
5. This system was created and designed by co-researcher Dr. Randal Pinkett.
6. The eight-week training course in succession included:

* Introduction to the Windows Operating System: overview of the icons, menus, and toolbars associated with Windows.
* Working with files and folders: how to create, delete, copy, backup, move and rename files and install software.
* Maintenance and troubleshooting: how to conduct scan disk and defrag, use the task scheduler, change Windows settings, and use anti-virus programs.
* Introduction to Internet Explorer 5.0: brief history and definitions of the Internet and World Wide Web, and review of icons, menus, and toolbars in Internet Explorer 5.0.
* Navigating the Internet: review of Internet address rules, how to use search engines, store bookmarks, subscribe to a web site, view browser history and surf the Web.
* Advanced file use: how to download files off the Internet, understand cookies, and work with temporary Internet files created by Internet Explorer.
* E-mail: overview of icons, menus, and toolbars in Outlook Express. How to configure an e-mail account, set up and use message rules, send and receive e-mail, manage incoming and outgoing messages, use Outlook Express address book and send e-mail attachments.
* Working with the hardware: how to set up a computer, connect printer and other peripherals.

7. Sociocultural constructionism is a theory, expanded by Dr. Randal Pinkett (2001), which argues that "individual and community development are reciprocally enhanced by independent and shared constructive activity that is resonant with both the social setting that encompasses a community of learners, as well as the culture of the learners themselves" (p. 29).
8. For the remainder of this manuscript the distinction between full participant and participant is intentional.

References

Beamish, A. (1999). Approaches to Community Computing: Bringing Technology to Low-Income Groups. In D. Schön, B. Sanyal, & W. J. Mitchell (Eds.), *High Technology in Low-Income Communities: Prospects for the Positive Use of Information Technology* (pp. 349–368). Cambridge, MA: MIT Press.

Bishop, A. P., Tidline, T. J., Shoemaker, S., & Salela, P. (1999). Public Libraries and Networked Information Services in Low-Income Communities. *Libraries & Information Science Research, 21*, 361–390.

Gaber, J., & Gaber, S. L. (1997). Utilizing Mixed-Method Research Designs in Planning: The Case of 14th Street, New York City. *Journal of Planning Education and Research, 17*(2), 95–103.

Mark, J., Cornebise, J., & Wahl, E. (1997). *Community Technology Centers: Impact on Individual*

Participants and Their Communities (Paper submitted to the Informal Science Division, National Science Foundation and Human Resources). Newton, MA: Educational Development Center.

Mead, L. M. (1991). *The New Politics of Poverty: The Non-Working Poor in America.* New York: Basic Books.

Miller, M. L., & Din, G. (1996). *A Practice Based Anti-Poverty Analysis* (Policy Brief Section I of III). San Francisco, CA: Asian Neighborhood Design Network.

Morino, M. (1994, May). *Assessment and Evolution of Community Networking.* Paper presented at the Ties That Bind Conference on Building Community Networks, Cupertino, CA.

O'Connor, A. (1999). Swimming against the Tide: A Brief History of Federal Policy in Poor Communities. In R. F. Ferguson & W. T. Dickens (Eds.), *Urban Problems and Community Development* (pp. 77–137). Washington, DC: The Brookings Institute.

Pinkett, R. D. (2001). *Creating Community Connections: Sociocultural Constructionism and an Asset-Based Approach to Community Technology and Community Building in a Low-Income Community.* Unpublished doctoral dissertation, Massachusetts Institute of Technology.

U.S. Department of Commerce (1995). *Falling through the Net: A Survey of the "Have Nots" in Rural and Urban America.* Washington, DC: National Telecommunications and Information Administration, U.S. Department of Commerce.

U.S. Department of Commerce (1998). *Falling through the Net II: New Data on the Digital Divide.* Washington, DC: National Telecommunication and Information Administration, U.S. Department of Commerce.

U.S. Department of Commerce (1999). *Falling through the Net: Defining the Digital Divide. A Report on the Telecommunications and Information Technology Gap in America.* Washington, DC: National Telecommunications and Information Administration, U.S. Department of Commerce.U.S. Department of Commerce (2000). *Falling through the Net: Toward Digital Inclusion. A Report on America's Access to Technology.* Washington, DC: National Telecommunications and Information Administration, U.S. Department of Commerce, Economic and Statistics Administration.

Wilson, W. J. (1987). *The Truly Disadvantaged: The Inner City, the Underclass and Public Policy.* Chicago: The University of Chicago Press.

Wilson, W. J. (1996). *When Work Disappears: The World of the New Urban Poor.* New York: Vintage Books.

Redefining the Academy for the Public Good

CHAPTER 11

Diversity and Social Justice in Higher Education

Jennifer E. Lerner

Abstract: Advocates of diversity in higher education claim that it benefits all students, while critics argue that public rejection of affirmative action reflects a rejection of diversity efforts. In-depth interviews with white college students about their experiences with diversity reveal that they value diversity but do not understand the connection between diversity efforts and racial inequality. This disjuncture leads students to enjoy and support only certain types of diverse encounters, rejecting those that emphasize issues of power and inequality. These findings help us identify future directions for diversity efforts in higher education.

The revival of debate over affirmative action in higher education surrounding the Hopwood decision and the two cases against the University of Michigan has refocused scholarly attention on how campus diversity affects student learning, racial attitudes, and civic engagement. A substantial body of research demonstrates that a diverse faculty, curriculum, extracurricular program, and student body produces better educational outcomes for all students. Nonetheless, the vigorous debate over the value and implementation of diversity continues, as critics point to widespread public rejection of its principal policy manifestation in the form of affirmative action and of certain approaches to diversity. Their data, too, are valid. How can we understand these conflicting perspectives?

Much of the debate about diversity in education stems from a conflict between the original intentions of multiculturalism and the way multiculturalism later developed. Early advocates saw multicultural education as a way to challenge racial/ethnic inequality. Controversies around curricular change toward this goal soon led to a watered-down multiculturalism in which the goal was mere exposure to diverse people and cultures. The goal become tolerance, not justice, and as racial inequality fell from focus, affirmative action measures stood out starkly, representing for many the only aspect of the tolerant world of education that still differentiated among students based on race.

In this chapter, I draw upon data gathered as part of a larger research project on how college students understand the meaning of diversity in American society. I argue that to reconcile the competing arguments about the impact of diversity, we must take a qualitative look at what students *mean* when they talk about the benefits (or costs) of diversity. To come to terms with this debate, we must reexamine the conflict between the initial goals of diversity and the ways it has been implemented—and understood by students—in the academy so far.

COMPETING RESEARCH ON DIVERSITY IN HIGHER EDUCATION

A large body of literature demonstrates the value of diversity in higher education.[1] This research shows that both white students and students of color benefit from diversity in the student body, in the faculty, in the curriculum, and as a goal of the institution. In particular, studies have identified benefits in civic attitudes (for example, greater openness to cross-racial interaction and more desire to improve race relations), in intellectual growth (improving, for example, students' ability to think actively and solve complex problems), and in satisfaction with the college experience (Astin, 1993; Gurin, Dey, Hurtado, & Gurin, 2002; Smith, 1997; Terenzini, Cabrera, Colbeck, Bjorklund, & Parente, 2001).

Although there are many scholars and commentators who critique this research (and diversity measures in general), one recent and controversial article is emblematic of the sorts of critiques raised. Stanley Rothman, Seymour Martin Lipset, and Neil Nevitte (2003) correctly point out that a major weakness of some of the pro-diversity literature is its reliance on survey measures that may not tell the whole story about the effects of diversity. In particular, the authors note that students and faculty are virtually unanimous in the position that diversity has helped rather than hindered higher education. They suggest that this unanimity reflects a social acceptability bias—supporting diversity is now seen as the only socially acceptable position to take—and that the survey data therefore reveal little about the actual impact of diversity. In fact, using measures that do not ask directly about diversity, Rothman, Lipset, and Nevitte find that students at more diverse campuses are less satisfied with their educational experiences and with the work ethic and preparedness of their peers, and that students at diverse schools personally experience more discrimination than do students at less diverse institutions.

This discrepancy is interesting, important, and should prompt further exploration of the basis for the students' dissatisfaction. Perhaps Rothman, Lipset, and Nevitte are correct that belief in the value of diversity is now the socially acceptable answer, leading students to report satisfaction with unsatisfying situations (or to be unaware that the diversity of their institutions is the source of their dissatisfaction). Rather than conducting further research to explore the possible meanings behind this discrepancy, however, Rothman, Lipset, and Nevitte rely on a significant leap in logic to argue that students at diverse schools have a less satisfactory experience because the students of color admitted through affirmative action are less qualified than other students. This unsupported conclusion reveals the axe so many have to grind about affirmative action and how it can lead to conclusions far beyond the scope of the actual data.

It is also worth noting that Rothman, Lipset, and Nevitte fail to consider a range of variables prominent in the rest of the literature on diversity in higher education. This literature consistently points out that the presence of diverse peers is a necessary but not sufficient condition for achieving the academic and civic benefits of diversity in college. A variety of institutional factors shape how diversity in the student body will or will not produce positive student outcomes (Smith, 1997). In other words, Rothman, Lipset, and Nevitte's critique targets only a small part of the research evidence on how diversity affects higher education, and the evidence they omit might have fully explained the findings they consider a rebuttal of the pro-diversity literature.

In this chapter, I want to explore these discrepant findings from another direction, using qualitative research to examine how students actually make sense of the diversity they encounter on campus. Rothman, Lipset, and Nevitte are correct that research reveals seemingly contradictory beliefs among college students—both support for diversity and rejection of affirmative action and other efforts that make diversity possible and meaningful. The best way to understand why students often hold these apparently conflicting views, and how they make sense of that conflict, is to hear from students directly how they experience and understand diversity. What do college students think "diversity" means, and how do they connect that abstract concept, which they overwhelmingly claim to value, with their larger set of attitudes, experiences, and understandings of how society works and their place in it? Understanding how students think about diversity in relation to their other views can help us clarify the source of the underlying tensions between advocates and critics of diversity efforts in higher education.

Data and Methods

The data reported here are part of a larger study examining how undergraduates respond to course curricula that challenge their positions of privilege in racial/ethnic, gender, and class hierarchies. This study involved semester-long observation of three introductory sociology courses at two research universities (one a second-tier, nationally-recognized university; the other a respected regional university) in a metropolitan area in the Southeast. I chose courses that made social inequality a central theme (spending at least half the semester on inequality issues) and that used different pedagogical approaches.

From each class, I recruited a sample of students to interview three times each, at the beginning, middle, and end of the course. Because my purpose in the larger project was to examine how students responded to challenges to their privilege, I selected students with various combinations of privileged social positions—for example, white men from both wealthy and working-class backgrounds, men of color, white women, etc. The students were mostly first- and second-year students, though a few were third-year students, and they reported a range of majors, including many still undecided. In all, the project involved approximately ninety-five hours of classroom observation and seventy-nine interviews with twenty-eight students. I coded the observational and interview data both inductively (looking for themes to emerge from the data) and deductively (identifying data relevant to previously identified themes).

In thirty- to sixty-minute tape-recorded interviews, I asked the students about their evolving thoughts about the course material as well as about their backgrounds and their college experiences overall. Although asking students about "diversity" was not a focus of the research, many of the interviews yielded comments that illuminate how students make sense of their experiences with diversity at college. In this paper, I examine the discussions I had about diversity and race with five of these students, all of whom are white.[2] I selected these students because their responses were the most revealing, but their views are also representative of common patterns among the white students I interviewed.

Student Views on Diversity
and Race Relations

My data support the widespread finding that college students see "diversity" as a core part of the college experience. Some students, however, are more enthusiastic and curious about diversity than others. Further, as they talk about their views on diversity, it becomes increasingly clear that in their minds, in contrast to the views of many of their teachers, "diversity" and its value are a very separate matter from questions of race and social inequality. It is students' views on this latter issue, I will argue, that tell us much more about how students really learn (or fail to learn) from the diversity they encounter in higher education. In this section of the paper, I will illustrate this point by analyzing students' responses to diversity, moving from students who are neutral toward diversity to students who excitedly welcome it, and examining how these views toward diversity correspond to their views about racial/ethnic inequality.

Matt[3] offers the most minimal acceptance of diversity possible. Explaining that he comes from an all-white community in the Northeast, he notes that college is much more diverse, but that the diversity doesn't bother him. Another student, Tom, expresses only slightly more positive feelings about diversity. He believes that diversity is preferable to the uniformity of his home town in the Midwest. It is not clear, however, *why* Tom has this preference. He shows little interest in actually exploring the diversity around him. The following exchange is the entirety of his comments on diversity:

> JL: So you enjoy having all the people around, or would you rather go back to a small setting?
>
> Tom: I like the smaller setting, knowing all the people, but everyone there was white, Christian, you know, small town. Here there's completely different diversity, which I like. Like my two roommates, one's Jewish, and the other's half...Persian, which is interesting.
>
> JL: Do you talk about that stuff a lot, like your different backgrounds?
>
> Tom (tersely): No.

This exchange begs the question: What does Tom see as the value of diversity? It seems that for Tom, its mere presence is enough. Tom's example might be the sort Rothman, Lipset, and Nevitte would use to illustrate the social acceptability effect. Tom knows he is "supposed" to say diversity is good, but when pressed, he does not seem to have reflected on its value. On the other hand, Tom did raise the issue of diversity on his own (I had only asked him to compare small town to city life), which indicates more than a mere socially required nod at diversity.

Like Matt and Tom, Angela also sees diversity as a key part of the college experience. But while Matt finds it neutral (at best) and Tom sees it as a mildly pleasant background characteristic of the school, Angela finds the diversity, along racial as well as class lines, somewhat uncomfortable. The first in her tight-knit Italian-American family to leave their New York City home to attend college, she says, "I felt like I was a very open-minded person back home. Then I came to college and see that I really don't know very much about the world." Like Tom, Angela is aware that diverse people and experiences surround her, but she is not interested in learning from this diversity. As she explains it, she prefers to "get around" the issue:

> I mean, my parents say that all the time, you know, "Don't be mean, we're all equal, but you can't marry one." That's something that—that's in a lot of my—I mean, I have friends whose parents are completely racist, completely bigots about everything. But then, we have my parents that like to get around it and I'm exactly the same way. I mean, I have friends from other cultures, but I would never think about dating them.

Angela's beliefs about racism support her "getting around" the issue approach as quite reasonable. She says:

> I don't know if it's something we can fix because I think it's in us. I think it's something that we've grown up with and I don't care what anyone says. Racism is in all of us. Ignorance about other cultures is in all of us. We grow up with it. That's just how I feel.

Given these comments, one could easily imagine Angela agreeing with survey items like, "Racism is still a problem today," and thus being considered a diversity "success story," whereas in fact, she has quite rigid beliefs about the intractability of racism (even though she seems to see it as learned) and the appropriateness of only surface cross-racial interactions. Although she originally saw herself as "open-minded," by which she seems to mean open to other cultures, she draws a very traditional line between friendships and acquaintances with people of color and romantic relationships with them. In Angela's view, there is a slippery slope from accepting people of color as equal to white people to accepting them as potential family members, so much so that she expresses her parents' lessons on the matter as one short sentence moving from "don't be mean" to "don't marry one."

Angela is also careful to separate her own views of race from those of people who are *completely* racist, seeming to recognize that her views *are* racist while at the same time claiming a non-racist status in comparison to others. She goes further by claiming that everyone is racist and that this racism cannot be eliminated, thereby explaining away any blameworthiness on her part—if everyone is racist, then her own views are unremarkable; and if these views cannot be eliminated, then she bears no responsibility for failing to reflect upon or change her views.

One noteworthy aspect of Angela's position is that her views on diversity (finding it a bit unpleasant and threatening) and her views on race (finding inequality and prejudice intractable) are consistent with each other. For many other students, in contrast, a positive view of diversity appears to conflict with more negative views of racial/ethnic "others." The students point out the value of diversity and express interest in engaging it in some way. The ways they engage with diverse peers or curricula, however, demonstrate that their general claims about valuing diversity do not fully reveal their views of racial/ethnic "others."

Abby seems to find her diverse interactions at college mildly interesting, but she disengages from them at the slightest provocation, and her views on racial inequalities, like Angela's, may help to explain her readiness to tune out. Sometimes, Abby describes the types of experiences we usually expect to come out of diversity. Although Abby's goal in choosing a college close to home was to minimize change and difference, once at school, Abby learned from and enjoyed her encounters with students different from herself. She says that her sociology class has helped her to notice social phenomena she did not see before, like "the hierarchy of people, things like that. And the stigmas that people place on others, like that. And things that—stereotypes that I put on people. It's like, 'Oh, I understand now.'" When I asked her for a specific example of a stereotype she had noticed in herself, she said:

> Um, I don't know. I sit with a person in class, and she was talking to me—it was funny, because she was talking about how she's in an accounting class. She's Vietnamese. And, um, she explained to me how usually people always think that Vietnamese people are very smart and very good in math. And, she goes, "It's not true because I stink at it." And, I was like, "Oh, you know, I kind of did think that." So, just little things like that, those little stereotypes that I always considered to be true, and now knowing they're not.

Abby seems to approach this new understanding as an interesting piece of trivia, one that provides the pleasures of self-discovery and worldly awareness. However, the pleasures associated with these new insights are, for Abby, contingent upon the absence of any negative pressures, including discomfort and any claims that might be "too extreme." For example, in the same discussion about new insights she gleans from her sociology course, Abby says that she has learned about "the different reactions of different people from different cultures," citing the split opinion between the Black and white communities in the city after Black suspects were named in connection with a major crime spree. Notice the way that her assessment of the difference shifts quickly from interest and understanding to rejection as she describes her reaction to the debate:

Abby: Like, with the whole [crime spree] thing, when they were putting up pictures, and they showed that they were Black people, there was a Black girl who reacted and said, "Of course they're Black, they're going after the Black people." And, the white people were like, "It would have happened the same way if it was a white person." So, I don't know. That was interesting.

JL: Why do you think there was that difference in reaction between Black and white people?

Abby: I think because Black people have had more of a background of being accused when they're innocent.

JL: So, you think that's a justified reaction of that girl to feel that way?

Abby: I can understand why she would, but then again, you know, we have progressed. We're not back in those days still, so I think she did overreact a little bit.

Abby goes through several steps in making sense of this encounter. Her first response to the difference of perspective is to find it "interesting." Then she tries out the new perspective, (correctly) providing the reason that many African Americans fear and distrust the police. But she quickly follows this insight with a boundary-setting move, making it clear that her appreciation for that point of view is limited. In particular, she argues that such claims about inequality, while they have some reality, are rooted in a different time and are less relevant to today's situation.

Abby's views on racism and social change are also relevant to her interpretations of diversity. She believes that racism, which appears in the form of individuals' beliefs and behaviors, can never be eliminated:

Abby: I think it's always been that way, but we've come a long way over hundreds of years. But, yeah, I think it's always been that way. I still think it will be like that, at least a little bit, pretty much forever. I mean, it shouldn't be. It should be equal, because they're all Americans, too. We all are. We all have our rights.

JL: Why do you think it's going to be like that forever?

Abby: Because there are those people out there who are stubborn and won't think any other way. Then, they, you know, influence others, and they influence others, and it just—unless you stop everybody from being stubborn, you know, it will never stop. There will always be one person out there who thinks that we should be segregated. I don't think that should be.

For Abby, we have made much progress with regard to race, and when we have not progressed, it is because some individuals are "stubborn" and spread their racism to others. Her views thus acknowledge that racism continues and at the same time compartmentalize it (it is the province of a stubborn few) and place it in the context of overall progress ("we've come a long way over hundreds of years"). She follows this same pattern in her analysis of racial bias during the crime spree. She notes that there is a history to the Black community's distrust of the police, then minimizes its contemporary impact by emphasizing that we are making progress toward racial equality.

Abby carries this understanding of positive change over time even further in her analysis of the class' study of the recent genocide in Rwanda. Her response to the book the class read on this topic also illustrates how little she is willing to endure discomfort in the service of greater awareness about diversity and inequality. Abby recognizes that the instructor included this book in the curriculum in part to educate students about diversity. Explaining what the professor wanted to them to learn from this topic, she says:

> Um, maybe to understand society and another culture. Like, that's so not like what's going on here, unless I'm completely oblivious to something going on in, like, Arizona or something. But, like, um, to just make us, you know, open our eyes and know that this is going on, because this is a huge, huge deal going on. I'm sure I'm not the only one who didn't know—or, maybe I am the only one, but—who didn't know this was going on. I think she just wants us to realize that there is another world outside of America and to pay attention.

Abby seems to understand a key part of the message of the curriculum, and the larger goals of a diverse education, in this statement. When we examine her views further, however, she reveals that she has learned little from the new awareness the book was supposed to bring her. Her major comment mid-semester, when we were just beginning the topic, was how much the subject made her want to "lose her lunch." After we had completed the unit and I discussed it with her again, even that level of "enthusiasm"—the shock and disgust at the horrors of a genocide— had waned, and she complained that it did not seem that important since it had happened so long ago. (The genocide began in 1994 and its results are ongoing; the book the class read was published in 1998, and the interview took place in 2002.)

She also complained that it was really sad. At this point, about a month after she had explained the topic's value in the curriculum, I had to prompt her to even say that she was glad to have learned about these events.

Abby thus began her approach to the material with an awareness that learning about it would teach her about people, places, and events she did not know about and increase her knowledge about the rest of the world. Most of what she learned seems to have stopped at the point of revulsion; her discomfort at what she heard became her main priority, and, in fact, led her to misunderstand the events that took place. In our final interview, she noted that she still did not understand why the two groups were "killing each other," when in fact, the curriculum described a genocide in which one ethnic group attempted to systematically eliminate the other. And in the end, Abby simply lost interest, withdrawing from the substance altogether and justifying her withdrawal by claiming that the material was outdated.

Abby's general approach to a larger set of issues may help explain her flip-flopping reactions to these two incidents. Abby is aware that she shows little sustained interest in anything she would consider "political." As she explains:

> I hate politics. If you talk politics with the wrong type of person you just offend them and they go off on tangents forever, and you're just like, "Shut up."...Um, I don't know, like when they say they want to change a stupid law, like a simple stupid law, I don't care. But, if it's a big, big thing, I'm like, "Why are you doing this?" and I start to get interested, but then, like two hours later, I'm bored. So, I stay out of it.

This lack of interest, including disinterest in sustained attention to even something "big," may explain why Abby changed her view on studying the genocide in Rwanda. In short, for Abby, "diversity" is interesting, but the political is not. The political is either unimportant (changing some "simple, stupid law"), unpleasant (from political people and their tangents to the discomfort of learning about genocide), or pointless (because these issues, like racism, will never be completely resolved).

This impulse to separate diversity from inequality and power is even clearer in Courtney's responses. Courtney feels more strongly than Abby about the value of diversity, citing it as one of the most important aspects of her college experience. At the same time, however, Courtney's discourse quickly and repeatedly shifts from pleasure in diversity to criticisms of people or behaviors that make racial *inequalities* apparent. When I ask her about her views on affirmative action, for example, she quickly shifts to discussing diversity:

> **Courtney:** I mean, [the college], I think, does a really good job of incorporating, you know, people of all types. I don't really think

[affirmative action is] right, but I don't really think it's wrong. I think that they need to find like a middle way. It should be, like, mixed really well. I don't want to go anywhere that's all white. I mean, I didn't know anything about society. I live in a small white town and everybody was the same where, when I came [here] it was just like one of every kind. Like, it might not be something you can learn in a book, but being surrounded by that, it does teach you a lot of the cultures and it does make you—like, when I came here, I was prejudiced, you know? But, being here and seeing that just because they're *that* doesn't mean they're *this*, you know? Just being around it teaches you a lesson in itself. So, I definitely think they do need to work to make sure everybody is mixed—fairly, though. Not just because, "oh, well, you're white, so you get in, but not her."

JL: Do you have anything specific in mind that, you know, since you've been here, anything specific that really changed your mind or that you learned from?

Courtney: Well, my first, like, running into the situation—I came here with my best friend from high school, which was white. It was just the two of us. But, next door—I lived in the dorms the first year, so it was just a floor of 40 girls, once again, of every single—I mean, things I hadn't even heard of, you know, countries that I didn't even know where they were. And there was a girl next door from Ghana and she came in halfway through the first semester, and when I first heard she was coming—I mean, this is really bad. I feel really bad. Her name was Melat, and we were like, "Oh, God. What is she going to be like? What if she does this?"....But once Melat came in, one night, [my friend] and I sat down and we were just like, "So, tell us about Ghana." And, she was like, well, "Tell me what do you think of when I tell you that I'm from there." And, I was like, "Well, when I hear that, my perception is like it's just a small, old town, not very established, blah, blah, blah." Come to find out, like, she told us a whole different story. It just made me realize that my perception of different people's cultures and stuff, you know, is just nothing that it really is. So, just listening to her one on one, she really opened up my eyes to a lot of stuff. And, from that point on, you know—and, I still talk to her now. Her dad's here from Ghana and she wants us to go out to dinner with him. Before, I probably would have been scared to death because she's different and it's not what I'm used to. And, when she sat down, I mean, she even told us, "Look, I was scared. I'm moving into a room with five girls and I'm the only one from another country, directly from another country." She's like, "But, you guys are awesome. You all taught me so much already." And, we always kid her, "Can you put our hair in cornrows?" Like, it's just like, by living in close quarters like that, like, I just learned stuff from being around her. So, she was the first person that really opened up my eyes, and then from there on, I just let myself see other things where before I was just like my way is the only way.

Courtney's comments are sincere, and it is clear in talking with her that she values this experience a great deal. Nonetheless, her understanding of the experience addresses only one part of the value of diversity. Courtney values diversity mainly as a change of pace, an engaging variety, and an opportunity for enjoyably (if sometimes somewhat nerve-wracking) "eye-opening" experiences. She states her preference for a campus that is not "all white" in much the same tone as one might praise a dining hall for offering variety rather than hamburgers every night. There is no sense that diversity on campus might be related to inequality or social justice, even though the issue arose in relation to the question of affirmative action. She thus expresses the watered-down multiculturalism that has predominated the educational landscape since the 1980s—the idea that diversity means the pleasure of learning some (surface) details about other cultures, not (as advocates originally intended) the difficult grappling with deep cross-cultural communication and the effort to make our interactions and institutions equally accessible to all.

Courtney's cross-cultural encounter with her Ghanaian hallmate is also a quite common way of engaging with the peer who is "other." To Courtney, this peer is slightly scary, a subject of curiosity, and, when she is found to be willing to play along by answering their questions, a friend with whom Courtney can make a joke of the idea of being in some way like the "other" (as, for example, in wearing her hair in cornrows). Although Courtney does seem to learn some valuable lessons from this cross-cultural encounter, her comments reveal some important remaining assumptions about racial difference.

A key part of the Ghanaian student's legitimacy to Courtney, what made her ultimately so interesting, was that she was successful in conventional American ways Courtney could make sense of. She feels guilty about assuming that countries she is unfamiliar with are poor and underdeveloped, but no compunction about celebrating how very similar she and the Ghanaian student are in their possessions and in certain values and aspirations. In other words, part of what makes this "other" safe and acceptable to Courtney is that she does not challenge the system in any way—she does not raise the specter of inequality, which, as Courtney's further comments reveal, shaped her fears and expectations about her new hallmate. When I ask her where she got her ideas about what Ghana might be like before meeting her hallmate, she says:

> Um, I don't really know. I mean, I was never really exposed to anything different. You know, in high school I just remember hearing, you know, there's all these countries that aren't developed, you know, and they aren't up with technology. And, I guess I just thought Ghana is really far away—and, that's really bad for me to say that, but I'm being honest. But, I was just like, "It's kind of poor, and it's far away." And, I told Melat this, you know, like dirt roads, you know, not houses like we have, not buildings like we have, not cars like we have. And, she's like, "Oh, my God." Come to find out both her parents are doctors and they have two houses and Lexuses and Mercedes. I'm just like, "You're kidding me?" You know, and she's like, "Yeah, but I just don't like to talk about it or else, you know, I would have told you before." It was kind of like a smack in the face, because inside, I was like, "Oh my God, I judged this girl to be some poor black girl coming from this far away country who's not going to know anything." She was like a biology major, 4.0, you know, it's just like a totally different person. And, I told her and she's like, you know, "Why did you think that?" And, I was like, "I guess because I had never been educated on anything different." I mean it's not like my parents were ever like, "Black people are bad." They were never like that, but they—not them, but just my school and the town. We're not exposed to anything at all. Like, it's very—like I said, it's very white. So, I was never told that's how it was, but I just put all the tidbits of information together and came up with that for myself.

Courtney makes some interesting and quite telling connections in this statement. She is clearly now aware that her ideas about Ghana were based on ignorant assumptions. But she also articulates a central part of the basis for those assumptions—her images of impoverished African Americans. She does not describe Melat as a poor immigrant who won't know anything; she describes her as a poor *Black girl* who won't know anything. And in reflecting upon where she got her ideas about Ghana, she notes that her parents never told her, "Black people are bad." She does not mention what her parents did or did not tell her about Ghanaians, Africans, or immigrants. Apparently, for Courtney, a Black person is a Black person—and it is amazing if she drives a Lexus or gets straight As.

Attending a diverse college also gave Courtney other opportunities to interact with students of color, sometimes with trepidation, and sometimes enjoyably. She gave me some examples:

> At first, [diversity on campus] really intimidated me. Like, an example, it might be really stupid, but I'm trying to get into this pre-med honors society and I just got an email about it and I went to the website and I was looking at pictures on line and the majority of it is like Indian, you know, other people, and I was like, God, you know, this is kind of intimidating. But, I was like, if they were to come to [my hometown]—like now I see how it feels to be, like, on that other side. So, it's intimidating, but it didn't make me—I'm still going to hopefully get in, you know, and I'll just mix in and don't make it awkward. It's only going to be as bad as I make it. So, that's just an example of one thing here. Um, like, my sorority, um, there's a bunch of different—there's six sororities, but mine happens to be the most mixed. Like, it's over half Asian, and I'm glad—like, that's just a small example, but I'm glad that I picked that one because, you know, like, the stereotype—you know, it's a bunch of different kinds of girls, and just from being with them, I've learned like all different kinds of things. They're like, "Oh, the Asians are over here," you know, at an event, they're like, "white people picture. Asian picture." I'm like, it's good that we can joke around with it and it's fine, you know, we don't have a problem. There are like dark-skinned people, white people, Asian. That's just a small example, but things I did at home—you know, there's no mix, nothing. I think in a way it really like shut down the way I saw things. Then I got here and was like, "Oh." It's good, though. I'm glad.

Courtney finds the prospect of joining a group of people of another race/ethnicity "intimidating," but also feels some control over it, noting that "it's only going to be as bad as I make it" (a statement which implies that she does not consider it likely that the interaction might be *good*). She clearly desires diverse interactions and values the fact that she belongs to what she believes is her college's most racially mixed sorority, and, as with her Ghanaian friend, she values the opportunity to joke about the presence of difference.

Again, however, Courtney's willingness to see (or perhaps simply her understanding of) racial difference is limited to the pleasurable aspects of that difference. Although she says that her experiences have shown her how a person of color might feel uncomfortable surrounded by white people, she does not extend this understanding to connect it to racial inequality, or how people of color might feel the need to band together at times for mutual support. Only a few minutes after laughing about her sorority sisters calling for an "Asian picture," Courtney shifts to frustration at racial separation. I asked her what she thought about our class discussion about the privileges white people experience in everyday life as a result of their whiteness,[4] and she quickly reveals the boundaries of her definition of "diversity."

> **Courtney**: Um, I thought [the discussion] was interesting. Some of the things that [the professor] read [from McIntosh's list of white privileges], I didn't really agree with. Not trying to be prejudiced, but I think it goes both ways a little bit. I understand that it's never going to be perfectly, um, equal. This may seem stupid, but one thing that really bothers me is, okay, like we have Black History Month, but if we ever tried to have a White History Month, oh, my God, it would be a disaster. Like, that's one thing that bothers me about, you know, they're like, "white people have all these privileges," and stuff, but yet, in the same way, you know, there's Black History Month, there's Black Counseling. Why can't it just all be history month and highlight different people? You know, are we going to have like every ethnic counseling? Just small stuff like that, like in a way, I feel like they want it all to be equal—I mean, white and Black and every other culture, too—but it still always gets separated. Like, if we want it to be equal, then we all need to act as one and stop all this, you know, "This is for whites, this is for Blacks, this is for so and so." It creates a line, you know? You can't just go to a counselor, you know, you have to decide to go to Black Counseling, you know, and stuff like that. I mean, I agree. I think that white people do have more privileges and those need to stop, but as well as, you know, all these small things on the other side that keep adding up. Because, like, you know, one group does one thing and the other group has to retaliate and feel like they've accomplished just as much. I don't know. That's just a personal picky thing. Even when I was little, I asked my mom—I remember watching Nickelodeon and it popped up on the screen, Black History Month, and I'm like, "We don't have White History Month at all, you know?" And, she didn't really know how to explain it because, you know, there's no explanation for it really. That's just how it is. So, I mean, even as a kid, those kinds of things do cross your mind. And, even

here, you know, I know here at school there's Black counseling and there's white counseling. You know, if we're all the same and we're all equal, then why do they have to have different—I know we have different issues, but you know, why not have a counseling office with Black and white people working where if you need to go to a Black person to talk about how you feel like you're being discriminated against, do that. Don't make it like separate. I don't know. That's just one of my things.

JL: Can you think of any arguments for why they should have it separate? Or, can you not think of any good reason?

Courtney: Well, I mean, I can see how they need it separate for the fact that how I said if a Black person, or even a white person, feels like they're being discriminated against, you know. Like, affirmative action, like, "Oh, so and so got in because she's Black." I wouldn't want to go to a Black counselor and say, "Oh, they got in because they're Black," or "They got an A just because they're Black." Like, that would be hard for me, because it's like saying the wrong thing to the wrong person. I mean, so I could see having it separate for that reason, just to meet the needs of everybody. But, if it was all under one roof, like one section, like student counseling, and if you wanted to specify, like, "I want to see so-and-so." You wouldn't have to go in and say, "I need to see a Black counselor." Say, "I need to talk about this issue and it would be great"—like, when you go to the doctor, "I'd like a woman." You know? Nothing against men, but that's just my personal thing. I want a woman. Like, I think if it was just all under the same, you know, roof, that it might—that's just one example. I'm sure there's other things. I mean, I guess I can see it being separate, but that could be changed under one roof and just branch that off from there. You know, all one, still, but to meet the needs of all the kids or whatever.

In these comments, Courtney struggles with the difference between acceptable and unacceptable racial separation. On the issue of White History Month, she cannot come up with any substantive difference between it and Black History Month, a confusion that indicates a shallow understanding of the motivation behind Black History Month, which is intended to compensate (in small part) for the systematic exclusion of Black contributions from the history studied during the rest of the year. On the other hand, Courtney does have some understanding of what might motivate a person of color to want to speak to another person of color for support, but she resists making that preference too apparent, making too much of a "line." Although she sees a parallel to her own preference, as a woman, for a female doctor, and believes that preference means "nothing against men," she wants to be sure, for a not fully articulated reason, that such choices are not institutionalized or overt.

It is also telling that the other example Courtney can come up with relevant to her own experiences is that she might want to complain about African Americans receiving extra privileges, and she would not want to "say the wrong thing to the wrong person." In this example, she reiterates her underlying resentment about the benefits building up on the "other side," and reveals a fear of certain types of encounters (also evoked in her claim that having a White History Month would be "a disaster") in discussing race and ethnicity. This fear is a common theme in the students' responses. Abby wants to avoid political discussions where people go off on frustrating tangents, Angela wants to "get around" the issue, and Courtney feels that certain types of views will result in uncomfortable turmoil.

All of the students I have discussed here might have been used as evidence, in one way or another, of the success of diversity in higher education. All but Angela say that they value the diversity of college life and prefer it to the racial/ethnic homogeneity of their hometowns. Even Angela, at least on the surface, believes in racial equality. For the students who most enjoyed and valued diversity, Abby and Courtney, opportunities to meet classmates and friends from different racial/ethnic backgrounds was exciting.

On the other hand, the further we explore the students' comments about race, the more evident it becomes that the diversity they value is limited to the pleasurable and non-threatening aspects of racial difference. Further, the students fear or reject most consideration of race issues as questions of inequality, injustice, or even debate. It is the students' approval of diverse encounters that the advocates of diversity value, and the students' rejection of questions of power and inequality that the opponents of diversity emphasize. To understand the impact and status of diversity in higher education, we must examine both of these impulses at the same time, rather than considering only one part or the other.

DIVERSITY AND SOCIAL JUSTICE

Critics like Rothman, Lipset, and Nevitt (2003), although they strongly underestimate the breadth and depth of the literature in support of diversity in the student body, the faculty, the curriculum, and institutional goals, do point to an important problem. There is an apparent disconnect between support for diversity and hostility toward the programs and efforts that create and sustain it. Because diversity *has* become such a socially desirable value, many students who report experiencing the benefits of diversity may not, in fact, be gaining the tolerance of difference and concern for racial equality that many educators and researchers intend.

In this paper, I have argued that a full understanding of the impact of diversity requires engaging students on how they make sense of their diverse college experiences. As we examine this sense-making, it becomes clear that along with believing in the value of diversity, white students have a variety of complex reactions to their ensuing encounters with students of color and with race-based curricula, including a range of emotions (pleasure, fear, frustration, curiosity) and a confusing mixture of attitudes about the place of racial and ethnic minorities in college and in the society at large.

It should not surprise us that students have internalized the value of "diversity" in its most general, abstract sense without seeming to connect that value to broader social questions of intergroup understanding, power, and inequality. The division between these two types of understanding and approaching racial difference has been built into multicultural education since its beginnings. Curricular changes originally intended to be systematic interventions into an entrenched dominant culture in education were soon watered down to a "celebration of diversity" model wholly divorced from questions of power and privilege. Today's college students grew up in these schools, where diversity means an annual "diverse" holiday assembly or a day for tasting ethnic foods. If this is the meaning of diversity, why wouldn't they value it?

At the same time, the college-level curriculum retained much of its focus on inequality (albeit still not as systematically as most advocates had hoped) through racial and ethnic studies programs and by other faculty bringing these concerns to traditional departments. As students arrive at college, often excited about the opportunity to experience greater diversity than they have ever been exposed to, they thus encounter a conflict. In college, diversity often no longer means the pleasures of entertaining discovery. It may, instead, mean painful misunderstandings between roommates, bewildering "self segregation," heated classroom discussions, and inexplicably angry and militant student activists.

Much of the literature on the benefits of diversity demonstrates that diverse curricula and social interaction produce in students a desire for greater racial understanding, a greater "awareness" of race issues, and a desire for more cross-cultural interaction (see Smith, 1997). But the meaning of these preferences is not always entirely clear. In my own classrooms, when I teach students about multicultural education, they find it self-evident and blasé (*of course* we should learn to interact with people of all cultures). But when we discuss issues of race and ethnicity, the apparent consensus suddenly disappears. Does this mean that their support for diversity is just the socially acceptable answer? I do not think so. Instead, I think that the gap we see between their two sets of views is not a gap to them at all, and our failure to understand why these views seem compatible to students is a key barrier to the future success of diversity efforts.

In the end, we need to face up to the fact that multicultural education is not simply about passing along a benign skill set ("the ability to function in a diverse workplace") like teaching students teamwork skills or writing. Too often we have relied on this claim to justify our efforts to those who resisted all such changes as "reverse discrimination" and weakening the canon. To a certain extent, this justification has worked. But Rothman, Lipset, and Nevitte, and other critics like them, are correct that a deep undercurrent of frustration and resentment remains about issues of racial and ethnic division, and to truly educate our students, we must address these feelings head-on rather than sweeping them under the rug.

Critics of diversity suggest that if we see student support for diversity but rejection of affirmative action and other attention to inequalities, this inconsistency reveals their true feelings about the diversity measures we have taken. And, the discrepancy indeed shows just that, but not in the way critics claim. The critics of diversity efforts in higher education believe that students reject these efforts because the efforts are unfair and because they degrade the quality of higher education. In fact, students have learned well what we have taught them. We have taught this generation, through multicultural education in primary and secondary schools, that "everyone is equal" and that differences (such as clothing and food preferences) should be occasionally explored as an enjoyable break from the everyday work of education. We have devoted far less attention to teaching them about the ongoing impact of racism in the United States today—about residential segregation, about the racial wealth gap, about environmental racism, about discrimination against people of color in hiring and in many everyday interactions, about race bias in the criminal justice system, about the ways teachers' expectations affect the academic performance of students of color.

Given these messages, the findings of the critics are completely predictable. The conclusion, however, should not be to indict diversity efforts, which clearly influence students positively when they are correctly implemented. Rather, the words of these students must prompt us to reconsider what we mean by diversity and what our goals are as we educate about race and ethnicity. The student voices heard here show a significant disconnect between what students see as "diversity" (read: good) and "race" (read: uncomfortable, overblown). If it is our goal as educators to teach students to merely celebrate diversity and desire more cross-racial interaction and dialogue, our current approach suffices. But if we want our students to do more—rather than just *desiring* cross-racial contact, actually working to integrate their peer groups, workplaces, and communities; or rather than only engaging the fun parts of diversity, also struggling with the inequalities of power and privilege that the equal sharing of ethnic foods covers up—we must reevaluate our approach.

It is much easier politically to paint diversity efforts with a broad brush (as we do when we describe them as preparing students for the diverse workplace), and to leave it to individual faculty in the trenches to broach the more difficult subjects. But while the easier road has earned us much progress in integrating diversity into higher education, it also leaves us at the impasse I have described in this paper. It is time for higher education to once again stand up boldly for a racially just future.

Endnotes

1. Although "diversity" may be defined in many ways, for the purposes of this chapter, I use the broadest possible definition, understanding diversity in higher education to include any measures to include people from all races/ethnicities, people of different nationalities, both men and women, people of different social class backgrounds, and a range of other forms of difference. "Diversity" includes both the physical presence of diverse people among the students, faculty, and staff of the academy, but also the inclusion of diverse points of view in the curriculum and in the policies of the institution. Empirically, however, this chapter focuses more narrowly on racial/ethnic diversity, as it is the form of diversity that has been the most heatedly debated in higher education.
2. This focus on white students is not meant to suggest that we should not examine how students of color view and experience diversity at college. Students of color, however, necessarily come to the experience of racial/ethnic diversity from a different perspective than white students do, and examining both of these sets of experiences is beyond the scope of this paper.
3. All student names have been replaced with pseudonyms, and a few identifying details have been changed to conceal the identities of the students and their universities.
4. This discussion was based on the list of white privileges in Peggy McIntosh's (1988) classic article "White Privilege and Male Privilege: A Personal Account of Coming to See Correspondences through Work in Women's Studies."

References

Astin, A. W. (1993). *What matters in college? Four critical years revisited.* San Francisco: Jossey-Bass.

Gurin, P., Dey, E. L., Hurtado, S., & Gurin, G. (2002). Diversity and higher education: Theory and impact on educational outcomes. *Harvard Educational Review, 72,* 330–366.

McIntosh, P. (2001). White privilege and male privilege: A personal account of coming to see correspondences through work in women's studies. In M. L. Anderson, & P. H. Collins (Eds.), *Race, class, and gender: An anthology* (4th ed., pp. 95–105). Belmont, CA: Wadsworth.

Rothman, S., Lipset, S. M., & Nevitte, N. (2003). Racial diversity reconsidered. *Public Interest, 151,* 25–38.

Smith, D. G. (1997). *Diversity works: The emerging picture of how students benefit.* Washington, DC: Association of American Colleges & Universities.

Terenzini, P. T., Cabrera, A. F., Colbeck, C. L., Bjorklund, S. A., & Parente, J. M. (2001). Racial and ethnic diversity in the classroom: Does it promote student learning? *Journal of Higher Education, 72,* 509–531.

CHAPTER 12

Ethical Conflicts and Public Responsibilities:

COMMERCIALIZATION IN THE ACADEMY

Joshua B. Powers

Abstract: The purpose of this study was to investigate ways that university technology commercialization may create ethical conflicts with social contract for science responsibilities. An analysis of 125 university licensing contracts with industry revealed substantial evidence of ethical conflicts undermining higher education's public good commitments and the norms of academic science.

In November of 1944, President Roosevelt wrote to his Director of Scientific Research and Development, Vannevar Bush, requesting his counsel on how peace-time science might be fostered in ways that mirrored the success of the industrial-scientific-government partnership of the war years. In his letter, Roosevelt (1944) wrote:

> There is…no reason why the lessons to be found in this experiment cannot be profitably employed in times of peace. The information, the techniques, and the research experience developed by the Office of Scientific Research and Development and by the thousands of scientists in the universities and in private industry, should be used in the days of peace ahead for the improvement of the national health, the creation of new enterprises bringing new jobs, and the betterment of the national standard of living.…New frontiers of the mind are before us, and if they are pioneered with

the same vision, boldness, and drive with which we have waged this war we can create a fuller and more fruitful employment and a fuller and more fruitful life (p. 1).

More than a half century after Bush submitted his now famous reply, *Science: The Endless Frontier*, the American scientific enterprise continues to be one that emphasizes a triple-helix like partnership between government, universities, and industry (Etzkowitz & Leydesdorff, 1997) for the discovery and dissemination of knowledge for the public good. The social contract for science that has been in place for 60 years is sourced in the belief that higher education can be entrusted to engage in programs of basic inquiry unfettered by the entrapments of the marketplace. Furthermore, the social contract as manifested for institutions and their faculty rests on the foundational values of free and open access to information and research findings, the pursuit of truth wherever it may lead, and the unimpeded and transparent dissemination of these results (Merton, 1942).

Many important advances have emerged from the social contract. Federal research investment in universities have led to breakthroughs in radar, semi-conductors, highway safety, crop production, and a myriad of human health advances, to name but a few. These important innovations occurred through incremental and paradigm shifting discoveries, aided by researcher access to data, replication/critique of findings, and a culture of altruism versus self-interest (Argyres & Liebeskind, 1998). In recent years, however, the forces of academic commercialization appear to be eroding the academic norms that undergird the social contract. Specifically, the free, open, and unfettered pursuit of truth and its dissemination is increasingly substituted by counter norms of secrecy, restrictions on the dissemination of new knowledge, and other self-interested behaviors (Anderson & Louis, 1994).

The roots of this change can be found in a variety of sources that took shape about 25 years ago. In 1980, out of concern that the United States was losing its economic competitiveness in the world, the federal government sought to incentivize institutional behavior by making it advantageous for higher education to privatize their most valued asset: the intellectual capital of the faculty. Specifically, universities could, for the first time, easily own the rights to technological innovations emerging from federally funded research. Having patents, federal policy makers felt, would stimulate industry to license more academic technologies, a key cog on the way to becoming a commercialized product for consumer consumption. This belief was borne out, given the enormous growth in academic patenting and industry licensing of academic-sourced technologies since 1980.

Prior to 1980, however, most academics and universities resisted efforts at privatizing knowledge ever since the first academic patent was obtained in 1917 by Frederick Cottrell, the University of California, Berkeley inventor of the breakthrough smokestack anti-pollution device, the electrostatic precipitator. The view was that commoditizing academic research in a way that limited access undermined higher education's social responsibilities, especially in the arena of medical science, a field central to advancing public health. Cottrell himself even warned against direct university involvement in patenting and licensing, believing that:

> A danger was involved, especially should the experiment prove highly profitable to the university and lead to a general emulation of the plan. University trustees are continually seeking for funds and in direct proportion to the success of our experiment its repetition might be expected elsewhere…the danger this suggested was the possibility of growing commercialism and competition between institutions and an accompanying tendency for secrecy in scientific work (Cottrell, 1932, p. 222).

Unfortunately, the combined influence of the changed policy environment described above, the rise of highly lucrative opportunities in the new field of biotechnology, and resource contraction from traditional sources (such as through state subsidies of public higher education) overcame this resistance. Today, many universities and their faculty are becoming deeply involved in commercialization. All are hoping to realize a blockbuster financial success story, such as Gatorade (the University of Florida—$100 million in royalty revenues to date), Google (Stanford University—$694 million in stock), or Taxol (a cancer-fighting compound from Florida State University—$350 million in royalty revenues to date).

A growing range of scholarly work has been documenting the ways in which privatizing the intellectual commons (Argyres & Liebeskind, 1998) has been manifested and undermines the social contract (e.g., Bok, 2003; Slaughter & Rhoades, 2004). A subset of this work has focused on the ethical conflicts that academic commercialization can engender, such as data withholding, industry influence on faculty research, and financial conflicts of interest. Yet, what has been learned about these conflicts has largely emerged from self-report studies, analyses of institutional policy documents, or corporate linkage disclosures in leading academic journals. Although these kinds of studies have made a valuable contribution to knowledge, the nature of the topic makes it possible that controversial practices are underreported and/or suggests that what is stated in conflict of interest policy materials or disclosures may not align with actual practice. What is missing is research evidence on what universities and faculty actually do rather than what they say they do or feel on various ethical conflict issues.

The purpose of this study is to investigate ways in which universities may engage in practices that represent ethical conflicts with their public social contract for science responsibilities. Unlike previous research, this study was the first of its kind to investigate on a national level what universities and faculty inventors actually do rather than what they say they do or what appears in policy statements. This was accomplished via a content analysis of contractual documents mined from Securities and Exchange Commission (SEC) materials of firms with linkages to universities. The analysis focused on four technology licensing practices with ethical implications affecting the social contract for science: transparency on licensing deal financials (i.e., full disclosure of financial terms), the awarding of exclusive licenses to single firms for technology development, university and faculty stock accepted in licensee companies, and the ceding of publication oversight rights to licensee companies. These investigations of interest led to the following research question: What licensing practices with social contract implications are manifested in contractual documents between universities and for-profit firms?

CONCEPTUAL FRAMEWORK

Slaughter and Leslie (1997) argue that the forces of commercialization in higher education—or what they label academic capitalism—have been driven by changes in national policies guiding academic research and declines in state support for higher education. The combined effect of these forces, they suggest, has been to incite universities to become more entrepreneurial in an effort to generate sufficient revenues to support its labor and increasingly capital-intensive enterprise. One outcome of this movement toward entrepreneurialism has been the erosion of the traditional culture of academic science that undergirds the social contract.

Merton (1942) codified the ethos of the pre-entrepreneurial era with his description of four fundamental norms associated with the conduct of academic research. The first of these, *universalism*, captured the importance of recognizing that science should be evaluated on its merits and not on subjective criteria such as the reputation or social standing of the researcher. The blind review process of publication is perhaps the most apparent manifestation of this value set. The second norm, *communality*, articulated as a value that no person "owns" knowledge; it is shared openly and freely with all. Thus, an academic scientist should be willing to freely share her/his data and discoveries with others, all in the name of advancing knowledge. The third norm was *disinterestedness*. The intent of this value was that a researcher should conduct their work separate from personal motives. In other words, the academic scientist should selflessly pursue truth wherever it may lead in the name of advancing science and not as a means of personal gain. The last norm, *organized skepticism*, captured the importance of public and open critique of research findings, allowing others to attempt to replicate results and/or to build on the ideas. The most readily apparent manifestation of this norm is the process of presenting papers at academic conferences where others can openly question and explore the merits, opportunities, and implications of new research findings.

While these four norms continue to be present in various forms today, others have suggested that there are new counter value sets in academic entrepreneurial science. Mitroff's (1974) study of the Apollo moon project offered a language to describe these "counter-norms." In contrast to universalism, for instance, he argued that the forces of *particularism* were also at work. Particularism, he suggested, led some to judge the quality of scientific work not on its own merits, but in part on the reputation of the individual or group presenting it. The fact that researchers with a known reputation tend to have enhanced chances at landing a major federal grant, for instance, is one high-profile example of particularism. A second counter-norm that Mitroff articulated was *solitariness*. In contrast with the belief that ideas and knowledge are universally shared and "owned" by all, solitariness suggested that scientists sometimes do seek to protect their findings jealously and not share their source data in order to safeguard a research stream and future credit. *Self-interestedness*, a third counter norm, this time in direct conflict with its traditional norm, disinterestedness, values the pursuit of new knowledge not for its own sake but to personally gain from such efforts in whatever form that might come—personal accolades, financial, and the like. Thus, particular streams of research might be pursued because it is perceived by the field to be more important, cutting edge, have potential financial gain opportunities, and/or lead to certain valued benefits like access to resources to built a larger and more complex lab. The final counter-norm, *organized dogmatism*, involves academic scientists promoting their own findings, theories, and innovations over those of others, and not for sound research-related reasons. Hence, this counter norm affirms that a researcher's key ally becomes their press agent who spins out regular releases to the popular press in the hopes of landing a feature story on their work and/or criticisms of their "competitors."

A growing body of literature has studied these forces and noted how they are manifested for academic faculty and their institutions in terms of a growing tolerance or ambivalence about conflicts of interest (Anderson & Louis, 1994; Slaughter, Campbell, Holleman, & Morgan, 2002). Campbell (1997) offers some useful examples such as faculty or institutional stock ownership in licensee companies, the powerful influence of corporate sponsors of research, faculty serving in company management posts while simultaneously serving as a researcher, and faculty and institutions placing profiting on intellectual property over the pursuit of research free of financial motives. Others have documented that some faculty are willing to accept company-imposed publication restrictions or delays, often so that patent protections for which they and an industry sponsor might ultimately benefit can be filed (Blumenthal et al., 1997). This practice has extended to pre-publication review or ghost writing by the contracting firm, especially for studies involving drug trials (Angell & Relman, 2002). Faculty also sometimes withhold data from colleagues, primarily to preserve their scientific "lead" (Louis, Jones, & Campbell, 2002) or to increase the chance of obtaining needed resources to advance their research (Kenny, 1986). Furthermore, it is common for faculty to have consulting arrangements, board positions, or an equity stake in a company that licensed their technology (Boyd & Bero, 2000). Other researchers have reported growing scientific misconduct (Swazey, Louis, & Anderson, 1994), calling into question the legitimacy of published findings and in some cases, even serious breaches in human subject protections. In summary, the body of work on the growing adoption of the counter-norms for academic science would suggest that the conflict of interest issues that they can engender would also be evident in the contractual documents that universities make with licensee firms.

METHODOLOGY

Data for this study were drawn from an analysis of public company documents that must be disclosed as part of the normal course of a public, or soon to be public, firm's activities. The documents include initial public offering prospectuses (detailed company information required to inform potential investors), annual company reports, and of other support filings, all of which are available on-line through the SEC. Although there is no uniform approach or method by which companies describe their licensing activities, risk information that is reflected in a licensing deal (e.g., company dependency on another firm or university for an important technology) generally requires that they at least report the existence of a particular licensing deal, the parties and contract dates involved, the type of license (exclusive vs. non-exclusive), and basic terms (e.g., financial arrangements, length of term, etc.). Furthermore, a full licensing contract is often attached as an exhibit/appendix.

Procedures and Sample

A three-step process was used to mine SEC reported licensing-deal information for major U.S. universities. First, the names of all 151 Carnegie Doctoral Extensive universities were extracted from the 2000 Carnegie Classification database, since the vast majority of academic commercialization occurs within this classification of institution. Second, a specialized search engine, 10kWizard.com, was used to extract the data of interest. This search engine specializes in mining useful information embedded in SEC documents via the use of Boolean search terms and the extraction of blocks of text. Furthermore, there is a section of the search engine that targets SEC filing exhibits (i.e., attachments or appendices to primary documents). In previous tests of the 10kWizard search engine, it was clear that filing exhibits are the most likely place to find detailed information on university-industry licensing deals, often including the actual licensing contract (Powers, 2003). Experimentation with the Boolean search capabilities revealed that searching these exhibits with the word "license" within ten words of a university name was a very effective way of selecting out university licensing contract information from other types of exhibits.

The second step of the procedure revealed 125 separate agreements between 52 universities and 83 companies between January 2000 and October 2005, the final sample used in this study. The universities and companies were geographically spread across the United States. The five-year timeframe was chosen to ensure that the sample included the most current licensing practices and was large enough to provide generalizable findings.

In step three, the data of interest was extracted from these 125 licensing deals. Information on the company involved, the nature of the filing, the date of the license, the industry code, the license type (exclusive vs. non exclusive), the inventor name, financial information (i.e., royalty and stock amounts), and publication restriction terms, if any, were downloaded into a separate spreadsheet for descriptive analysis (e.g., number and percentage of license types, days of allowable publication restriction, etc.). Blocks of textual language around the issues of interest were then downloaded in their entirety into a separate file for analysis and used to identify themes/concepts that emerged related to issues of ethical conflicts.

Data analysis

Following the data extraction, two forms of content analysis methodology were employed. Classical content analysis (Carney, 1972) was used to conduct numeric and word counts as well as frequency of theme or phrase occurrences. Theoretical content analysis (Marino, Castaldi, & Dollinger, 1989) was utilized to classify themes into categories. Thus, for instance, the number of licenses that were exclusive versus non-exclusive in nature, the number of licensing deals that involved stock equity to a university and/or the faculty inventor(s), and the number of times that financial information on stock ownership or royalty percentages was masked were investigated. Furthermore, language around the issues of interest, including on the topic of publication restrictions, were analyzed and grouped.

RESULTS

As mentioned previously, 125 licensing contracts between a university and a for-profit firm were identified from SEC documents between January 2000 and October 2005. Fifty-two universities were represented in the sample, some with only one licensing deal represented and others with more, the highest being 20. The median number of licensing deals per university was two, while the modal number of licensing deals per university was one (23 of 52). On the firm side, 83 companies were represented. The range of licensing deals with a university was between one and four, with a median and modal number of deals per firm of one (53 of 83), with a mean of 1.5 deals per firm. Figure 1 shows the breakdown of the nature of these licenses by industry of the licensee firm.

Figure 1. University Licensed Technologies by Industry Type

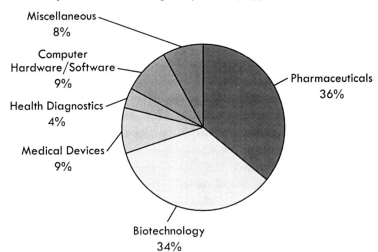

Approximately 1/3 of the licensed technologies were to the pharmaceutical industry, typically in the form of new chemical compounds that show medicinal promise for the treatment or prevention of disease. Another 1/3 were licensed to the biotechnology industry, broadly defined to capture new biologic products, living substances, and biological research with potential promise for improving health and health care. Medical devices, typically surgical or orthopedic devices/ apparatuses, represented 9% of the total technologies, while health diagnostics, generally new instruments useful for the diagnosis of disease and genetic processes, made up 4% of the total. In sum, technologies with some direct connection to the health sciences fields made up over 80% of the licensed technologies in the sample. Given the lopsided financial support afforded to the health sciences in federal research funding, along with the fact that life science related patenting represents at least 40% of all patenting that emerges from higher education (National Science Board, 2004), it is not surprising that most licensed technologies in the sample came from the health science disciplines. The other 17% of technologies in the sample were in the computer hardware and software arenas (9% of sample) as well as a variety of other miscellaneous fields (8%) such as manufacturing, chemicals, and business services.

As mentioned at the outset of this study, the focus of the research was to use content analysis methodology to investigate four technology licensing practices with potential ethical implications affecting the social contract for science: transparency on the financial terms of licensing deals, the awarding of exclusive licenses to single firms for technology development, the acceptance of university and faculty stock in licensee companies, and the ceding of publication oversight rights to licensee companies. The results of both the classic and theoretical content analyses are described in the sections that follow, each preceded by a brief discussion of the larger ethical context in which it is embedded.

Transparency in Licensing Activities

One of the historic bedrock values of academic science in support of the social contract has been transparency. In other words, researchers are to fully disclose findings as well their source data and methodologies so that others can then engage in replication activities and follow-up analyses. By doing so, good ideas are affirmed, mistakes or non-generalizable findings are revealed, and new extensions/applications are identified. Furthermore, academic researchers are expected to disclose potential conflicts of interest that might call into question the veracity of their findings. For example, the federal government requires principal investigator disclosure of significant financial interests[1] in a company in grant applications when it could affect the design, conduct, or reporting of research activities. Some academic journals require disclosure of company-funded research projects that are reported with the article at the time of publication. Efforts such as these help to affirm the integrity of the system and public confidence that resource investment in academic research is being handled responsibly.

Thus far, however, compliance reporting of potential financial conflicts of interest are self-evaluated and disclosed such that no independent confirmation is required. Furthermore, the requirement extends only to academic researchers and not their affiliate institutions, despite the fact that the latter may also fall prey to conflicts of interest. Hence, an investigation of financial transparency in academic licensing activity is a useful first independent assessment of both faculty and institutional financial involvements with licensee companies.

Of the 125 licensing agreements investigated for this study, 82 masked the royalty terms (66% of the total). In other words, there were clearly financial terms associated with licensing royalty arrangements, but none were disclosed or were simply edited out of the documents. Those that did disclose ($N = 43$) provided amounts ranging from 2.5–10% of net sales and often with a set minimum of $5,000–100,000 per year; these figures could easily exceed the federal conflict of interest disclosure threshold of $10,000 per year, even with relatively modest sales or no sales at all. By law, universities must share a percentage of royalties with inventors, most commonly about 1/3 of the total received. Thus, it is clear that royalties are a potential source of financial conflict of interest for both universities and inventors.

In the case of the university or faculty inventor(s) receiving stock, it was clear that one or both received stock in 51 of the licenses. Of those 51 cases involving the transfer of stock, however, only 31 of them disclosed the terms with some degree of comprehensiveness (61%), the rest choosing to mask the arrangements. Of those that did disclose, it was clear that at least 12 of them would exceed the federal conflict of interest disclosure limit of either $10,000 in value or 5% ownership of a company, some many times over.

These combined findings indicate a considerable lack of transparency in university licensing regarding financial terms. On one level, this could be attributed to firms that may naturally wish not to disclose certain terms for business secrecy reasons. The SEC recognizes this fact by giving companies the ability to file a confidential treatment request on certain tightly prescribed financial and related information that could harm the company if it was disclosed in the marketplace. However, there was a critical mass of licensing deals in this sample in which full disclosure was made on royalty and/or stock elements (34% and 61% respectively). This finding suggests that some companies do not see disclosure of royalty and stock financials causing them material harm. By extension, then, it implies that the masking of key financial deal data may sometimes be driven by university desires for confidentiality rather than the firm's. Furthermore, it also suggests that if universities insisted on full financial disclosure in licensing deals, any firm resistance might be reduced or eliminated.

Licensing Exclusivity

Much commentary has been offered regarding the wisdom and efficacy of ceding broad rights to the development of a university-licensed technology to a single firm (e.g., Press & Washburn, 2000). These concerns have been especially acute around the licensing of basic technologies for which no clear application is evident. Some have argued, for example, that the patenting and exclusive licensing of gene sequences and stem cell lines to one company is not in the public interest, since it limits rather than enhances the potential development of broad-based applications in any number of health-oriented areas (Rai & Eisenberg, 2003). Technology transfer practitioners argue, however, that no company would ever risk licensing a basic technology with a very long, expensive, and risky incubation period without exclusivity protections. Thus, universities and faculty are left in a quandary. Social contract for science obligations would suggest the need to make emergent technologies widely available so that the ideas can both advance science and be transformed into products of societal benefit. Yet, precisely because many of these technologies have unknown applications, companies are at times unwilling to license the technologies without at least some protection against others' easily producing a competitive product. Furthermore, if a university cannot license the technology, no revenues are realized to at least offset patenting costs.

An analysis of the study data revealed that 112 of the 125 licensing deals (90% of the total) were made exclusively with a single firm, and often with rights that extended worldwide. The rest were made either non-exclusively (i.e., other firms could have access to the technology) or, in four of the cases, co-exclusively (i.e., with one other firm). Careful reading of licensing documents, however, revealed that in about 1/2 of the cases in which a technology was licensed exclusively, the term was defined to delineate a particular "field of use," ostensibly to allow the technology to be licensed to another firm for a use not covered by the terms of the license. Yet, the definition used varied widely among the license contracts. For example, in one license deal, field of use was defined as "cancers of the gastro-intestinal track," while in another to "all human and veterinary applications." Clearly, this standard differed between the two licensing deals in terms of breadth of exclusivity. Furthermore, while most universities included language indicating their unimpeded right to conduct their own follow-up research using the technology,[2] relatively few clearly extended that right to academic researchers outside of their affiliate university. As a result, access to others' work—a central building block of academic research—appears in these cases to be possible at best only through complex and time-consuming material transfer agreements, likely with some degree of company oversight.

In many of the licenses, whether exclusive or non-exclusive, it was also clear that universities allowed a firm to do sublicensing (i.e., license the original technology to a third party). In this case, though, most appeared to do so with a higher value placed on its ability to generate more revenues for the university than for the purposes of seeing the technology reach the marketplace as quickly as possible for consumer benefit. This inference was drawn from the nature of university "reach through provision"[3] language that included generally tight prescriptions on the original licensee firm; specifically, these prescriptions pertained to revenue flows from third parties and university rights to royalties on new patents or products based on the original technology and subsequently licensed to or developed by a third party. Some have criticized this practice as impeding the pace of innovation, since it creates potential barriers to access and acts as a disincentive for third parties to sub-license a previously developed technology.

Stock Acceptance Practices

A central conflict of interest issue in university technology licensing involves the controversial practice of universities and faculty accepting stock in a licensee firm. Those that oppose the practice see it undermining disinterested inquiry when a faculty member stands to profit from the application of her/his research, which could potentially undermine the legitimacy of research findings surrounding that technology (Boyd & Bero, 2000). Others argue that accepting equity in lieu of up-front fees from typically cash-starved young firms shows institutional commitment to the partnership and creates mutual incentives for firm success (Bray & Lee, 2000).

As discussed under the transparency topic above, it was evident that 51 of 125 licenses (41% of the licenses) involved some form of stock equity for the university and often for the faculty inventor as well. For those that did disclose the amounts (31 of 51), the number of shares provided was quite varied, ranging from a low of 3,000 shares to a high of 800,000 shares. Furthermore, in at least eight of the cases, the amount of shares given equaled or surpassed a 5% company ownership stake. This proportion surpasses not only the federal government's threshold of a possible conflict of interest, but also a universally accepted norm for a controlling company interest. In addition, a number of the disclosed deals provided healthy stock options for the university and/or the inventor(s) in which either had a window of opportunity to purchase company shares at a pre-determined discounted rate. Evidence of whether or not this option was ever exercised would not be disclosed in these documents, unless those amounts led to an individual or the institution owning more than 5% of the company. However, it is quite common for persons to exercise such an option if they believe the stock to be a good investment.

Considering the fact that almost 1/2 of the licensing deals involved stock, it is clear that universities must view the practice as important and potentially lucrative, despite the risks that stock shares will fall in value or only appreciate over a very long period of time, as is especially true for the biotechnology sector. The concern, of course, is that this form of corporate entanglement may undermine the integrity of the research process. Recent research has shown, for instance, that some high profile breaches of human subjects protections have been attributable in part to the compromised integrity of researchers who had a financial stake in the company for whom the researcher is testing a new therapy (Thompson, 2000).

Firm Oversight of Publication

Previous research indicates that increased partnerships with industry can lead to company encroachment on the publication process (Blumenthal et al., 1997).

Although the extent of company control remains unclear, it is not uncommon for companies to expect a delay in publication to afford them time to consider patent applications prior to a technology being released into the public domain via academic publication (Cho, Shohara, Schissel, & Rennie, 2000). Given that the free exchange of ideas has been a bedrock value of academic science for advancing knowledge, impediments to this process are considered by many to be troubling at best and fundamentally wrong at worst.

The data mined from university licensing contracts revealed that 39 of 125 deals involved restrictions on publication. Restrictions were typically built around allowing a firm time to evaluate if an academic researcher's article/paper breached any confidentiality restriction built into the licensing contract and/or as a means of evaluating a new development from the original technology (i.e., right of first refusal on a new patent or license). Sixteen of the 39 deals allowed for a 30-day publication moratorium, while seven deals were set at 45 days, five at 60 days, and nine at 90 days. Of those contracts with predetermined moratoriums, the average number of delay days was 52, just under two months. Two of the 39 licensing deals also indicated a firm right to publication delay, but the number of days was masked. Within the set of 39 licensing contracts, the range of language and explicitness over the rights of each party varied. For example, some contract language simply stated a number of days of restriction and that all the university needed to do was notify the licensee of an impeding publication that would meet this timetable. Other contracts, however, made clear that the university must "submit for review and comment any impending publications" within a stated timeframe. Others included language that articulated what was allowable in publications, namely those that "were only for noncommercial educational and research purposes," with the implication that the company determined what met this standard. Still other contracts added closing clauses that affirmed final institutional authority on this matter.

It is important to note that 36 other licensing contracts explicitly made it clear that there were to be no restrictions on a faculty member's right to publication, and nearly as many as had noted some kind of allowable company restriction on publication. These universities appeared to have made clear that universities and their faculty researchers retained the full, unimpeded, and uninfluenced right to publish, irrespective of the source of funding or the possible desires of a company around secrecy and technology control.

The remaining 50 licensing deals in the dataset (40% of the entire sample), though, made no mention of restriction on publication. This could imply that companies were not afforded any rights in this regard. However, it could also mean that universities were not adequately proactive in asserting this important right for preserving the integrity of the academic research process. By extension, then, it may be that at least some of the universities involved in these deals are ceding substantive rights to companies over the nature and pace of university research publication.

Discussion and Recommendations

The purpose of this study was to investigate ways in which universities may engage in practices that represent ethical conflicts with their public responsibilities and which may serve to undermine the social contract for science responsibilities. Using data mined from 125 licensing contracts between universities and firms, the extent and nature of four technology licensing practices with potential ethical implications were investigated. These practices included transparency on the financial terms of licensing deals, the use of exclusive licensing to single firms for technology development, university and faculty acceptance of stock in a licensee company, and publication oversight rights by licensee companies. The results indicated substantive deviation from the norms that have historically undergirded academic science, as evidenced by considerable non-transparency, barriers to access to university patented technologies by both follow-on researchers and non-licensee firms, university and faculty stock equity acceptance practices that may represent conflicts of interest, and a degree of company control of the academic publication process at some institutions. The individual and combined effects of these practices raise concerns for the discovery and dissemination of new knowledge for the public good and the integrity of the academic research process.

In light of these findings, four recommendations are warranted to preserve, if not rebuild, the integrity of academic research in support of the social contract for science. First, universities should consider a refinement of mission and purpose for technology commercialization that eliminates, or largely relegates low on the list, the importance of revenue generation. Few universities even enjoy substantial revenue flows and many have been losing money on their technology transfer programs for years (Campbell, Powers, Blumenthal, & Biles, 2004; Powers, 2005). In an era of high attention to economic development, a de-emphasis on revenues could be achieved by raising in importance the value of industry partnerships rather than technology commercialization per se. Universities have always been an important source of basic innovation for industry and have typically disseminated information through the open and public presentation of research at academic conferences and in scholarly publications. However, universities have also functioned more or less in an ivory tower fashion, such that linkages with business and industry for many faculty and universities are indirect and fleeting. The concern has often been that close ties to industry could influence academia to adopt an applied rather than a basic research model. However, this is largely an unfounded concern, given that basic R&D has remained around 70% of all academic R&D for decades (National

Science Board, 2004). A small but growing cadre of university technology transfer professionals has begun speaking to the need for a greater emphasis on partnerships with industry over revenue maximization as a way of best stimulating national innovation while also staying true to the social contract mission of higher education (Blumenstyk, 2004). Doing so can also help to rekindle the importance of openness and transparency, bedrock facilitators of the social contract for science.

Second, and in support of industry-university partnering, universities need to rethink exclusive licensing. In regard to basic technologies emerging from universities, serious consideration should be given to making them freely available or to licensing them on a non-exclusive basis. Stem cells and gene sequences are excellent case examples. Should a university be patenting and exclusively licensing these technologies (as some like the University of Wisconsin have done) when their applications are clearly broad but currently unclear? Given the potential impact on health care, multiple research teams and companies should have access to these technologies for research and development purposes for potentially broad applications, and via simplified processes such as streamlined material transfer agreements. Teams of university-industry scientists could then be more easily and broadly formed with each playing its respective role (academics examining broad application possibilities and industry investigating specific, targeted application work). As a company begins to "own" a particular application, more formalized agreements could then be established for the firm's profitable exploitation of the technology. However, the university should not let financial return considerations be a central driver of technology commercialization considerations, especially since few ever realize significant financial gains. An approach such as this helps to preserve the integrity of the academic science enterprise.

Third, government policy makers should become more actively involved in facilitating reforms. Thus, for example, federal financial conflict of interest guidelines should be established for faculty *and* institutions, such that universities are expected to disclose in the same manner as faculty investigators. While it may be that threshold points might be raised for universities, it should nevertheless be clear the extent to which institutions are financially entwined with their industry partners. Policy makers might also expect institutions to adopt a policy in which university and faculty stock in licensee companies are escrowed for a period of years so that it can be liquidated only at particular pre-arranged moments. Doing so allows stock ownership to continue, but removes some of the incentive for short-term thinking and influence that may taint either faculty or institutional judgment. In addition, policy makers ought to press universities to allow for certain prescribed activities that support their industry partnership mission. For example, faculty could apply for leaves of absence to work for a licensee company, even one they founded, and/or be allowed to use a sabbatical for this purpose.

Appropriately legitimizing these activities has the potential for speeding the processes of innovation, an important governmental goal. However, they must be evaluated in a way that does not compromise the core responsibilities of a faculty member: teaching, research, and service.

Lastly, careful attention to the encroaching controls of industry in the publication process is needed. Bok (2003) and Angell (2004) speak eloquently to the ways in which academe has allowed corporate influence to encroach the university. Especially worrisome is the way that major pharmaceutical companies are influencing the medical sciences and undermining higher education's integrity as an impartial source of accurate data on matters of human health and safety. Academic institutions need to assert their social responsibilities and remain as free from market forces as possible, especially as it regards their unimpeded right to publish research, even when it criticizes company-funded research.

LIMITATIONS AND OPPORTUNITIES FOR FUTURE RESEARCH

While this study advances knowledge on the ethical conflicts of academic commercialization, it is not without limitations. First, the sample of companies chosen does not represent all of the licensing deals that are made with industry. For example, SEC rules allow some firm flexibility in defining the level of detail needed to make an adequate disclosure of investor risks. Thus, there were some licensing deals in the public domain that could not be used in this study because they lacked the details needed to be included in the analysis. In addition, many companies with university licenses are private and thus not bound by SEC reporting requirements. Although there is no reason to believe that universities would approach licensing with private companies differently than with public firms, surveys of universities or private companies regarding their licensing contracts and practices would be a valuable next research step. Second, the study was a cross-sectional investigation and did not explore how practices may be changing over time. Finally, a qualitative study in which university and industry licensing officers are engaged on issues raised in their own contracts would provide useful insights behind decision processes and orientations toward technology commercialization, something that could not be explored in this study.

CONCLUSION

In today's entrepreneurial climate for higher education, it is difficult to imagine a return to a pre-1980 period given the systemic changes and pressures confronting the industry. Nevertheless, this study offers a unique, evidentiary window into what actually occurs with technology commercialization and not simply what professionals involved say occurs. Most importantly, it offers instructive insights into what might be done to stop—indeed reverse—the erosion in higher education's social contract obligations so that the public good can best be advanced in this developing arena of university activity.

Endnotes

1. Defined as when an investigator, including his or her spouse and dependent children, will receive anything of monetary value, typically including salaries, payment for services, consulting fees, stocks, bonds, stock options, patents, copyrights, royalties, or similar items, that could affect the design, conduct, or reporting of the research activities proposed. A significant interest is defined as exceeding $10,000 in any year or more than 5% ownership interest in any single entity.
2. The primary exception being as a function of the right of a company to first-refusal on new patent opportunities based on refinements of the original technology.
3. A reach-through provision is defined as property rights in products developed by the licensee or sub-licensee through the use of the transferred technology.

References

Anderson, M. S., & Louis, K. S. (1994). The graduate student experience and subscription to the norms of science. *Research in Higher Education, 35*, 273–299.

Angell, M. A. (2004). *The truth about the drug companies.* New York: Random House.

Angell, M. & Relman, A. S. (2002). Patents, profits, & American medicine: Conflicts of interest in the testing & marketing of a new drug. *Daedalus, 131*(2), 102–111.

Argyres, N. S., & Liebeskind, J. P. (1998). Privatizing the intellectual commons: Universities and the commercialization of biotechnology. *Journal of Economic Behavior & Organization 35,* 427–454.

Blumenstyk, G. (2004, March 12). A contrarian approach to technology transfer. *The Chronicle of Higher Education,* pp. A27, 28.

Blumenthal, D., Campbell, E. G., Anderson, M. S., Causino, N., & Louis, K. S. (1997). Withholding research results in academic life science. *Journal of the American Medical Association, 277,* 1224–1228.

Bok, D. (2003). *Universities in the marketplace: The commercialization of higher education.* Princeton, NJ: Princeton University Press.

Boyd, E. A., & Bero, L. A. (2000). Assessing faculty financial relationships with industry. *Journal of the American Medical Association, 284,* 2209–2214.

Bray, M. J., & Lee, J. N. (2000). University revenues from technology transfer: Licensing fees vs. equity positions. *Journal of Business Venturing, 15,* 385–392.

Campbell, E. G., Powers, J. B., Blumenthal, D., & Biles, B. (2004). Inside the triple helix: Technology transfer and commercialization in the life sciences. *Health Affairs, 23,* 64–76.

Campbell, T. I. D. (1997). Public policy for the 21st century: Addressing potential conflicts in university-industry collaboration. *The Review of Higher Education, 20,* 357–379.

Carney, T. F. (1972). *Content analysis.* Winnipeg: University of Manitoba.

Cho, M. K., Shohara, R., Schissel, A., & Rennie, D. (2000). Policies on faculty conflict of interest at U.S. universities. *Journal of the American Medical Association, 284*, 2203–2208.

Cottrell, F. (1932). Patent experience of the research corporation. *Transactions of the American Institute of Chemical Engineers, 26*, 222–225.

Etzkowitz, H. & Leydesdorff, L. (1997). *Universities and the global knowledge economy: A triple helix of university-industry-government relations*. Trowbridge, UK: Redwood.

Kenny, M. (1986). *Biotechnology: The university-industrial complex*. London: Yale University Press.

Louis, K. S., Jones, L. M., & Campbell, E. G. (2002). Sharing in science. *American Scientist, 90*, 304–307.

Marino, K. E., Castaldi, R. M., & Dollinger, M. J. (1989). Content analysis in entrepreneurship research: The case of initial public offerings. *Entrepreneurship Theory and Practice, 14*, 51–66.

Merton, R. K. (1942). A note on science and democracy. *Journal of Legal and Political Sociology, 1*, 115–126.

Mitroff, I. I. (1974). *The subjective side of science: A philosophical inquiry into the psychology*. New York: Elsevier.

National Science Board. (2004). *Science & Engineering Indicators 2004*. Washington, DC: National Science Foundation.

Powers, J. (2003). Commercializing academic research: Resource effects on performance of university technology transfer. *Journal of Higher Education, 74*, 26–50.

Powers, J. (2005). *Profits and losses in university technology transfer*. Paper presented at the annual meeting of the Association for the Study of Higher Education, Philadelphia, PA.

Press, E., & Washburn, J. (2000, March). The kept university. *Atlantic Monthly, 285*, pp. 39–54.

Rai, A. K., & Eisenberg, R. S. (2003). Bayh-Dole reform and the progress of biomedicine. *American Scientist, 91*, 52–59.

Roosevelt, F. D. (1944, November 17). *President Roosevelt's letter*. Retrieved November 28, 2005, from http://www.nsf.gov/od/lpa/nsf50/vbush1945.htm#letter

Slaughter, S., Campbell, T., Holleman, M., & Morgan, E. (2002). The "traffic" in graduate students: Graduate students as tokens of exchange between academe and industry. *Science, Technology, & Human Values, 27*, 282–312.

Slaughter, S., & Leslie, D. (1997). *Academic capitalism: Politics, policies, and the entrepreneurial university*. Baltimore, MD: Johns-Hopkins.

Slaughter, S., & Rhoades, G. (2004). *Academic capitalism and the new economy*. Baltimore: Johns-Hopkins.

Swazey, J. P., Louis, K. S., & Anderson, M. S. (1994). Ethical problems in academic research. *American Scientist, 81*, 542–553.

Thompson, L. (2000, September-October). Human gene therapy: Harsh lessons, high hopes. *FDA Consumer, 34*(5), 12–18.

CHAPTER 13

Chicana/o Professors
and the Public Good:

COMMUNITY COMMITMENT, ACTIVIST SCHOLARSHIP,
AND THE PRACTICE OF CONSCIOUSNESS

Luis Urrieta, Jr.

Abstract: This chapter explores ten Chicana/o professors of education's sense-making about their role in the academy in terms of community commitments, activist scholarship, and the practices of consciousness in their struggle for their version of the public good. An inductive and domain analysis was used to analyze the observation, document, and narrative data used in this study. Chicana/o consciousness in practice involved not only active awareness of their agency in moment-to-moment interactions, but also the responsibility to seize those moments to act for change. These Chicana/o professors consciously exercised their agency not only in reaction to white supremacy (i.e., White hegemony) in the academy, but also in proactive, enduring ways through day-to-day practices to subvert and challenge the whitestream (i.e., traditional, Euro-centric) norms and practices of higher education. The practices of Chicana/o consciousness, I argue, can contribute to further developing a common understanding of higher education for the public good.

I would like to believe that institutions of higher education were meant to be public spaces for the betterment of society and that their product, higher education, is meant to produce engaged citizens committed to active participation for the public good. But, do all communities define the "public good" in the same way? Is someone's good another person's bad? Is someone's good fortune another's misfortune?

I would argue that higher education for the public good as a broad concept should be the pursuit of knowledge(s) that prepare all individuals for active participation in society; thus, it should not just function as a concept, but also manifest in practice (pedagogy). Higher education for the public good should be the active pursuit to produce people with a consciousness inclined toward social justice, including through activism for equality, equity, and true democratic engagement.

Higher education for the public good should promote not simply individual gain and competition for mass accumulation, but also people becoming involved in community building and mutual support. The products of higher education for the public good should model and teach with and about a different way to be a citizen. This includes moving beyond a procedural, individualistic, and spectator form of citizenship into a collaborative effort with a high sense of social responsibility to serve the public interest for all people.

This chapter explores how ten Chicana/o professors of Education make sense of their role in the academy in terms of community commitment, activist scholarship, and the practices (pedagogy) of consciousness in their struggle for their version of the public good. Important in this study is the social-cultural, as well as the historical, individual, and collective, context from which this understanding of self as Chicana/o emerges in relation to the hegemony of white supremacy in the U.S. Urrieta and Reidel (2006) define "white supremacy" as the official and unofficial practices, principles, morals, norms, values, history, and overall culture that privileges Whites in U.S. society.

This study was guided by the following research questions:

1. How are community commitments embedded into the ideology and practice of Chicana/o academics in education?
2. How does the intellectualism of Chicana/o scholars contribute to, and/or disrupt the social and political hegemony of the Euro-American academy?
3. How does personal experience and collective memory, through the Chicana/o identity framework, inform the practices that either sustain or challenge traditional educational institutional practices in higher education?

The agency in practice of these Chicana/o professors of education will be defined as Chicana/o consciousness. Chicana/o consciousness in practice involves not only active awareness of their agency in moment-to-moment interactions in the struggle for social justice, but also their felt responsibility to seize those moments to act in the world. In this chapter, I will provide an overview of the close relationship between Chicana/o identity and consciousness, and how the Chicana/o professors in this study describe their work as activist pedagogy for the public good.

THEORETICAL FRAMEWORKS AND BACKGROUND

Social Theory and Agency

Social and cultural reproduction theories proposed relatively closed reproductive processes (Morrow & Torres, 1995). From this perspective, individual agency was relatively absent within the structures of social and cultural systems. Culture itself was essentialized as static collective bodies of knowledge and norms, passed down from generation to generation (Levinson, Foley, & Holland, 1996).

Resistance theories later challenged the idea that subjects did not have the agency to respond to the structures and institutions (Morrow & Torres, 1995) of whitestream[1] society. In Chicana/o scholarship, Solórzano & Delgado Bernal (2001) examine Chicana/o agency in education as a form of "transformational resistance" using a Critical Race and Latino Critical Race (Latcrit) theoretical framework and have defined it as:

> behavior illustrating both a critique of oppression and a desire for social justice...the student holds some level of awareness and critique of her or his oppressive conditions and structures of domination and must be at least somewhat motivated by a sense of social justice. With a deeper level of understanding and a social justice orientation, transformational resistance offers the greatest possibility for social change (p. 319).

Transformational resistance, however, is articulated within the constraints of resistance theoretical frameworks that often disable and delimit the potential of agency (Holland & Lave, 2001), and frame action as reactive rather than proactive.

Bourdieu (1977) challenges stagnant views of culture and the dichotomy of structure and resistance by redirecting attention to the constant improvisation of cultural forms. According to Bourdieu, although there are certain behavioral expectations in society that constrain, no action in the interaction process between dominants and subordinates is complete until the entire "moment" of interaction has transpired. Bourdieu states: "But even the most strictly ritualized exchanges, in which all the moments of the action, and their unfolding, are rigorously foreseen, have room for strategies" (p. 15).

Holland, Lachicotte, Skinner, and Cain (1998) also highlight the importance of improvisations of cultural forms as a manifestation of agency. When improvisation is seen as agency, there is the potential for a local or full-scale new social movement as "improvisation can become the basis for a reformed subjectivity" (p. 18) and has the potential for collective action. Chicana/o consciousness in practice has this potential.

To think about Chicana/o professors' strategic roles in the academy as a practice of their identity, or as informed, orchestrated action (Holland, 2003), it is necessary to revisit the concept of agency. Inden (1990, p. 23) defines human agency as:

> the realized capacity of people to act upon their world and not only to know about or give personal or intersubjective significance to it. That capacity is the power of people to act purposively and reflectively, in more or less complex interrelationships with one another, to reiterate and remake the world in which they live, in circumstances where they may consider different courses of action possible and desirable, though not necessarily from the same point of view.

Holland et al. (1998) aptly add that personal agency exists within a seeming contradiction between humans as social producers and humans as social products. Chicana/o consciousness in practice is this "realized" awareness of knowing of their ability *and* responsibility to act critically in the world, knowing well that there are structural and inherent contradictions to limit their social practice.

Agency, as understood in this chapter, also incorporates the concept of cultural production. Cultural production focuses on how human agency is maneuvered under the structures of the system (Levinson et al., 1996). According to Levinson et al. (1996), cultural production "indexes" a dialectic between structure and agency, "[f]or while the educated person is culturally *produced* in definite sites, the educated person also culturally *produces* cultural forms" (p. 14, original emphasis). Chicana/o professors' practices in the academy in this study are under this self-awareness or conscious understanding of agency, culturally *produced* in formal educational institutions and working within them to *produce* new and trans/formative cultural forms.

The following section addresses historical, social, and philosophical aspects of the Chicana/o identity and the quest to challenge U.S. White supremacy. This quest for change involves a re/definition of activism when working within whitestream institutions for higher education with the aim of creating trans/formational, democratic, more socially just spaces.

Chicana/o Identity and the
Practice of Consciousness

Chicana/o identity officially emerged in the 1960s. This new understanding of the self as "Chicana/o" claimed legitimacy as a "U.S. citizen" group with equal rights. Yet, Chicana/o was also product of the oppressive structures of historical colonial institutions such as whitestream schooling (Urrieta, 2004b) due to the military invasion and subsequent continuous occupation of Northern Mexico (today known as the U.S. Southwest) (Acuña, 2000; Gallegos, 2000). This new identity actively denounced a long history of educational practices embedded in the federal educational system that denied equal access and treatment to children of Mexican descent.

The ideology behind the Chicana/o *movimientos* of the 1960s was not monolithic, yet a general ideology often referred to as Chicanismo emerged. According to Acuña (2000), generally anger and reaction to an unjust system, whether macro or micro, was being acted out. There was a call for Chicanismo that took on different meanings for different people. Chicanismo generally meant to have "pride of identity, and self-determination" (pp. 357–358). Self-determination included a strong sense of "community commitment" (Delgado Bernal, 2001) that was later attributed to having a Chicana/o, or *mestiza/o* consciousness (Anzaldúa, 1987; Delgado Bernal, 2001).

Activism usually revolved around community-based organizations, efforts that sought to "better" the conditions of the *barrio* (neighborhood). Gutiérrez (2001) concurs by alluding to community in terms of *raza* and of the brotherhood of Chicanos as *carnales*. "*Chicanismo* meant identifying with *la raza* (the people), and collectively promoting the interests of *carnales* (brothers) with whom they shared a common language, culture, and religion" (Gutiérrez, 2001, p. 214). García (1998) similarly writes about Chicanismo as a philosophy surrounded by historical symbols and active attempts to fight against racism through activism. Chicanismo is thus the broad ideology behind the identity politics of the self-proclaimed Chicana/o. Participants in these politics (practices) were often perceived as activists, or members of a new social movement called the Chicana/o Movement.

Having a Chicana/o consciousness often meant engaging in activism of various sorts, with the aim of creating a "better world"—another interpretation of the public good. In the 1960s, Chicana/o activism took on more physical acts of protest (García, 1998) and was associated with other protest movements of the '60s (Maciel & Ortiz, 1996). Thus a new and unique perspective, drawn from a Mexican-American past, yet different than any other previously espoused, emerged with the advent of Chicanismo.

Institutionalization and Chicana/o Professors

Certain sectors of the Chicana/o *movimientos* were infiltrated by the end of the 1970s and the notion that the movement had become "institutionalized" emerged (García, 1996). With the implementation of Chicana/o Studies Programs and of MEChA's (*Movimiento Estudiantil Chicano de Aztlán*)[2] on different university campuses, feelings of distance emerged from the original grass-roots organizing of earlier times. A different form of participation or "professional activism" (Padilla, 2003) emerged.

Institutional "penetration" is evident in institutions for higher education. García (1996) asserts that "[o]ne development from the period of the Chicano Movement is the 'penetration' of Chicanos in decision-making institutions" (p. 95). Acuña (2000) documents, for example, that, in 1967, only three percent of the teachers in California had Spanish surnames. In 2000, the percentage of Hispanic teachers was 13.5% (California Department of Education, 2000). The number of Hispanic university faculty members is not as promising, yet is also growing. Although these numbers do not reflect the proportion of the Latina/o population, there is a growing number of Chicanas/os penetrating into institutions that were formerly closed. García (1996) states, "One can suggest that the political times may be different and that institutionalization of the movement calls for different strategies and approaches" (p. 103).

Not all Chicanos/as see institutionalization as good, but rather as costly compromises. Some activists of the '60s lament the changes and distancing from the tactics and activism of that time (García, 1996; Muñoz, 1989). Scholars like Acuña (2000) have called the '80s and '90s the "Hispanic" generations, full of negotiations and compromises. The notion of the institutional "sell-out" is often conjured up as the ultimate compromise in these negotiations for institutional recognition and power (Urrieta, in press). However, such accusations are not deterministic or dichotomous as many have made them seem. The experiences of Chicana/o, Latina/o educators in higher education highlight some of the contradictions.

Chicana/o, Latina/o faculty document the personal struggles with covert and overt forms of racism and marginality experienced when dealing with or overcoming dominant gate-keeping institutional practices (Padilla & Chávez, 1995). Studies have found that academic success for Chicanas/os is an alienating process at institutions of higher education that are rarely welcoming environments for students or faculty (Gonzáles, 2001; Urrieta, 2003). Alemán (1995) states:

> As Latina/o professors, we are newcomers to a world defined and controlled by discourses that do not address our realities, that do not affirm our intellectual contributions, that do not seriously examine our worlds. Can I be both professor and Latina without compromise?" (p. 75).

Such *testimonios* speak broadly to the experiences of Chicanas/os in higher education. With reference to identity, there is an orchestration of selves that emerges as a person acquires a more enduring identity—Chicana/o—and learns to negotiate roles, languages, and scripts according to the social/cultural spaces entered (Urrieta, 2003). The institutionalization of Chicana/o professional activism in the Post-Civil Rights era is the context for this study.

METHODOLOGY

This study further develops my previous research conducted in California from 2001–2003 (Urrieta, 2003). My previous study builds on Gándara's (1995) seminal work on low-income Chicana/o educational success, as well as Delgado Bernal's (1999) work on Chicana/o activism. It is a study of the experiences of twenty-four Chicana/o educators, including undergraduates planning careers in education, as well as current teachers, graduate students in education, and professors of education. I explore how identity and agency manifest in activism for these particular Chicana/o educators. In further analysis of this work, I also explored how Chicanos/as achieve educational success through strategic practices of identity and ideological negotiation and orchestration by "playing the game," and yet maintain activist commitments for change (Urrieta, 2005).

In this study I focus specifically on Chicana/o professors of education. Ten Chicana/o faculty members (five woman and five men) at different universities in the Southwest were interviewed. The faculty members interviewed had tenure-track appointments in public universities; five had experience working in Tier 1 Research Universities, and five were affiliated with Teaching Institutions. This sample included two full professors, two associate professors, and six assistant professors, with each of these rankings being gender equal.

With this research, I wanted to further understand how Chicana/o professors of education make sense of their role in the academy as it relates to community commitments, their scholarship, and in particular, their individual and collective agency, or practices (pedagogy), in their struggle for their version of the public good. The participants in this study were treated as consultants or as "experts" (Hinson, 2000). Autobiographical narratives were privileged as the epistemological foundation (Reed-Danahay, 1997). Observations were also conducted and documents collected for limited forms of discourse analysis (Freeman, 1996).

To participate, consultants had to strongly self-identify as Chicana/o and be employed as tenure track faculty in schools and/or colleges of education in accredited universities in the U.S. Professors were contacted using a purposeful sampling method (Gall, Borg, & Gall, 1996) using personal contacts, professional organizations, and professional contacts. An in-depth, semi-structured (Davies,

2001) interview was conducted with each professor as well as five hours of observations at their host institution. Two documents were requested from each professor: an example of personal writing such as a journal entry, poetry, etc., and a formal writing sample such as curriculum vitae, syllabus, or professional statement.

The data were analyzed using an inductive analysis (Lincoln & Guba, 1985). Interview transcripts were actively used to triangulate observation and document data and to substantiate and/or refute claims (Davies, 2001). After themes were identified and data sorted into domains (LeCompte & Schensul, 1999), representative examples from the interviews were cited to support each of the emergent themes. Pseudonyms are used for all people and institutions. In the following sections I discuss briefly the overall findings and later focus particularly on the themes of:

1. community commitment,
2. activist scholarship, and
3. the practice (or agency) of consciousness.

Overall Findings

Generally the Chicana/o professors expressed feeling isolated and alienated at their institutions. The degree of isolation for some was greater than for others due to the setting and number of supportive colleagues directly available with whom to network. The isolation of Chicana/o professors, however, was not a deterrent in their active attempts to present to all of their students a more critical and multi-perspective curriculum, as evidenced through course syllabi as well as by their use of instructional pedagogies to raise students' critical consciousness. Equitable student evaluation, support for learning, and mentorship were important to Chicana/o professors. Mentorship was especially important when working with graduate students where pseudo-familial metaphors were used to refer to these relationships.

All professors expressed a strong and equal commitment to both their teaching and research in areas that support and present alternative epistemologies and perspectives. This commitment involved raising awareness about social justice education, equity issues, resources allocation, and critical analysis of policy and language issues, immigration, race/ethnicity, and affirmative action. Several professors were doing this by incorporating these issues to their course syllabi; others, however, were teaching small seminars for which they were not getting paid and not receiving university credit for teaching. Professors doing research expressed a "political twist" to their research agendas as well as a controversial element to their "debunking of myths" in whitestream research previously used to stereotype minority communities.

All of the professors, in particular, saw themselves as a resource to Chicana/o students on their respective campuses (undergraduate and graduate) as well as to Chicana/o students nationally that often sought their assistance. Their commitments to "opening doors" and to mentor students in the graduate school socialization process were taken very seriously. Opening doors often involved maintaining Chicana/o networks across different university contexts, locally and nationally, that enabled for the flow of students through what some called "pipelines." This was done with the goal of increasing Chicana/o student representation at all levels of the educational system.

Chicana/o networks were not limited to other scholars in four-year universities, but included professors at the community colleges as well as graduate students, teachers, and community members at all levels and in different fields or disciplines. Such connections also included networks in government organizations; legal organizations, such as MALDEF (Mexican American Legal Defense and Education Fund) and LULAC (League of United Latin American Citizens); NCLR (National Council of La Raza); and other policy forums created to address community issues, especially relating to Latina/o educational attainment and access to higher education. Such networks often provided social, emotional, academic, legal, political, and other forms of support.

Part of professors' activist commitments also involved the creation of trans/formative spaces for Chicana/o, Latina/o students and their allies (of other races/ethnic groups). Trans/formative spaces included research opportunities, classroom discussions, office space for meaningful interaction, centers to gather, after school programs, migrant education summer programs, and minority new student orientation programs. Research and teaching were thus seen as very important in both creating these spaces and securing funding sources that would enable these professors to have these spaces and fund students through their graduate and undergraduate programs, while also doing community related research. Professors who worked in teacher education programs and with terminal Master's students focused on:

1. teaching students how to use critical pedagogy to make the K–12 classroom a site of trans/formation, and
2. preparing students to attend elite universities to do doctoral-level work.

Conveying the public "voice" was also of great importance to activist Chicana/o professors; they did so not only through presentations at academic conferences, but also by talking to a variety of different groups, including community organizations—even when they did not receive "official" university credit for their service. Many were actively involved in writing for local newspapers, radio, and television in order to present a more critical perspective on issues affecting the community. All felt that their connections to K–12 education, K–12 teachers, and community educators were important and, in many cases, helped to keep them grounded, honest, and humble in their professional and personal lives. With the hope of influencing the direction of the academic and policy conversation, many also engaged audiences as keynote speakers and "experts," even when the label made them feel uneasy.

A few undertook positions locally and nationally that gave them the agency to make informed policy decisions regarding educational issues affecting the Latina/o community. One professor served as a high official in the national government, for example, while others worked in policy circles and/or gave expert testimony in court. Through their research, several sought to raise awareness about issues such as standardized testing, the validity of the SAT, minority student access to higher education, and the efficiency of K–12 instructional programs. In some cases, professors' involvement in faculty search committees was also perceived as being instrumental in hiring more Chicana/o, Latina/o faculty in their departments. Their positions as faculty members gave them the agency to recruit and, in many cases, admit—or commit to working with— Chicana/o, Latina/o students and other students committed to their vision for a better world.

"We can make a difference…we can!"

The above quote illustrates the enthusiasm for change expressed by most of the professors interviewed, and although some talked about their discomfort in predominantly White working environments, all were committed to work for a better world. In the following section I will discuss the themes of:

1. community commitment,
2. activist scholarship, and
3. the practice (or agency) of consciousness.

These themes were particularly salient for all of the professors interviewed. Representative quotes are used to illustrate the concepts.

Comunidad

Whether it was with Latina/o communities outside of the university or with student communities within it, community commitment was central to the work of Chicana/o professors in education. Adriana said:

I am incredibly grateful and I feel this very strong sense of responsibility that I need to turn that into opportunities for other people. And because I have a particular connection to the Chicano community, it allows me to do that there.

Not only was this an important component of professors' research, teaching, and service agendas, but most, like Adriana, also expressed a sense of responsibility to work on Chicana/o, Latina/o issues in education, even when these issues were devalued by the institution. Andi stated:

The reason lots of us get into this business [education] is because we have this felt need, we have a community in crisis, we see it and we wanna get in there and do something. It's not something that you wait to get tenure for and then you do it.... It is fundamental to why we got into the academy. It is...fundamental to our work. It's not...we don't have the luxury [to wait for tenure to begin to work on Chicana/o, Latina/o issues].... I can't do it after tenure. We don't have that luxury.

Like Andi and Adriana, other professors interviewed expressed their commitment to raise awareness about the issues affecting the larger Latina/o community, even if they had to pay an institutional price—tenure and/or promotion—for this commitment. Andi's statements are representative of other professors' motivations for entering the field of education in the first place. Part of that motivation is not just to work for the physical benefit of the Latina/o community, but also to raise the consciousness of *all* of the students they teach. Miguel, for example, stated:

My goal as an educator is to make people think critically about the reality that they live in. Because I am convinced that if they do that, they will want a different world than the one we are in.... I see that, that practice in a classroom as activism. It is the space in which I am politically working toward... a better world, it is a more humane world and that's where I do it.

As Miguel states, commitment to community for these Chicana/o professors was not exclusively about the Chicana/o community per se (although there were strong commitments expressed), but also a commitment to the greater good—one could say the public good—of all people. It was understood that when inequality and discrimination exist in a society, it affects not just the oppressed, but everyone in that society in negative ways.

Although the field of education is one that especially draws the interests of Chicana/o, Latina/o students, the Chicana/o faculty in this study were not unconditionally committed to "brown" students simply because they identified as Chicana/o or Latina/o. Felipe expressed this well:

> I'm not interested in just having brown faces with White middle-class dreams. I'm not interested in working with students who just wanna get a nice cushy job and make a whole lot of money. I'm interested in working with students who come from communities where they had to overcome a lot of barriers to even get to college. Poor working families who've been able to overcome that and to help them to go to college so that they can then go back and help those kinds of Mexican communities, Chicano communities, and not necessarily just prepare middle class "Highspanics."

Community commitment, for Felipe, therefore related to addressing the pressing issues affecting and afflicting the broader Chicana/o, Latina/o community outside and within the university. However, it was not just about an undisputed ethnic/cultural alliance, but also an ideological commitment to and for social justice—the pursuit of a better world, a more humane world that includes everyone living in it.

Activist Scholarship

The literature on intellectualism highlights that interpretations of intellectualism and the role and responsibilities of intellectuals in society vary (Gramsci, 1971; Said, 1994; West, 1999). The Chicana/o professors in this study did not see their scholarship simply as an expected practice of their career, but as form of activism or activist scholarship. Felipe stated this well:

> I would consider an activist agenda [in research] doing the kind of work that's gonna shake things up. They're not doing the safe kind of research, they're doing research and producing the kind of knowledge that's gonna be very controversial, that's gonna have some resistance. Uhm, that's gonna have strong critique against it. But I think that's one way of determining of whether your work is making a difference or not. If it causes some resistance then you know you must be having something that's threatening change, 'cause people don't like change. So it's a good measure.

Activist scholarship is not unsound or un-rigorous research, but rather scholarship about issues undervalued or misunderstood in the whitestream academy and by whitestream researchers. Because activist scholarship challenges previously misunderstood or misguided research, it is often perceived by the whitestream, like Felipe says, as "controversial" and also "causes come resistance."

Activist scholarship is often associated with the tradition of social criticism. Social criticism poses difficult, but necessary questions that encourage intellectual debate fundamental to furthering the cause of democracy. Although the voices of intellectual dissent are necessary to the goals of deliberation, dialogue, and democracy, the activist scholarship of the Chicanas/os interviewed was not social criticism. Chicana/o activist scholarship is the active and valuable knowledge production, through empirical research, that validates the epistemologies of those outside the whitestream in U.S. society. Adriana stated:

> Our role is to codify and give credibility to certain kinds of knowledge and then to codify and give credibility to people who have that knowledge. And of course it's a huge tension because there are people within the academy who believe that there's one kind of knowledge. And that kind of knowledge of course is privileged in this setting. And I think our job, people like me, people like you Luis is I think to always call it into question.

Giving credibility to "certain kinds of knowledge" and the people that possess that knowledge is fundamental to the scholarship of Chicana/o professors. The production of knowledge for these Chicana/o professors is not knowledge for knowledge's sake, but an active agenda to reverse the wrongs and erasure of people of color that result from white supremacy and whitestream indoctrination.

The Practice of Consciousness

The practice of Chicana/o consciousness involves not only active awareness of one's agency to challenge white supremacy in moment-to-moment interactions in the struggle for social justice, but also the responsibility to seize those moments to act in the world (Urrieta, 2003). All of the Chicana/o professors interviewed were aware of their agency and sought "moments" where they could exert this agency in proactive and practical (rather than reactive and reductive) ways. Andrés stated:

> I want more people with experiences like mine and like other Latinos, in positions where they can either acquire or utilize the assets of the academy to make a difference. And that's broadly defined, intellectually, politically, and on a day-to-day practical basis.

Andrés' reference to the "assets of the academy" illustrates that for these Chicana/o professors, academic culture and the artifacts of this culture (such as writing, teaching, public speaking, etc.) were not only tools for domination, but could also be tools for liberation—to make a difference—in proactive ways. Agency, as understood in Andrés' statements, is also not about mass revolution (that is not what proaction means here), but about change "on a day-to-day practical basis."

The practice of consciousness, especially the practical aspects of change, was especially important in the field of education for these Chicana/o professors. Education was seen as a place for emancipation, although for others, education is the very site of whitestream indoctrination. Felipe stated:

> It's a place of liberation when you think about activism. Education is the most fertile ground to liberate yourself. Liberate yourself, your mind and liberate yourself economically, socially, spiritually, every way, through education. I think you can totally liberate yourself in many ways by the power of writing, by the power of thinking.

Because the field of education was already seen as a potential place to bring about change, the Chicana/o professors in this study used their positions to practice their consciousness in several ways. The practices of consciousness included forming individual and collective networks of support for their efforts, mentoring students, teaching, and using their public voice to raise awareness about issues they considered important.

Mentoring students was probably considered one of the most important practices of consciousness for the Chicana/o professors in this study. This was especially true when it involved mentoring graduate students. Laura, for example, stated:

> I think we have that responsibility to be mentors, mentors to other Latinos. I think one of the things, I think once you earn your doctorate, once you've done a qualitative study or statistical study, it doesn't make a difference, that you always have to help the next person that is doing a doctoral study.

Although mentoring students is part of academic culture in graduate school, the ways that Chicana/o professors spoke about their responsibility to mentor and specifically about their mentoring relationships was significant. The practice of consciousness through mentoring relationships evoked familial and kinship ties that were captured well by Andrés:

> Once you're in a position where you can help others, then you ought to do it. You have to do it. That's just the responsibility you have. And mainly because there may not be that support for those individuals elsewhere. It's the old you know *padrino, madrina* syndrome. When you baptize someone, you have a responsibility.

> The devil is not supposed to take that person. Should anything
> happen to the parents, you're supposed to do it. When you marry
> someone, you're the *padrino* in some sense, you have responsibility.
> You know to help them, nurture them, support them, not just, it's
> not just an honorific relationship it's a responsible relationship.

Andrés specifically uses the metaphor of Catholic sacramental sponsorship to make his point about mentoring. In this cultural context, the mentoring relationship has a more familial and also sacred commitment to have a "responsible relationship" and part of that relationship is to nurture and support, and most importantly protect, the *ahijada/o* (mentee/student) from harm (the devil).

The Practice of Chicana/o Consciousness and the Public Good

Chicana/o consciousness in practice, in this study, similar to Villenas' (1996) colonizer/colonized ethnographer dilemma, is about Chicanas/os working, as professors, in educational institutions that would have them contribute to the educational colonizing enterprise, but with the personal counter-intent and motivation to trans/form these institutions into more accessible and democratic spaces. Villenas (1996) attempts to locate herself within the problematic dichotomy of the colonizer (whitestream ethnographer) and the colonized (Chicana), and ultimately resolves the dilemma by seeing her own agency as a *Chicana ethnographer*. She concludes:

> My answer to the ethnographer-as-colonizer dilemma is that
> I will not stop at being the public translator and facilitator for
> my communities, but that I am my own voice, an activist seeking
> liberation from my own historical oppression in relation to my
> communities (p. 730).

The Chicana/o consciousness in practice of these professors, like Villenas, is about finding and expressing an alternative voice. Exercising agency consciously for Chicana/o professors is not only in reaction to white supremacy in the academy, but also in proactive, enduring ways through their day-to-day practices to subvert and challenge the whitestream norms and practices of higher education. Chicana/o consciousness is thus formed on the basis of cultural, collective, and community memory (Delgado Bernal, 2001), but is negotiated and manifests in seized moments of opportunity for change in institutions for higher education. When these opportunities arise, improvisation, whether planned or unplanned, is key.

Overall, the practice of consciousness by these Chicana/o professors was seen as strategic and opportunistic in a positive sense. By being strategic and opportunistic, they were aware of their agency and their positions of power to bring about change. The Chicana/o professors in this study were careful about seizing the moments when they could make, or improvise, changes into the system. All of the Chicanas/os in this study felt fortunate and satisfied with their contributions to their vision of a greater good. All felt they were contributing to the cause of social justice in one way or another. Adriana, with a radiant smile and enthusiastic tone of voice, said:

> I just get enormous, just enormous gratification out of doing what I do. I mean I just, I can't tell you how happy I am that things have worked out the way they have because one of those major sources of grat....There's two sources of that gratification. And one is...this network of Chicano scholars that it is such a really wonderful part of my life. And the other is being able to work with students...I mean I get to chose who I'm going to work with and I chose to work with people who think similarly to me and who will make a difference, you know?

Adriana expresses the gratification she enjoys in doing the work she does as a professor with the purpose of making a difference. The sources of this gratification include the network of Chicana/o scholars she works with and the mentoring relationship she has with students who think like her and are committed to making a difference—the public good. Elogio, a professor and administrator, similarly responded with enthusiasm:

> I've been fortunate. I've been in positions where I can make policies, where I can make decisions, everything from this position, to other positions, to department chair, to even faculty member where I could make decisions about students.... I've been fortunate to be in those positions where you can do that. You can make gains, 'cause you can.

Elogio, like Adriana, and the other professors in this study, was proud and confident about his accomplishments and contributions to a greater good—one could argue, the public good. Elogio's consciousness in practice was especially important due to his position and awareness of his agency and ability to make positive, more democratic changes.

IMPLICATIONS FOR THE WHITESTREAM PUBLIC GOOD

The practices of Chicana/o consciousness, for those committed to dismantling white supremacy and the whitestream norms of higher education institutions, can contribute to further developing a common understanding of higher education for the public good. That common understanding should be geared toward creating engaged citizens committed to the goals of social justice that include equality, equity, and democratic engagement. As a point of departure toward that goal, however, it is important to understand with clarity that we live in a white supremacist and patriarchal society from which our notions of whitestream as *the* mainstream emerge.

In terms of the practices of Chicana/o consciousness, in this chapter, I focused on community commitments, activist scholarship, and practices such as teaching, the public voice, networking, and especially mentoring; however, there are many other practices that need to be further studied in constructive ways. From community commitments, it is important to understand that there has to be an active institutional commitment to diversity, like that of the Chicana/o professors in this study, that goes beyond mission statements and actually involves the active pursuit and commitment to communities of color and other underrepresented groups in higher education. This study also highlights that scholarship is political and that the activist scholarship of the professors studied is no different in rigor or in political inclination than is any other scholarship. The difference is that whitestream scholarship is blinded by its normalized status. For the Chicana/o professors in this study, knowledge for knowledge's sake is not as innocent, or as objective, as whitestream scholars claim it to be. Finally, the practices of consciousness are important—voice, networking with those committed to social justice, teaching as a tool for consciousness raising, and mentoring, especially students of color, involves a responsible and respectful—not just an honorific—relationship.

The practice of Chicana/o consciousness has important insights to offer our broader conceptions of higher education for the public good in terms of the social responsibility *all* faculty members have in their positions of power. Faculty members committed to the public good should model a different way of being a citizen with actions, not just with concepts, and should especially focus their energies to serve the public interest. U.S. society is changing rapidly, demographically and otherwise. Dismantling white supremacy and whitestream practices as the mainstream in higher education is timely and in the public interest—it's for the public good.

Reprinted by permission: Urrieta, Jr., L. and Méndez Benavídez, L.R. (2007). Community Commitment and Activist Scholarship: Chicana/o Professors and the Practice of Consciousness. *The Journal of Hispanic Higher Education*, 6(3). 222–236.

Endnotes

1. Sandy Grande (2000) refers to "whitestream" as the cultural capital of whites in almost every facet of U.S. society. Grande uses the term whitestream as opposed to mainstream in an effort to decenter whiteness as dominant. Whitestream, according to Denis (1997), is a term which plays on the feminist notion of "malestream." Denis defines Whitestream as the idea that while (Canadian) society is not completely White in socio-demographic terms, it remains principally and fundamentally structured on the basis of the Anglo-European white experience. Whitestream in this article refers to the official and unofficial texts used in U.S. society that are founded on the practices, principles, morals, values, and history of white supremacy and that has been normalized as natural, or "mainstream." Whitestream indoctrination is not exclusively the domain of Whites in U.S. society, but of any person actively promoting white supremacy as "standard."
2. MEChA in English translates to *The Chicano Student Movement of Aztlan*. MEChA was officially created as the official student organization of the Movement by faculty, staff, students, administrators, and community members gathered by the Chicano Council on Higher Education at the University of California at Santa Barbara in 1969 (Urrieta, 2004a).

References

Acuña, R. (2000). *Occupied America: A history of Chicanos* (4th ed.). New York: Longman Press.

Alemán, A. M. M. (1995). Actuando. In R. Padilla, & R. C. Chávez (Eds.), *The leaning ivory tower: Latino professors in American universities*. Albany, NY: State University of New York Press.

Anzaldúa, G. (1987). *Borderlands/La Frontera: The new mestiza*. San Francisco: AuntLute Books.

Bourdieu, P. (1977). *Outline of a theory of practice* (R. Nice, Trans.). Cambridge: Cambridge University Press.

Davies, C. A. (2001). *Reflexive ethnography, A guide to researching selves and others*. London: Routledge.

Delgado Bernal, D. (1999). Chicana/o education from the civil rights era to the present. In J. F. Moreno (Ed.), *The elusive quest for equality: 150 Years of Chicana/Chicano education*. Cambridge, MA: Harvard Educational Review.

Delgado Bernal, D. (2001). Learning and living pedagogies of the home: The mestiza consciousness of Chicana Students. *International Journal of Qualitative Studies in Education*, 14, 623–639.

Denis, J. C. (1997). *We are not you: First nations and Canadian modernity*. Calgary, Canada: Broadview Press, Collection Terra Incognita.

Freeman, D. (1996). "To take them at their word": Language data in the study of teachers' knowledge. *Harvard Educational Review*, 66, 732–761.

Gall, M. D., Borg, W. R., & Gall, J. P. (1996). Educational research: *An introduction*. New York: Longman Publishers.

Gallegos, B. (2000). Postcolonialism. In D. A. Gobbard, (Ed.), *Knowledge and power in the global economy: Politics and the rhetoric of school reform*. Mahwah, NJ: Lawrence Erlbaum Associates.

Gándara, P. (1995). *Over the ivy walls: The educational mobility of low-income Chicanos*. Albany, NY: State University of New York Press.

García, I. M. (1998). *Chicanismo: The forging of a militant ethos among Mexican Americans.* Tucson, AZ: University of Arizona Press.

García, J. A. (1996). The Chicano Movement: Its legacy for politics and policy. In D. R. Maciel, & I. D. Ortiz (Eds.), *Chicanas/Chicanos at the crossroads: Social, economic, and political change.* Tucson, AZ: University of Arizona Press.

González, K. P. (2001). Inquiry as a process of learning about the other and the self. *Qualitative Studies in Education,* 14, 543–562.

Gramsci, A. (1971). *Selections from the prison notebooks.* New York: International Publishers.

Grande, S. M. A. (2000). *American Indian geographies of identity and power: At the crossroads of indígena and mestizaje.* Harvard Educational Review, 70, 467–498.

Gutiérrez, R. (2001). Historical and social science research on Mexican Americans.J. Banks, & C. Banks (Eds.), *Handbook of research on multicultural education.* San Francisco: Jossey-Bass.

Hinson, G. (2000). *Fire in my bones.* Philadelphia: University of Pennsylvania Press.

Holland, D. C. (2003, April). *People-in-activity: A cultural historical approach to identity, agency, and social change.* Invited lecture presented at the annual meeting of the American Educational Research Association, Chicago, IL.

Holland, D. C., & Lave, J. (Eds.). (2001). *History in person: Enduring struggles, contentious practice, intimate identities.* Santa Fe, NM: School of American Research Press.

Holland, D. C., Lachicotte, W., Jr., Skinner, D., & Cain, C. (1998). *Identity and agency in cultural worlds.* Cambridge, MA: Harvard University Press.

Inden, R. (1990). *Imagining India.* Oxford: Blackwell.

LeCompte, M., & Schensul, J. (1999). *Designing and conducting ethnographic research: The ethnographer's toolkit* (Book 1). Walnut Creek, CA: Sage Publications.

Levinson, B., Foley, D. E., & Holland, D. C. (Eds.). (1996). *The cultural production of the education person: Critical ethnographies of schooling and local practice.* Albany, NY: State University of New York Press.

Lincoln, Y. & Guba, E. (1985). *Naturalistic inquiry.* Beverly Hills, CA: Sage Publications.

Maciel, D. R., & Ortiz, I. D. (Eds.). (1996). *Chicanas/Chicanos at the crossroads: Social, economic, and political change.* Tucson, AZ: University of Arizona Press.

Morrow, R. A., & Torres, C. A. (1995). *Social theory and education: A critique of theories of social and cultural reproduction.* Albany, NY: State University of New York Press.

Muñoz, C., Jr. (1989). Youth, identity, and power: The Chicano Movement. New York: Verso.

Padilla, R. (2003, August). *The landscape in higher education.* Paper presented at the inaugural meeting of the American Association for Hispanics in Higher Education, Pomona, CA.

Padilla, R., & Chávez, R. C. (Eds.). (1995). *The leaning ivory tower: Latino professors in American universities.* Albany, NY: State University of New York Press.

Reed-Danahay, D. (1997). *Auto/ethnography: Rewriting the self and the social.* Oxford: Berg.

Said, E. (1994). *Representations of the intellectual.* New York: Pantheon Books.

Solórzano, D. G., & Delgado Bernal, D. (2001). *Examining transformational resistance through a critical race and latcrit theory framework: Chicana and Chicano students in urban context.* Urban Education, 36, 308–342.

Urrieta, L., Jr. (2003). Orchestrating the selves: Chicana and Chicano negotiations of identity, ideology, and activism in education. Unpublished dissertation, The University of North Carolina at Chapel Hill.

Urrieta, L., Jr. (2004a). Chicana/o activism and education: An introduction to the special issue. *The High School Journal,* 87(4), 1–9.

Urrieta, L., Jr. (2004b). Dis-connections in "American" citizenship and the post/neocolonial: People of Mexican descent and whitestream pedagogy and curriculum. *Theory and Research in Social Education, 32*, 433–458.

Urrieta, L., Jr. (2005). "Playing the game" versus "selling out": Chicanas and Chicanos' relationship to whitestream schools. In B. K. Alexander, G. Anderson, & B. Gallegos (Eds.), *Performance theories in education: Power, pedagogy, and the politics of identity*. Mahwah, NJ: Lawrence Erlbaum and Associates.

Urrieta, L., Jr. (in press). Sell outs. In W. A. Darity (Ed.), *International Encyclopedia of the Social Sciences* (2nd ed.) New York: Macmillan.

Urrieta, L., Jr., & Reidel, M. (2006). Avoidance, anger, and convenient amnesia: White supremacy and self-reflection in social studies teacher education. In E. W. Ross (Ed.), *Race, Ethnicity, and Education*. Westport, CT: Praeger Press.

Villenas, S. (1996). *The colonizer/colonized Chicana ethnographer: Identity, marginalization, and co-optation in the field*. Harvard Educational Review, 66, 711–731.

West, C. (1999). *The Cornel West reader*. New York: Basic Civitas Books.

CHAPTER 14

Toward the Engaged Institution:

RHETORIC, PRACTICE, AND VALIDATION

David J. Weerts

Abstract: This multi-case study of land grant institutions examines how campus executives, faculty, and staff at large research universities articulate and demonstrate their commitment to outreach and engagement. This study also sheds light on how community partners validate and make sense of this commitment. Findings suggest that community partner perceptions of institutional engagement are informed by rhetoric and behavior of top university leaders, and the extent to which faculty and staff successfully form community-university partnerships built on mutual respect, trust, and shared goals. The impact of various organizational structures on community perceptions of engagement is also discussed. The study provides implications for how land grant universities might better align their leadership, organizational structures, practices, and policies to be more responsive to societal needs.

During the last decade, a number of forces have challenged public colleges and universities to be more committed to serving societal needs. One of the most high profile challenges came from the Kellogg Commission on the Future of State and Land Grant Universities established in 1996. In their third report, *Returning to Our Roots: The Engaged Institution*, the Kellogg Commission argued that colleges and universities will face multiple challenges in the decades ahead, and at the center of these challenges is the public perception that higher education institutions are out-of-touch and unresponsive to the needs of society (Kellogg Commission on the Future of State and Land Grant Universities, 1999).

The Commission's stinging assertions have been supported by other studies conducted in the late 1990s suggesting that land grant institutions have drifted from their missions to be universities of the people. Among them, Bonnen's (1998) extensive critique of the modern land grant institution argued that university outreach and public service "is poorly focused and not well internalized in the value system of the modern university" (p. 39). His analysis led him to conclude, "We must face the fact that the covenant that has governed the university's relationship with society since World War II has dissolved" (p. 45).

In response to these criticisms and growing accountability pressures from legislators and the public, various national organizations have emerged to steer colleges and universities toward a more public agenda. Among them, a national clearinghouse has been established to help faculty members evaluate the quality of outreach scholarship as they seek promotion and tenure (Scholarship of Engagement, 2004) and organizations such as the National Forum on Higher Education for the Public Good have been established to "significantly increase awareness, understanding, commitment, and action relative to the public service role of higher education in the United States" (National Forum on Higher Education for the Public Good, 2004, para. 1).

The movement to create more publicly engaged institutions has gained momentum due to key scholarly contributions that have placed outreach scholarship in a more prominent light. Important works such as *Scholarship Reconsidered* (Boyer, 1990), *Scholarship Assessed* (Glassick, Huber & Maeroff, 1997) and *Making the Case for Professional Service* (Lynton, 1995) have been especially important influences on how faculty work might be reconceptualized to focus on serving broad public interests (Knox, 2001).

PURPOSE OF THE STUDY
AND RESEARCH QUESTIONS

The purpose of this study is to contribute to an understanding of how land grant universities might better align their leadership, organizational structures, practices, and policies to be more responsive to societal needs. A unique aspect of this study is that it is concerned with the perspectives of community stakeholders and the factors that these partners believe are key to demonstrating a university's commitment to outreach and engagement.

Stemming from this rationale, two primary research questions guide this study. First, what are the factors that shape or characterize a land grant institution's commitment to outreach and engagement? Stated another way, what is the rhetoric and practice that defines and guides institutional efforts in outreach and engagement? Second, in what ways and to what extent do these institutional factors inform community partners' perceptions about institutional commitment to outreach and engagement? In other words, how do important stakeholders outside the institution validate and make sense of a land grant university's commitment to outreach and engagement?

Before these questions can be investigated, it is first important to clearly define two key terms in this study: "community" and "engagement." This study recognizes the challenges of defining both terms, as their interpretations are often nebulous and far-reaching in scope. In this study, community refers to geographical regions within states linked by common experiences and concerns (Anderson & Jayakumar, 2002). As for the term, "engagement," this study borrows from a definition as articulated by the American Association of State Colleges and Universities (AASCU) Task Force on Public Engagement. According to AASCU, "The publicly engaged institution is fully committed to direct, two-way interaction with communities and other external constituencies through the development, exchange, and application of knowledge, information, and expertise for mutual benefit" (American Association of State Colleges and Universities, 2002, p. 7).

LITERATURE AND CONCEPTUAL FRAMEWORK

The concept of engagement as it is defined by AASCU is best understood through the lens of open systems theory, which provides the theoretical orientations for this paper. Organizational theorists suggest that higher education institutions face multiple organizational and structural challenges as they attempt to respond to a broad and diverse public agenda. Fundamentally, colleges and universities have been described as "organized anarchies" because they operate with ambiguous goals, unclear procedures, and are vulnerable to changes in their environment (Cohen & March, 1974). Open systems theory applies well to organized anarchies like colleges and universities that are made up of complex and loosely connected coalitions of shifting interest groups (Pfeffer & Salancik, 1978) capable of autonomous actions (Glassman, 1973).

Recognizing these organizational characteristics of colleges and universities, open systems theory provides a compelling framework for thinking about the forces that guide institutions to move toward establishing a two-way, mutually beneficial relationship with their communities. From an open systems perspective, engagement with the environment is essential for the survival and functioning of the system:

> The interdependence of the organization and its environment receives primary attention in the open systems perspective. Rather than overlooking the environment, the open systems perspective stresses the reciprocal ties that bind and relate the organization with those elements that surround and penetrate

it. The environment is perceived to be the ultimate source of materials, energy, and information, all of which are vital to the continuation of the system. Indeed, the environment is seen to be the source of order itself (Scott, 1992, p. 93).

Within this framework, an interdependent relationship between the university and its external stakeholders is especially important, because the survival of an institution is viewed as dependent on information and resources from these stakeholders. The present movement for public colleges and universities to "reengage" with societal needs has stemmed from threatening information from outside institutions that has pushed colleges and universities to be more responsive to their constituents. Challenged by increased demands for accountability, a skeptical media, and an intense demographic shift in the U.S. population, the leaders of the Kellogg Commission warned, "Institutions ignore a changing environment at their peril. Like dinosaurs, they risk becoming exhibits in a kind of cultural Jurassic Park: places of great interest and curiosity, increasingly irrelevant in a world that has passed them by." (Kellogg Commission on the Future of State and Land Grant Universities, 1996, p. 2).

Open systems theory assumes that loosely coupled organizations (Weick, 1976) like colleges and universities are capable of self-maintenance and that they have the ability to reconnect with societal demands to ensure their survival. The literature review that follows relies on this framework to understand organizational challenges facing colleges and universities as they attempt to be more engaged with community partners.

FACTORS ASSOCIATED WITH INSTITUTIONAL COMMITMENT TO ENGAGEMENT

Scholars have noted that institutional commitment to outreach and engagement varies significantly across colleges and universities. While most campuses have rhetoric that speaks of their commitment to outreach and engagement, the breadth, depth, and richness of engagement vary significantly across postsecondary education institutions (American Association of State Colleges and Universities, 2002; Holland, 1997; National Association for State Universities and Land Grant Colleges, 2002). The true test of understanding institutional commitment to outreach and engagement is to investigate the attributes of campuses that characterize these activities (Holland, 1997).

The literature reviewed for this study provides a broad conceptual framework for mapping the complex set of factors that explain institutional commitment to service and outreach. These factors can be grouped into the following four categories:

1. institutional history and culture;
2. leadership, organizational structure and policies;
3. faculty and staff involvement; and
4. campus communications.

Institutional history plays an important role in shaping campus culture, mission, and future directions for outreach and engagement activities on campus. For example, in Wisconsin, the University of Wisconsin–Madison's commitment to service can be traced back to the Wisconsin Idea, the early 20th Century concept of leveraging the expertise of the university to directly improve the lives of state residents (Berry, 1972). This concept continues to shape UW–Madison's mission and vision for serving the state as the institution strives to update the idea for the 21st Century (Ward, 1999).

Leadership has been identified in many studies as a key factor predicting institutional commitment to outreach and engagement (e.g., Maurrasse, 2001; Votruba, 1996; Walshok, 1999; Ward, 1996; Zlotkowski, 1998). It is known that presidential leaders are critical to legitimizing service activities (Ward, 1996) and that the intellectual and political support of charismatic leaders are important to sustaining institutional commitment to service (Walshok, 1999). In addition, leaders are vital to providing a public face of engagement by hosting events, providing contacts, and playing other roles to support the effort (Walshok, 1999) and are central to sustaining engagement efforts since these individuals are charged with making key decisions about funding outreach programs (Ward, 1996).

A foundational work informing the organizational aspects of this literature review was conducted by Holland (1997), who investigated institutional commitment to service learning. Drawing on 23 case studies conducted between 1994 and 1997, Holland identified and evaluated seven organizational factors strongly associated with institutional commitment to service learning programs: mission, promotion, tenure, hiring, organizational structure, student involvement and curriculum, faculty involvement, community involvement, and campus publications.

As Holland (1997) suggests, organizational structure is important to understanding how an institution views the status of outreach or engagement programs. A recent study suggested that centralized outreach structures are more effective than decentralized structures as they are used to help research universities track, coordinate, and communicate its service to the state and local communities (Weerts, 2002). Similarly, it is known that outreach and engagement projects housed in a president or chancellor's office can give a clear signal to campus partners that such projects are high priority (Weiwel & Lieber, 1998) and that such organizational arrangements help to recruit faculty to take on projects such as service learning (Bringle & Hatcher, 2000).

Organizational structure is also important at the community level, as community participation in the leadership—shared governance, shared staff positions, and committee work—is continually negotiated and restructured among partners (Bringle & Hatcher, 2000). Evaluation of these partnerships is critical to establishing a sense of ongoing commitment to engagement among participants (Walshok, 1999).

Faculty and staff involvement is also essential to analyzing institutional commitment to outreach and engagement. A strong core of committed faculty and staff is essential to institutionalizing values of service (Zlotkowski, 1998) and their commitment is shaped by organizational rewards and mechanisms that promote or inhibit their participation.

Rigid structures of academic departments can stymie outreach and engagement because they often place intense fiscal and structural constraints on faculty who seek to undertake these activities (Ewell, 1998), and limited funding and poor faculty reward systems are barriers to faculty members' involvement with off-campus service programs (Seldin, 1982). Holland (1997) reports that clarity of public service mission; degree of support for public service in logistics, planning, and evaluation; faculty development; and rewards and incentives were good predictors of whether faculty would be involved in service learning. The extent to which faculty and staff involve students in planning service activities and curriculum is also an important indicator of campus commitment to service (Ward, 1996).

Finally, the cultural aspects of faculty and staff ability to work with community members and among disciplines must not be overlooked. Faculty are socialized within traditional views of higher education and place boundaries on what constitutes "appropriate academic behavior" and thus advance restrictive definitions of research and promotion that inhibit community based work (Dickson, Gallacher, Longden, & Bartlett, 1985). Similarly, the two-way interaction as proposed by leaders of engagement initiatives is often hampered because university research is designed narrowly, with community partners acting as passive participants, not partners in discovery (Corrigan, 2000). Also, effective outreach and engagement initiatives require cooperation among a variety of disciplinary fields to address societal problems, and breaking down academic barriers requires significant attention to organizational structures, management, and budgeting (Amey, Brown, & Sandmann, 2002). The ability of faculty to represent service-related work as scholarship is key to legitimizing these activities (Lynton & Elman, 1987).

Another important piece of analyzing institutional commitment to service is understanding internal and external communication practices of colleges and universities. Internally, studies suggest that strong centralized communications—supported by a centralized database of service activities—can promote campus collaboration in developing outreach programs and reduce duplication of activities (Mankin, 2000). Outside of the institution, community partners need access to "entry points" where they can obtain information about opportunities for collaboration with university partners (Lynton & Elman, 1987). Campus publications that target external stakeholders and articulate the service aspects of their universities can also serve to advance the institution's public relations efforts (Holland, 1997).

The multi-faceted factors identified in this conceptual framework might be easily lost in a strictly narrative form. Thus, the relationships among these factors are visually presented in the fishbone or cause and effect diagram illustrated in Figure 1. A fishbone diagram is useful because it makes clear the relationships between dependent and independent variables and provides a format for documenting verified causal relationships (Scholtes, 1994). Applied to the conceptual framework of this study, the head of the fish (dependent variable) is labeled "institutional commitment to outreach and engagement." The large and small bones of the fish represent the macro and micro independent variables affecting commitment to outreach and engagement.

Figure 2. Study Contributions to Conceptual Framework

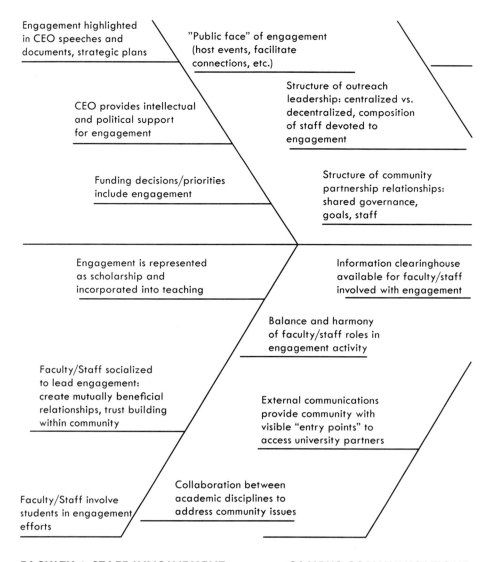

LEADERSHIP

ORGANIZATIONAL STRUCTURE

Engagement highlighted in CEO speeches and documents, strategic plans

"Public face" of engagement (host events, facilitate connections, etc.)

CEO provides intellectual and political support for engagement

Structure of outreach leadership: centralized vs. decentralized, composition of staff devoted to engagement

Funding decisions/priorities include engagement

Structure of community partnership relationships: shared governance, goals, staff

Engagement is represented as scholarship and incorporated into teaching

Information clearinghouse available for faculty/staff involved with engagement

Balance and harmony of faculty/staff roles in engagement activity

Faculty/Staff socialized to lead engagement: create mutually beneficial relationships, trust building within community

External communications provide community with visible "entry points" to access university partners

Faculty/Staff involve students in engagement efforts

Collaboration between academic disciplines to address community issues

FACULTY & STAFF INVOLVEMENT

CAMPUS COMMUNICATIONS

AND POLICIES

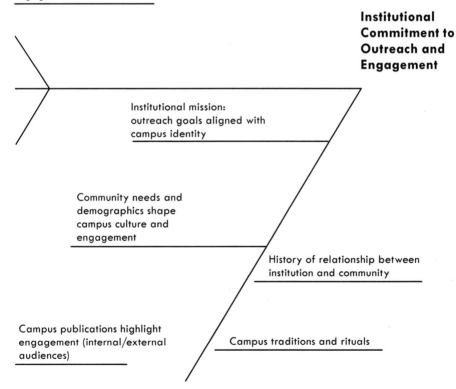

Organizational supports:
rewards, incentives,
promotion, hiring practices,
professional development,
and technical support

Formal and informal
assessment and evaluation
of outreach and
engagement

**Institutional
Commitment to
Outreach and
Engagement**

Institutional mission:
outreach goals aligned with
campus identity

Community needs and
demographics shape
campus culture and
engagement

History of relationship between
institution and community

Campus publications highlight
engagement (internal/external
audiences)

Campus traditions and rituals

INSTITUTIONAL HISTORY, CULTURE

Methodology

The research questions in this study are addressed through a multi-case study of three land grant universities that have historically been active leaders in community outreach and engagement: the University of Illinois at Urbana/Champaign (UIUC), the University of Georgia (UGA), and the University of Wisconsin–Madison (UW). These institutions were selected for investigation primarily due to their strong reputation for supporting outreach and engagement. The reason for selecting a multi-case method for this study is to show generalizability of data (Bogdan & Bicklen, 1992). In other words, data from the three institutions are analyzed and used to make broader conclusions about the link between organizational factors and community perceptions of outreach and engagement at land grant institutions.

Interviews and document review were the primary methods in all three phases of data collection for this study. In the first phase, the campus provost and chief officers overseeing outreach programs were interviewed to get a sense of the history, mission, and culture that guide outreach and engagement at their institutions. Using snowball sampling (Bogdan & Bicklen, 1992), these interviewees provided names of other key informants and documents that could help shed light on institutional efforts to promote outreach and engagement. In phase one, interviewees were asked to name three to five community partnerships underway on their campus that typified the institution's practices in outreach and engagement. Based on these interviews, two engagement initiatives were selected on each campus for further investigation and leaders of these initiatives were interviewed in phase two of the project.

Upon being interviewed, campus leaders of the engagement initiatives under investigation were asked to provide the names and contact information for three to six community partners who would be willing to be interviewed for the project. In phase three of my interviewing process, these community partners were interviewed to gain their perspective on issues of university-community partnerships. Measures were taken to ensure confidentiality of respondents and all data were coded using the procedures outlined by Bogdan and Bicklen (1992). Interview protocol stemmed from this study's conceptual framework. Table 1 provides a breakdown of the 44 interviews conducted for this project.

Table 1: Interviews by campus and stakeholder group

	University of Georgia (UGA)	University of Wisconsin–Madison (UW)	University of Illinois –Urbana, Champaign (UIUC)
Phase 1: Campus executives (provost, outreach senior executives)	3	3	2
Phase 2: Faculty & staff leaders of engagement initiative	4	7	6
Phase 3: Community partners affiliated with engagement initiative	6	7	6
Total interviews	13	17	14

Rhetoric and Practice of Outreach and Engagement at Land Grant Universities

UGA, UIUC, and UW share similar histories as major research universities that are defined by their land grant traditions. This theme was heavily referenced throughout campus interviews as respondents resonated to their historic missions to be "universities of the people." Among the three institutions, Wisconsin is especially linked to its famous organizing principle called the Wisconsin Idea. The century-old concept stems from UW's early leadership in linking university knowledge to public policy, economic development, and agricultural improvements across the state.

Corresponding to their histories, the missions of all three institutions point to their commitment to public service and outreach in terms of their obligation to "bring resources in the form of professional knowledge to improve quality of life," as one interviewee put it. The campus mission statements at the three institutions largely reflect an extension type model where the institutions view themselves as widening their borders of expertise to transfer technology and knowledge to the far corners of their states. One provost summarized a general conception of a land grant institution's role in connecting to societal needs: "The original articulation of the land grant mission is to bring the knowledge of the university to the state. Now we extend this idea nationally and internationally, literally reaching out to anyone with our products of scholarly and creative work." My review of campus documents suggests that the concept of engagement on these campuses is still emerging, and that the rhetoric and practice leading the institution toward a two-way relationship with states and communities is largely dependent on the philosophy of campus leaders overseeing outreach activities.

Leadership and organizational structure for outreach and engagement vary significantly across the three institutions. UW has the most decentralized structure and defines outreach broadly across all the schools and colleges. The Provost and the Vice Chancellor for Continuing Programs loosely oversee the programs, but outreach programs are managed, governed, and communicated by schools, colleges, and institutes across the university. Most importantly, a separate UW System campus named UW–Extension (UWEX) controls the budget for outreach across the UW System and shares faculty and staff appointments with UW–Madison and other UW campuses to engage campus faculty in extension work.

The leadership, structure, and culture of UW lend itself to a "hands off" approach toward outreach and engagement by allowing various units to determine their appropriate role in linking their activities to the Wisconsin Idea. Said one campus executive, "Outreach lives in many places at UW, and commitment to this activity varies from department to department." In this context, it is important to make clear that the face of public service and outreach at UW is shared with the UW–Extension campus, since both institutions share land grant status in Wisconsin. UW–Extension's explicit mission is to work with the UW–Madison and all the other UW System campuses to make the research and other resources of the University available to Wisconsin residents throughout the state. In this sense, outreach is very high profile in Wisconsin because it has been elevated to the level of being its own institution through the UW–Extension campus, but this may consequently lessen the profile of outreach on the UW–Madison campus.

UIUC and UGA are similar to UW in that the work of outreach on these campuses is conducted in schools, colleges, and institutes across the institutions. The difference, however, is that the UIUC and UGA campuses each operate a high profile office *within their institutions* as the "public face" of outreach and engagement. UIUC, for example, has an office of public engagement that acts as a broker between outside partners and UIUC on programs important to the state. Led by a Vice Chancellor for Public Engagement, UIUC has a strong presence and support for the concept of engagement. Central to this presence was the leadership of former Chancellor Nancy Cantor, who spoke about the values of engagement in speeches, published articles, and vision points on her webpage. Said one interviewee, "Nancy Cantor is committed to the concept of engagement—the concept of shared decision making versus the expert model. She recognizes the failures of the one-way approach that have historically defined our institutions."

At UGA, leadership for outreach is the responsibility of a Vice President for Public Service and Outreach. As evidenced by communications on the UGA website, the Vice President uses his position and authority to position outreach and engagement as an important strategic priority for the institution. The Office of Public Service and Outreach is set up to promote visibility and emphasize stewardship of UGA resources aimed to help Georgia communities. The structure reportedly aims to help the institution be responsive to public needs and act in more flexible ways to connect UGA personnel and community partners.

Across UW, UGA, and UIUC, rewards and incentives are beginning to be put in place to encourage traditional faculty to be involved in outreach. For example, UGA has service awards that provide recognition and support for faculty who are engaged in outreach. Similarly, the UW Chancellor hosts an event at his home to recognize those involved with service activities. UIUC also sponsors events to honor and recognize outreach work conducted by UIUC faculty.

While these reward mechanisms are viewed as important, interview data suggests that faculty involvement in outreach and engagement is ultimately contingent upon how this work will benefit their teaching and research. For some traditional faculty members in applied programs, the link can be made more easily. One associate professor in urban and regional planning at UW explained, "The partnership with the community benefits my teaching. Graduate students get a great experience in designing community workshops to study these issues—the community is a perfect laboratory for my students to learn."

Despite the efforts of some faculty, this study suggests that outreach and engagement at land grant universities is largely happening due to the work of outreach and academic staff, not traditional faculty. For example, UGA operates a separate public service career ladder housing over 800 UGA employees who are solely devoted to this effort. At UW, outreach appointments through UWEX are similar in scope and responsibility. In addition, UWEX buys time from faculty specialists across the UW System who devote a part of their work to outreach. Still, there is evidence that in some cases there is a divide between the "two classes" of employees. One outreach staff member when asked about working with traditional faculty on outreach projects said, "I'm glad that [the faculty] aren't involved with outreach. Most faculty have academic envy and are chasing Harvard instead of recognizing our charter to serve the people of this state."

In all cases, it was clear that traditional faculty would not be hired on the quality of their service, but that there is increasing support for engagement scholarship in some pockets of land grant universities. The challenge for all the institutions is that faculty have difficulty knowing how to evaluate this work and thus give it real consideration in promotion and tenure decisions. Still, tenure guidelines are being updated to "unpack and differentiate" outreach scholarship, as one campus executive put it, so that engagement work gains legitimacy among faculty throughout the institution. For example, the UWEX created a model to assess outreach scholarship for use in tenure and promotion decisions for outreach faculty (Wise, Retzleff, & Reilly, 2002). Despite these efforts, a challenge to assessing outreach is that it has many meanings across land grant institutions and can often be defined as almost anything outside of teaching and research.

Assisting the outreach and engagement effort at these institutions is student involvement through service learning programs and volunteer activities. Students on the three campuses are involved in this work to the extent that faculty in their major/minor areas are involved with engagement scholarship. Interview data suggests that among the three campuses, UGA is in the earliest stages of involving students through service learning, while UW's efforts in this area have been accelerated by the formation of the Morgridge Center for Public Service. Funded by an endowment from the Morgridge family in 1996, the Center "promotes citizenship and learning through service within local, national and global communities," (Morgridge Center for Public Service, 2004). At UIUC, the Office of Volunteer Services helps match students with service learning and volunteer activities throughout Illinois, most notably the East St. Louis Action Research Project (ESLARP), which involves over 400 student volunteers each year.

All three institutions investigated in this multi-case study are struggling with establishing useful measurements to demonstrate the impact of outreach and engagement activities. One campus executive staff member summarized it best:

> It is hard to measure the quality of public service because we have less consensus about what the outcomes are and should be. It is easy to evaluate the research area because we can look at the quality of the journal, number of citations of the author, etc. A lot of evaluation for service is applied to clinical aspects or the development of patents or total volumes sold.

Campus respondents all acknowledged that they primarily relied on input measures to understand impact of outreach but are trying to move to more qualitative outcome measures. UGA and UWEX have seemingly led the way in developing new benchmarks to measure impact of services and economic impact on clients. However, these techniques are not widespread among the institutions.

At all the institutions, communication pieces promoting outreach and engagement heavily compete for print and air time with many other university programs, especially in the area of research. A documents review suggested that UIUC had the most comprehensive coverage of outreach and engagement activities that were often integrated into the research and instructional missions of their institutions. The review suggested that publications pertaining to public service seem to have a more unified message when directed through centralized offices that have a public face for engagement (UGA and UIUC vs. UW).

Validation: Community Partner Perspectives of Outreach and Engagement

In this section, the voices of community partners shed light on factors perceived as key to understanding and validating institutional commitment to outreach and engagement. To limit the scope of this paper, interview data from community partners representing one engagement initiative from each campus will be summarized and presented within this study's conceptual framework. These initiatives include the UW Villager Mall project; Clarke County School District–UGA–Athens-Clarke County (ACC) Partnership; and the Office for Mathematics, Science and Technology Education (MSTE) at UIUC.

Responding to failing marks of schools in Athens, UGA's five-year partnership with Athens-Clarke County schools was developed in 2001 to establish at-risk schools as community learning centers "where leadership, resources and accountability are shared among all the partners, parents, and most importantly, students" (CCSD/UGA/Athens Community Partnership for Community Learning Centers, 2003). A wide range of school administrators, community partners, and UGA faculty, staff, and students collaborate in problem solving through action teams that address curriculum, community and parent involvement, educator preparation, and other components of education.

In Madison, Wisconsin, the UW joined a group of neighborhood associations called the South Metropolitan Planning Council (SMPC) to improve quality of life on South Park Street, an area of the city troubled by significant urban problems related to lack of affordable housing and persistent poverty. In 1998, the UW made a five-year commitment to lease space in the Park Street Villager Mall to play a role in training the community, providing expertise and resources to build capacity in neighborhoods, and to mobilize community teams to work on key issues such as housing and transportation. The initiative involves a large group of community partners and UW faculty, staff and students.

Finally, the University of Illinois' MSTE program was established in 1993 to support technology-based teaching and learning at the K–16 level. The MSTE program facilitates education reform in mathematics, science, and technology through a set of high-tech networks and communities (Reese, 2002). Innovative web-based modules provide standards-based, technology-intensive math and science instruction for students, teachers and faculty at all levels. The MSTE website receives over 100,000 hits per month to access its programs. The program is guided by an advisory board consisting of UIUC faculty, staff, and K–16 teachers and administrators who assist in program design.<Head/Subhead>Leadership. This study suggests that community perceptions about institutional commitment to outreach and engagement are informed by the rhetoric and behaviors of top executives at each of the institutions. One community member involved with the UW Villager Mall explained: "There is a sense among us that commitment to this project runs deep. The Chancellor's Office has highlighted this initiative in a special event and the university can use this initiative to its credit." A community member in Georgia also recognized the role of formal institutional leadership saying, "It took the Deans level leadership to change the culture—the feeling that [the faculty] were doing service work despite their real duties of research."

Most importantly, community members from all the institutions felt that top-level leadership was crucial to sustaining their particular initiative. At UIUC, some community partners involved with the MSTE program were worried about institutional leaders applying pressure to make the program primarily a research-oriented office and its implications for the unit's mission and sustainability. In Athens, one community partner said, "How long will UGA fund staff to do this work? What if the Dean of the College of Education moves or if the superintendent takes a new job?" At both the community partner and institutional levels, campus leadership was viewed as key to understanding the sustainability and commitment to engagement initiatives.

In sum, the study suggests that institutional responsiveness is best understood by observing top-level leadership, and that responsiveness is often the result of threatening action outside the institution. For example, in the Villager Mall (UW) and Athens-Clark County (UGA) case studies, outside forces propelled institutional leaders to take collective action in response to adverse conditions outside the institution. At UW, the declining state of Park Street threatened the vibrancy of the gateway to the campus, igniting action at the UW Chancellor's Office to address the issue. Similarly, the ACC–UGA initiative was spurred on by the pending risk of closing two area elementary schools.

Faculty and staff attitudes and involvement. The findings of this study support previous literature suggesting that structure, promotion and tenure, and organizational issues are important factors enabling faculty and staff to take on leadership roles in outreach and engagement. However, from the perspective of community partners interviewed in this study, socializing faculty and staff to work effectively with community members is just as important as building organizational mechanisms and policies to encourage faculty and staff participation. In other words, community partners informed me that one must go beyond analyzing structural and organizational factors when studying commitment to engagement and more carefully investigate the cultural and social factors that underlie these structures and organizational. For example, when asked what factors were most important to building productive working relationships with the university, the most common answer was "mutual respect and communication."

There is evidence that faculty and staff can, at times, be both the best evidence of institutional commitment to outreach and engagement, or the most damning evidence against it. The cases of successful faculty and staff involvement with the community were primarily evident at the level of providing expertise and service to the community on a particular project, such as housing, transportation, or educational issues. As the ACC–UGA example demonstrated, faculty and staff made trips to the school and offered expertise and personal support in a way that "inspired success," as one community partner put it. Others alluded to the strong personal relationships that some faculty members have built with the community over time and how this impacts the perception of the institution's commitment to engagement. As one community partner involved with the MSTE program pointed out, "[The MSTE staff] are good people who got into education for the right reasons and they are passionate and believe that their work will improve education. The partnership with MSTE works because [the MSTE staff] care about being successful for the kids versus protecting their own curriculum."

The most obvious barriers to successful engagement in these case studies are governance centered—how the faculty and staff relate to community partners in setting up the partnerships. It was clear that power issues are constantly being negotiated throughout the formation of the partnerships, and that trust may wax and wane during their formation. Evidence of conflict arose in two of the three partnerships. Said one frustrated community member:

> The university must do what they say they are doing… if this is an initiative of equals, act like equals. Turn off your cell phone. Don't take the call in front of all of us. If you are that important have someone else join us.

Similarly, use of language was important, as some community partners smirked that the university typically lists "university" first when describing "university-community" partnerships. However, some leaders of these initiatives are aware of the importance of language and have made efforts to ensure the evenhandedness of the university's profile with the community.

Organizational structure. Reviewing data from this study, it is clear that organizational structure is a challenge to facilitating engagement. The organized anarchy (Cohen & March, 1974) of complex land grant universities was acknowledged at all levels of interviews, but especially from community partners. As the previous analysis revealed, organizational structure of outreach varies across the campuses and had some effect on how community members viewed the accessibility of the institution.

One community respondent summarized:

> It is hard to get to know a place as complex as the UW. We often don't know what is available on campus to even ask for help. Our council is still trying to figure out how we can access the entire UW as a resource and this is difficult given complexity of the institution.

Said another who expressed frustration with the organizational structure of the decentralized nature of campus, "I felt like I was sent through this maze to the point that I almost lost interest [in participating in the program]. It is overwhelming in size and we didn't know who to talk to first." On the other hand, community partners in Illinois noted that participation in UIUC programs was enhanced through the formal creation of the Partnership Illinois program facilitated by the Vice Chancellor for Public Engagement. One community member said, "We tried for two years for people to work with us and nobody would even talk to us. Our opportunities expanded when the Vice Chancellor [for Public Engagement] got involved."

Despite these successes, a central challenge to engagement is that outreach and engagement is happening far beyond the boundaries of a central administrative unit, even within the most centralized outreach structures like UGA. Subsequently, the complex web of outreach and engagement activities makes it difficult to harness and understand the breadth and depth of these activities, even at the highest levels of leadership. As one community member put it, "The truth is, even the Chancellor's Office doesn't know what is all going on throughout campus and who has what expertise."

CONCLUSIONS AND IMPLICATIONS

In this study, organizational factors most strongly associated with community partner perceptions of institutional commitment to outreach and engagement were best understood through the domains of leadership, organizational structures, and faculty and staff involvement.

An important finding of this study is that leadership at the top levels of the institution is critical to demonstrating commitment to outreach and engagement—both in the institutional context and the community partner context. As much of the literature suggests, top-level leadership serves to legitimize and reward engagement activities among university participants. This study further suggests that leaders at the executive level have an important role in assuring community partners that the initiative is sustainable, important, and valued within the institution. Leaders demonstrate this commitment in rhetoric and by providing a public, high profile face to these activities. An implication of this finding is for institutions to increase the visibility of campus leaders in communities where engagement is a high priority.

However, while leadership is important, this study suggests that work at the ground level is essential to backing up the rhetoric of institutional leaders. For example, in addition to providing formal infrastructures and rewards to foster engagement activities, professional development programs must carefully prepare university personnel to build trust and mutually beneficial relationships with community partners. A main finding of this study is that developing an academic culture to support community work is critical to developing successful partnerships and plays an important role in demonstrating institutional commitment to engagement. One possible strategy is to develop an Outreach and Engagement Academy whereby faculty and staff are trained by experienced leaders of engagement representing both the campus and community. Such a program has been recommended by members of NASULGC's Extension Committee on Organizational Policy (National Association of State Universities and Land Grant Colleges, 2002). In Wisconsin, UWEX has developed a training program called the Extension Administrative Leadership Program (EALP) whereby faculty and staff who are a part of engagement work on UW campuses can enhance their professional competence and prospects for moving up the career ladder.

This study also provides implications for organizational structure. Findings suggest that community members examine the governance and organizational structure of the community-university partnerships to understand the power dynamics that define the institution's role in the community. Building collaborative structures was often cited as a critical piece of facilitating joint problem solving, community-based solutions, and fostering trust with community partners.

In addition, this study cautiously supports other literature (Weerts, 2002) suggesting that a centralized outreach structure such as the Office of Public Service and Outreach at UGA or Office of the Vice Chancellor for Public Engagement at UIUC may help facilitate access into the institution and provide community members with a recognizable structure that legitimizes outreach and engagement activity. This finding supports neo-institutional theorists who contend that organizational structures themselves can serve as an important signaling mechanism to the organization's constituencies about the values of an organization (Scott, 1992).

Figure 2 revisits the fishbone diagram from Figure 1 and illustrates how the findings from this study contribute to its conceptual framework. Marked by asterisks and bold type, the revised framework highlights key influences within leadership, organizational structure, faculty staff involvement, and communication that play an important role in validating commitment to outreach and engagement.

Figure 2. Study Contributions to Conceptual Framework

LEADERSHIP **ORGANIZATIONAL STRUCTURE**

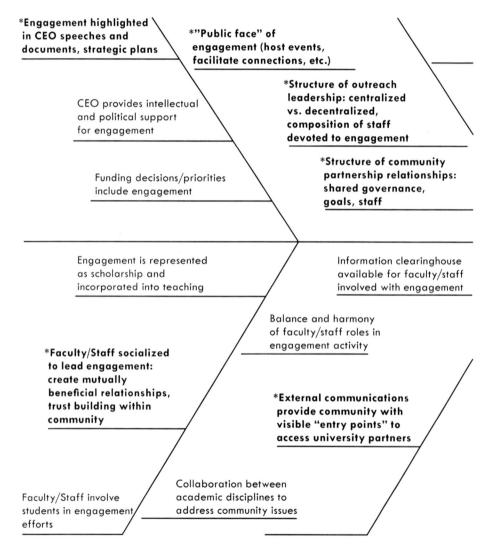

*Engagement highlighted in CEO speeches and documents, strategic plans

*"Public face" of engagement (host events, facilitate connections, etc.)

CEO provides intellectual and political support for engagement

*Structure of outreach leadership: centralized vs. decentralized, composition of staff devoted to engagement

Funding decisions/priorities include engagement

*Structure of community partnership relationships: shared governance, goals, staff

Engagement is represented as scholarship and incorporated into teaching

Information clearinghouse available for faculty/staff involved with engagement

Balance and harmony of faculty/staff roles in engagement activity

*Faculty/Staff socialized to lead engagement: create mutually beneficial relationships, trust building within community

*External communications provide community with visible "entry points" to access university partners

Faculty/Staff involve students in engagement efforts

Collaboration between academic disciplines to address community issues

FACULTY & STAFF INVOLVEMENT **CAMPUS COMMUNICATIONS**

AND POLICIES

Organizational supports:
rewards, incentives,
promotion, hiring practices,
professional development,
and technical support

***Factors identified by
community partner as
a key to validating
campus commitment to
outreach and engagement**

Formal and informal
assessment and evaluation
of outreach and
engagement

**Institutional
Commitment to
Outreach and
Engagement**

Institutional mission:
outreach goals aligned with
campus identity

Community needs and
demographics shape
campus culture and
engagement

History of relationship between
institution and community

Campus publications highlight
engagement (internal/external
audiences)

Campus traditions and rituals

INSTITUTIONAL HISTORY, CULTURE

LIMITATIONS AND FUTURE RESEARCH

Finally, some limitations are important to address at the conclusion of this study. Most importantly, this study recognizes the many complexities associated with studying the public service and outreach mission of colleges and universities. While an attempt was made to place parameters on this study, it is understood that organizational systems and definitions associated with outreach and engagement opportunities are multifaceted and often defined in a variety of ways. Put simply, this study offers one perspective on a very large issue that deserves more in-depth analysis.

Furthermore, this emerging model requires more data before firm conclusions and implications can be made that affect institutional policy and strategy. Additional interviews and case study sites would provide richer perspectives into the issues raised in this study and would strengthen its conclusions.

There is a wealth of opportunity for future research building on this study. This research suggests that the organizational structure of outreach and engagement be studied in more detail so that firmer conclusions might be made about the effects of centralized vs. decentralized structures on how community partners perceive institutional commitment to engagement.

Finally, an important area of research is to investigate the effect of outreach programs on public and political support for the institution. As the introduction to this paper suggested, engagement is viewed as vital to the future of public higher education, and institutions must be committed to this activity in order to remain relevant and deemed worthy of public investment. Additional research in this area would provide multiple benefits to practitioners, policymakers and interested scholars committed to aligning institutions to be responsive to their public service roles.

ACKNOWLEDGMENTS

The author wishes to thank the National Forum on Higher Education for the Public Good for their support of this project and gratefully acknowledges the thoughtful feedback of Alan Knox, Lorilee Sandmann, Kevin Reilly, Nicholas Hawkins, and Carole Kolb in completing this article.

References

American Association of State Colleges and Universities (2002). *Stepping forward as stewards of place*. Washington, DC: Author.

Amey, M. J., Brown, D. F., & Sandmann, L. R. (2002). A multi-disciplinary collaborative approach to a university-community partnership: Lessons learned. *Journal of Higher Education Outreach and Engagement, 7*(3), 19–26.

Anderson, J. L. & Jayakumar, U. M. (2002). *An intergenerational research symposium on higher education for the public good: Areas of research and collaboration.* Los Angeles, CA: Higher Education Research Institute.

Berry, R. (1972). *The Wisconsin idea...then and now.* Madison, WI: The University of Wisconsin.

Bogdan, R. C., & Bicklen, S. K. (1992). *Qualitative research for education: An introduction to theory and methods.* Needham Heights, MA: Simon & Schuster.

Bonnen, J. T. (1998). The land grant idea and the evolving outreach university. In R. M Lerner & L. A. Simon (Eds.), *University-community collaborations for the 21st century: Outreach to scholarship for youth and families* (pp. 25–70). New York: Garland Press.

Boyer, E. L. (1990). *Scholarship reconsidered.* Princeton, NJ: Carnegie Foundation for the Advancement of Teaching.

Bringle, R. G. & Hatcher, J. A. (2000). Institutionalization of service learning in higher education. *Journal of Higher Education, 71*, 273–290.

CCSD/UGA/Athens Community Partnership for Community Learning Centers. (2003). Retrieved August 6, 2003, from http://www.clarke.k12.ga.us/ccsduga/index.html

Cohen, M. D. & March, J. C. (1974). *Leadership in an organized anarchy.* Cambridge, MA: Harvard Business School Publishing.

Corrigan, D. (2000). The changing role of schools and higher education institutions with respect to community-based interagency collaboration and interprofessional partnerships. *Peabody Journal of Education, 75* (3), 176–195.

Dickson A., Gallacher J., Longden, B. & Bartlett, P. (1985). Higher education and the community. *Higher Education Review. 17*, 49–58.

Ewell, P. T. (1998). Achieving high performance: The policy dimension. In W. G. Tierney (Ed.), *The responsive university: Restructuring for high performance* (pp. 120–161). Baltimore: The Johns Hopkins Press.

Glassick, D. C., Huber, M. T., and Maeroff, G. I. (1997). *Scholarship assessed: Evaluation of the professorate.* San Francisco: Jossey-Bass.

Glassman, R. (1973). Persistence and loose coupling in living systems. *Behavioral Science, 18*, 83–98.

Holland, B. A. (1997). Analyzing institutional commitment to service: A model of key organizational factors. *Michigan Journal of Community Service Learning, 4*, 30–41.

Kellogg Commission on the Future of State and Land Grant Universities (1996). *Taking charge of change: Renewing the promise of state and land grant universities.* Retrieved June 30, 2003, from http://www.nasulgc.org/publications/Kellogg/Kellogg2000_Change.pdf

Kellogg Commission on the Future of State and Land-Grant Universities (1999). *Returning to our roots: The engaged institution.* Washington, DC: National Association of State Universities and Land Grant Colleges. Retrieved June 30, 2003, from http://www.nasulgc.org/publications/Kellogg/Kellogg1999_Engage.pdf

Knox, A. B. (2001). Assessing university faculty outreach performance. *College Teaching, 49*, 71–74.

Lynton, E. A. (1995). *Making the case for professional service.* Washington, DC: American Association for Higher Education.

Lynton, E. A., & Elman, S. E. (1987). *New priorities for the university: Meeting society's needs for applied knowledge and competent individuals.* San Francisco: Jossey-Bass.

Mankin, L. (2000). Gearing up for community service: Overcoming informational barriers. *Journal of Public Service and Outreach, 5*(1), 45–49.

Maurrasse, D. J. (2001). *Beyond the campus: How colleges and universities form partnerships with their communities.* New York: Routledge.

Morgridge Center for Public Service, University of Wisconsin Madison. (2004). Retrieved July 7, 2003, from http://www.morgridge.wisc.edu/about.html

National Association of State Universities and Land Grant Colleges. (2002). *The extension system: A vision for the 21st century. Report of the Extension Committee on Organization and Policy.* Washington, DC: Author. Retrieved June 30, 2003, from http://www.nasulgc.org/publications/ Agriculture/ECOP2002_Vision.pdf

National Forum on Higher Education for the Public Good. (2004). Retrieved June 5, 2003, from http://www.thenationalforum.org/mission.shtml

Pfeffer, J. S., & Salancik G. R. (1978). *The external control of organizations.* New York: Harper & Row.

Reese, G. C. (2002). *Technology-enhanced education reform: An historical analysis of a learning system—the evolution of the Office for Mathematics, Science and Technology Education at the University of Illinois, 1993-2002.* Unpublished doctoral dissertation, University of Illinois, Urbana–Champaign.

Scott, W. R. (1992). *Organizations: Rational, natural, and open systems.* Englewood Cliffs, NJ: Prentice Hall.

Scholarship of Engagement: The National Clearinghouse for Engagement Scholarship. (2004). Retrieved June 30, 2004, from www.scholarshipofengagement.org

Seldin, C. A. (1982). Off campus in-service activities: A status report. *Educational Research Quarterly, 7*(2), 31–41.

Scholtes, P. R. (1994). *The team handbook for educators: How to use teams to improve quality.* Madison, WI: Joiner Associates.

Votruba, J. C. (1996). Strengthening the university's alignment with society: Challenges and strategies. *Journal of Public Service and Outreach, 1*(1), 29–36.

Ward, D. (1999). The challenges of irreversible change in higher education: The University of Wisconsin-Madison in the 1990s. In D. Ward & N. Radomski (Eds.), *Proud traditions and future challenges: The University of Wisconsin–Madison celebrates 150 years* (pp. 1–24). Madison, WI: UW–Madison Office of University Publications.

Ward, K (1996). Service learning and student volunteerism: Reflections on institutional commitment. *Michigan Journal of Community Service Learning, 3,* 55–65.

Walshok, M. L. (1999). Strategies for building the infrastructure that supports the engaged campus. In R. G. Bingle, R. Games, & E. A. Malloy (Eds.), *Colleges and universities as citizens* (pp. 74–95). Boston, MA: Allyn & Bacon.

Weerts, D. J. (2002). *State governments and research universities: A framework for a renewed partnership.* New York: Routledge.

Weerts, D. J., (2000). Outreach as a critical link to state support for research universities. *Journal of Higher Education Outreach and Engagement, 6*(1), 49–56.

Weiwel, W., & Lieber, M. (1998). Goal achievement, relationship building, and incrementalism: The challenges of university-community partnerships. *Journal of Planning Education and Research, 17,* 291–301.

Wise, G., Retzleff, D., & Reilly, K. (2002). Adapting "Scholarship Reconsidered" and "Scholarship Assessed" to evaluate University of Wisconsin-Extension outreach faculty for tenure and promotion. *Journal of Higher Education Outreach and Engagement, 7*(3), 5–17.

Weick, K. (1976). Educational organizations as loosely coupled systems. *Administrative Science Quarterly, 26,* 22–36.

Zlotkowski, E. (1998). (Ed.). *Successful service-learning programs: New models of excellence in higher education.* Bolton, MA: Anker Publishing Company, Inc.

CHAPTER 15

Progressing Toward the Public Good:

CURRENT CONCEPTIONS, FUTURE DIRECTIONS, AND POTENTIAL CHALLENGES

Anthony Chambers and Nicholas A. Bowman

Abstract: In this concluding chapter, we provide our perspectives on the preceding chapters authored by the participants in the Rising Scholars program and discuss the future of higher education for the public good as a line of inquiry for early career scholars in higher education. First, we provide an analysis of the work presented by the authors, showing how these chapters convey the myriad relationships between higher education and society. Then, we discuss future directions for scholarship on higher education for the public good. Finally, we highlight a few noteworthy challenges in achieving higher education for the public good.

TAKING ON THE PUBLIC GOOD: RESEARCH PERSPECTIVES OF THE RISING SCHOLARS

In defining research on higher education for the public good, the authors in this edited volume explored critical issues and topics that have traditionally been core elements of higher education scholarship, in addition to areas that are less frequently examined. This section will both examine how the treatment of more "traditional" topics are imbued with social significance and how scholars examined, head on, the direct relationship between broader systems of higher education and the society of which they are a part. The topics presented below are organized differently from the three sections that were put forth in this volume so as to provide our perspective on these chapters and their place within research on higher education.

Access and Persistence

Goldrick-Rab examined factors that are related to college attendance patterns and persistence to graduation. She provides separate analyses within working-class and professional-class students, finding numerous differences in predictors between these groups. This recognition of the disparate forces operating at different social class levels merits further attention. Furthermore, she attempts to move toward causal claims for these decision processes: Are students "being pushed" toward certain decisions by their financial and academic situations, or are they "jumping" on their own?

Impact of the College Experience

Hundreds of studies have been conducted on how college impacts students (see Pascarella & Terenzini, 1991, 2005). Kerrigan, Dolby, and Lerner each use detailed interviews to focus on students' perceptions of society-related outcomes of particular experiences. For example, Dolby notes that most research on study abroad programs explores students' development of global awareness. However, particularly in the post-9/11 world, she argues that the development of one's own American identity becomes a critical (and salient) component of the study abroad learning experience; thus, students' study abroad experience can constitute a significant event in their identity development. In another chapter, Kerrigan discusses the impact of a capstone service-learning program at Portland State University. She finds that graduates perceived their service-learning experience as contributing to civic outcomes (i.e., leadership skills, community involvement/volunteerism, and appreciation of social diversity) and vocational outcomes (i.e., communication skills and career development). However, many of these graduates did not draw connections between their service projects and broader political issues.

Finally, whereas the first two studies (and most higher education literature) focus on clear outcomes and antecedents, Lerner argues that the relationship between White students' interactions with diverse peers and their conceptions of diversity efforts are reciprocal. Specifically, she shows that White students do not perceive a relationship between diversity efforts and racial inequality, which causes them to seek out and enjoy certain types of interactions with diversity (i.e., those that do not highlight issues of power), which in turn reinforces certain pre-existing notions of diversity. Thus, efforts to alter students' attitudes and behavior must challenge this self-perpetuating cycle.

Civic Engagement

Preparing students to engage in civic life has long been considered a function of higher education (Rudolph, 1962/1990). Flowers' analysis of volunteerism in African American college graduates follows in this tradition. He finds that it is difficult to predict the amount of time spent volunteering; in fact, the amount of time spent volunteering in college is *negatively* related to time spent volunteering four years after graduation. The only other significant relationship in his study seems more intuitive: social science and business majors spend more time volunteering after college than do science, engineering, and other technical majors. In other words, consistent with the goals of liberal arts education (American Association of Colleges and Universities, 2002), the fields of study that tend toward providing liberal arts education succeed in creating more civically engaged individuals.

On a micro-level, Brayboy and Urrieta provide nuanced analyses of how college graduates practice civic engagement through service to particular communities or constituencies. Brayboy explores how, for some American Indian tribes, a bachelor's or professional degree is primarily seen as a tool not for individual gain, but for enhancing the well-being of one's community. College graduates are expected to use their specialized training as doctors and lawyers to assist with remedying the ongoing struggles of their communities. Simultaneously, these highly-educated individuals must navigate the expectations and values of their communities, along with the time-consuming demands of their current occupations.

Similarly, in his study of Latina/o, Chicana/o faculty, Urrieta delineates the obligation to one's native culture and the dichotomy between community expectations and the academy's expectations. As a result of doing both academic and community work (which these professors attempt to link whenever possible), Latina/o, Chicana/o faculty have a greater workload than their White peers. However, these faculty strongly feel that they must serve as agents who challenge the current norms of academe to effect social change. By providing these detailed cultural analyses, Brayboy and Urrieta convincingly highlight the complex connections between individuals and communities, and how these college graduates use their education to serve specific aspects of the public good.

Community-Campus Partnerships

Whereas some chapters focus on the relationship of individuals to their communities, others describe how higher education institutions have partnered with their surrounding communities. Weerts provides a multi-case study examining the rhetoric and practice of outreach and engagement at three land-grant universities. He finds that community-campus partnerships are most likely to thrive when the partnership is supported not only by top-level leadership, but also by work within communities. In other words, universities can build initial support by using the appropriate rhetoric, but these efforts cannot succeed without the appropriate follow-through. He notes that two of the three campuses that he analyzed had centralized outreach structures, which seemed to be effective in supporting these relationships.

Two other chapters provided insight into other connections between campuses and communities. O'Bryant described the Camfield Estates-MIT Creating Community Connections (C3) Project, which sponsored in-home use of computers and internet access for two years, along with training sessions on the C3 system website and basic computer skills. The Massachusetts Institute of Technology was involved primarily in the research aspects, with the primary funder, technology contractor and consultant, and the tenants' association working collaboratively to enhance community-building efforts and provide useful internet services and skills. The focus of this research was not the community-campus partnership per se, but the outcomes that resulted from these efforts. Furthermore, in Garbus' chapter, she depicts Vida Scudder's College Extension as being (at most) loosely affiliated with any particular college, with undergraduates teaching some of the Extension courses. According to Garbus, Scudder was not attempting to create a "partnership" per se, but was attempting to bring college "culture" and knowledge to the community. Today, most scholars and community leaders would agree that such an arrangement is one-sided and often does not meet the needs and desires of community members (e.g., Pasque, Smerek, Dwyer, Bowman, & Mallory, 2005). Indeed, Garbus suggests that this dynamic may have caused College Extension's failure.

University-Industry Relationships

The commercialization of today's higher education institutions has recently garnered attention from commentators both inside and outside of the academy (e.g., Bok, 2003; Slaughter & Rhoades, 2004). While many of these works broadly consider the role of colleges in American society, Powers focuses on how relationships with industry affect research within universities. Specifically, he examines contracts listed with the Securities and Exchange Commission between public companies and universities, and he finds that a fair number of these arrangements pose ethical conflicts that undermine the norms of academic science.

Legal and Public Considerations in Institutional Policy

Finally, Green and Moses both examine affirmative action in the context of societal pressures. In her analysis, Green argues that the University of Michigan's decision to argue for the positive impact of diversity—as opposed to addressing racial inequality—was based on legal precedent as well as the palatable nature of this argument. Through this strategy, the University managed to garner broad support for its policy and simultaneously curtail arguments about racial preferences. This conclusion fits nicely with Moses' chapter, which suggests that the public generally agrees on the need for "equality" and "justice," but holds vastly different opinions on what these words mean and what policies would be appropriate for facilitating these outcomes. She argues that policy discussions of affirmative action must consider these divergent underlying conceptions of equality and justice. This line of inquiry, along with university-industry and campus-community partnerships, is particularly important for higher education for the public good, since it directly considers the intersection between higher education and society.

Synthesis

In various ways, the majority of these chapters dealt with interconnections of class, gender, culture, and/or race. Some of the chapters examined dynamics within groups (e.g., Flowers), whereas some examined interactions across groups (e.g., Lerner), and others examined policies pertaining to various groups (e.g., Green). A couple of chapters in particular cut across these categories. For example, Brayboy simultaneously highlighted the dynamics within some American Indian communities and how these values and norms influenced community members' pursuit, and subsequent use, of higher education. This emphasis is crucial—a defining piece of higher education for the public good is providing benefits to *all* members of the public.

It is also important to consider, methodologically speaking, how to best examine issues of higher education for the public good. Two of the chapters have used large secondary datasets to explore factors related to African American college graduates' volunteerism (Flowers) and transfer and persistence patterns across social class (Goldrick-Rab). These analyses' strengths are in their use of representative samples, consideration of myriad factors, and generalizability to national populations. However, even with advanced statistical techniques, establishing causality can be difficult. Why is time spent volunteering in college *negatively* related to time spent volunteering after college? Why are students who transfer to another four-year institution more likely to graduate than those who remain at the same institution? The available data are not sufficient to explain the reasons for these patterns.

The majority of the chapters in this volume have taken qualitative approaches, using interviews, document analyses, field observations, or some combination. These techniques are useful in highlighting the specific context and nuances of a given situation, relationship, or series of events. Interviews may be used to incorporate the perspectives of the actors (e.g., students, administrators, community members) in ways that are often not possible with secondary data analysis. Ideally, whenever possible, it is best to triangulate participants' own perspectives with other forms of data (e.g., document analyses) to strengthen the validity of one's claims, particularly when one's research is openly ideological (Lather, 2003).

FUTURE DIRECTIONS FOR SCHOLARSHIP ON HIGHER EDUCATION FOR THE PUBLIC GOOD

As political, economic, demographic and technological shifts in societies occur, the relationships between higher education and the publics that sustain and benefit from them follow suit. Higher education structures are often accused of resisting change, or moving at such a slow pace that change is imperceptible to the human eye. However, what changes regularly is how and what scholars in higher education choose (or are guided) to attend to in their work. Much of the change in society can be credited with the shaping of scholars' intellectual work, and the scholarship on higher education's public good roles and responsibilities is no different. As we postulate in the preceding pages, early career scholars in higher education are both challenged and driven by real and perceived inequities in society, socio-historical interpretations of events that offer new perspectives on contemporary social challenges, prophetic insights into the positionality of historically marginalized populations in American culture, and a growing validation of multiple ways of seeking and knowing truths and social phenomena. Scholars that point their lens of inquiry toward socially inspired and socially beneficial ends, often live (and sometimes die) on the razors edge of what Burton Clark (1987) metaphorically called "small worlds, different worlds." "Small worlds" refer to the norms that are developed and sustained by disciplinary peer groups, such as disciplinary guilds, institutional type classification systems (i.e., Carnegie classifications, etc.) or membership (invitational or application) in exclusive educational consortia (such as the AAU). Small worlds could be viewed as those externally positioned norms that impact the internal behaviors of scholars. "Different worlds" are the norms, values and expectations that are specific to particular types of higher education institutions. The balance and type of scholarship, teaching and service are determined locally (in different worlds), though with recognized influence from external forces (small worlds). Clark's "small worlds, different worlds" conception sets the stage for the tension experienced by some scholars who are committed to researching and teaching about socially inspired and socially beneficial matters, when their institution (different world) may not value such a focus in its reward structure, yet its professional guild or institutional affiliations (small world) may support, at least rhetorically, the need for higher education to use its resources for social improvement. The growing voice of the "public" has entered the equation through its elected and appointed proxies—such as legislators and policy makers—to demand tangible outcomes for its investments in systems and institutions of higher education. The outcomes of higher education must serve some public good!

What then might the future of scholarship on higher education's public good role look like? How then might scholars navigate the sometimes conflicting voices of the small worlds, different worlds, and demanding publics in their choices of intellectual topics of inquiry? Which of the existing normative structures (internal and external) must change, and how? And which of the existing normative structures should remain, and why? What voices should early career scholars who want to build sustained academic careers pay most attention to? Here are a few brief observations about the factors impacting the future of scholarship and scholars attending to higher education's public good role in society.

Impact of the Knowledge Economy on Public Good Scholarship

Positioning higher education as a vital contributor to economic development is not new. What appears to be emerging across several domestic and international fronts is the shifting context of higher educations economic role within the so-called "knowledge economy." Higher education is increasingly being viewed as a major player in the economic system where knowledge is heavily commodified, where market demands for certain skilled and knowledgeable higher education graduates escalates, and knowledge production—or in some cases higher education graduation rates as a "knowledge proxy"—is directly linked to regional and national economic growth (Jones, McCarney, & Skolnik, 2005). This shift in the relationship between higher education and economic forces has important implications for scholars who focus their scholarship on higher education for the public good. As demonstrated by the scholars writing in this book, what constitutes research, how it is done, and what ties it has to economic and social improvement is constantly evolving. As Jones (2006) reminds us, the changes within this evolution are complex and multifaceted: "they include an increasing emphasis on interdisciplinarity, applied problem-based initiatives, and programs of research that involve direct (contractual) collaborations with industry" (p. 319). While these "collaborations" have been lauded as appropriate and sometimes desired ways of acquiring needed (and otherwise unavailable) resources to conduct research, concerns exist regarding the retailing of academic freedom from scholars to industry in these arrangements. This transfer of faculties' defining professional quality (academic freedom) essentially redefines faculty scholars as "knowledge labor," positioning them dangerously close to employees of the commercial market. Again, Jones (2006) cautions us that "the critical role of faculty in terms of knowledge creation and dissemination related to social (public good), and not just economic, development must be more clearly understood" (p. 319).

Academic Freedom, Social Obligation, and Tenure

For early career scholars who focus their scholarship and teaching on higher education's public roles and responsibilities, do the concepts of academic freedom, social obligation, and tenure acquisition pose an uneasy triumvirate (at best), or a mutually exclusive values set (at worse)? What are the values and behaviors that govern faculty life and guides successful scholarly careers? In some institutions, does socially focused (public good) scholarship and teaching (as a reflection of one's academic freedom) inhibit or support one's path to tenure? Early career scholars and doctoral students, who aspire to be academic scholars, express deep concerns about the resistance from the academy to their commitment to combine quality scholarship and active public engagement that address serious social problems. Paul Sabin's article in *The Chronicle of Higher Education* (February 8, 2002) summarized the condition of many emerging scholar-citizens in American higher education:

> Assistant Professors have to keep quiet and seek tenure before they safely take on a significant public role...academe as well as society lose out by forcing young scholars to avoid public affairs while they pursue tenure....The studied silence and subtle disapproval regarding public service, advocacy, and community work leave many young scholars discouraged....Systemically undermining the relationship between scholars and the broader public audiences stifles badly needed dialogue on problems facing society as a whole (p. B24).

Academic freedom, as articulated in the 1940 Statement of Principles on Academic Freedom and Tenure issued jointly by the American Association of University Professors (AAUP) and the Association of American Colleges (now the American Association of Colleges and Universities [AAC&U]), positions this value as strictly a procedural value, with little ties to the actual issuance of tenure or faculty continuation at an institution. According to the 1940 document, academic freedom means that:

1. Teachers are entitled to full freedom in research and in the publication of the results, subject to the adequate performance of their other academic duties; but research for pecuniary return should be based upon an understanding with the authorities of the institution.
2. Teachers are entitled to freedom in the classroom in discussing their subject, but they should be careful not to introduce into their teaching controversial matter which has no relation to their subject. Limitations of academic freedom because of religious or other aims of the institution should be clearly stated in writing at the time of the appointment.
3. College and university teachers are citizens, members of a learned profession, and officers of an educational institution. When they speak or write as citizens, they should be free from institutional censorship or discipline, but their special position in the community imposes special obligations. As scholars and educational officers, they should remember that the public may judge their profession and their institution by their utterances. Hence they should at all times be accurate, should exercise appropriate restraint, should show respect for the opinions of others, and should make every effort to indicate that they are not speaking for the institution (pp. 3–4).

The institution of tenure has stimulated contentious debate within and outside of higher education for decades. The arguments have centered on the purposes, effects and institutional legitimacy of tenure in its current form. Since the official codification of tenure under the auspices of the American Association of University Professors in 1940, academic tenure in higher education was intended to "protect academic freedom—the freedom to teach and write without fear of retribution for expressing heterodox ideas" (*Grimes v. Eastern*, 1983, as cited in Copeland & Murry, 1996, n52).

Over the years, some have questioned its value, arguing that the issuance of tenure encourages faculty mediocrity on one hand, and, on the other hand, is the ultimate protector of academic freedom and unfettered intellectual exploration. Some institutions have opted out of the issuance of tenure all together. Others have replaced the traditional tenure process with "tenure-like" or "tenure-light" processes that tie faculty longevity (and to some degree, academic freedom) to regular performance evaluations.

Early career scholars specifically, and all scholars generally, who commit themselves to the exploration of socially inspired and relevant issues and knowledge, would do well to attend to the alignment between institutional and personal notions of academic freedom and social obligations. Ultimately, scholars are encouraged to consistently assess the degree to which a reasonable balance exists between these tensions (i.e., institutional and personal notions of academic freedom and social obligations) in order to facilitate the acquisition of tenure and longevity.

Globalization of Social Issues, Professional Mobility, and Geographic Fidelity

For early career scholars, it has become clear that the issues they choose to explore have implications far beyond the contexts in which they are studied. Issues of social justice in the United States, for example, have broad implications for victims of social injustice abroad. Likewise, issues of injustice toward women impacts the lives of those victimized because of race, religion, or sexual orientation, both domestically and internationally. Another emerging dynamic is the growing recognition of interconnectivity among problems explored by scholars. These public problems are not those of a single social domain, nor are there singular solutions to the vast cluster of problems embedded in each identified problem (Chambers, 2005). Networks of all types of people and institutions need to confront the problems with the same complex, systemic and interconnected frame that inspired and prolonged the problems. According to Vartan Gregorian, President of the Carnegie Corporation in New York:

> As a society, we tend to pay lip service to the complexity of problems and then continue to gamble on simplistic solutions, such as building prisons to solve the crime and drug problems. But as Bela H. Banathy, a systems theorist, writes: "A technical problem of transportation, such as the building of a freeway, becomes a land use problem, linked with economics, environmental, conservation, ethical, and political issues. Can we really draw a boundary? When we ask to improve a situation, particularly if it is a public one, we find ourselves facing not a problem, but a cluster of problems…and none of these problems can be tackled using linear or sequential methods" (2004, p. B12).

Early career scholars are faced with the challenge of considering the multiple dimensions and connections of issues they choose to explore and the related impacts these various dimensions have on their methodological choices, selection of research participants, types of analyses, interpretations of findings, and perspectives on what their work means in terms of its potential applications.

With this added complexity in the process of scholarship, the locality work plays a less significant role in terms of where one does the research, or, in some cases, the teaching. Early career scholars, and indeed, higher education scholars generally, are presented the options and challenges of professional mobility. That is, because of technological options and the demand for knowledge and data in real time, anywhere, scholars can "do what they do" anywhere, generally situating themselves in any kind of environment, educational or otherwise. This dynamic raises all kinds of questions about the real and perceived purposes of higher education institutions as physical places/spaces. While much of the debate about the physicality of higher education institutions has centered around the impact on students, we would argue that the debate should clearly position itself around the impact on teaching and scholarship. Finally, with the expansion of the notion of academic mobility, the concern about geographic and institutional fidelity seems appropriate and potentially acute. Will scholars commit to a place, community, region as a contributing member, or will the options for mobility dilute (or transform) the ethos of commitment to place? As the 1960s song lyrics suggest, will scholars, in their relation to institutions, embrace the notion that "if you can't be with the one you love, love the one you're with"? Additionally, the potential dilution of geographic and institutional fidelity raises concerns about what it means to be in a community of scholars; what constitutes one's academic home; who one's "colleagues" and "students" are; and what this transformation has to do with the process of tenure, which has traditionally been seen as an "institutional" decision.

These observations are more complex than simply negative or positive forces that impede or advance scholarship on higher education for the public good. They are reflections of the larger social shifts that, depending on the alignment or misalignment of institutional (different world), professional (small world), and social values and pressures, can present opportunities and/or challenges to scholars who focus their work on particular social outcomes. Scholars generally—and early career scholars, in particular—would do well to pay attention to these emerging dynamics.

CHALLENGES AND ISSUES FOR HIGHER EDUCATION FOR THE PUBLIC GOOD

There are significant barriers to enacting the vision of an expanded focus of scholarship on higher education for the public good in today's higher education institutions. As noted earlier, many observations regarding future changes in higher education, and society, will impact the work of early career scholars. Although a long list of challenges or potential obstacles could be presented here, we've chosen to focus on three areas of immediate concern: non-tenure-track (NTT) faculty, interdisciplinarity, and internationalization. It is worth noting some of the issues that may impede inquiry overlap with those that would provide fruitful directions for future inquiry (e.g., those pertaining to tenure and globalization/internationalization).

Non-Tenure-Track Faculty

Oftentimes, when people talk about "faculty," they are referring (implicitly or explicitly) to professors in tenure-track positions. Discussions of the need for research productivity, along with the concomitant tension between "traditional research" and research for the public good (Ward, 2005), primarily applies to this group of faculty. However, in recent years, the number of full-time non-tenure-track (FTNTT) faculty has quickly increased (Benjamin, 1997; Kirshstein, Matheson, & Jing, 1997), even surpassing the number of untenured tenure-track faculty (Benjamin, 1997). There are a variety of reasons for this trend, including cost savings, long-term staffing flexibility, providing specialized faculty resources, or as a viable—and, for some faculty, a preferable—alternative to traditional tenure-track positions (Baldwin & Chronister, 2001).

Although there are some general differences between FTNTT and tenure-track faculty (Baldwin & Chronister, 2001; Gansneder, Harper, & Baldwin, 2001), it makes sense to think about the diverse amalgamation of FTNTT faculty in terms of their primary role on campus. Gansneder et al. (2001) describe four types of faculty members: teachers (64% of FTNTT faculty), researchers (10%), administrators (11%), and other academic professionals (15%). Faculty members in the teachers group have far fewer publications and more in-class teaching time per week than do tenured or tenure-track professors. Despite their lighter teaching loads, faculty in the administrators group also have extensive responsibilities that leave little time for research; their level of research productivity is also quite low, when compared to tenured or tenure-track faculty. Taken together, faculty whose primary role is teaching or administration comprises three-quarters of all full-time non-tenure-track faculty members. This percentage is probably even higher for part-time faculty who are not on a tenure track.

Since FTNTT faculty teach such a large number of students (especially at large universities), there must be creative ways of involving non-tenure-track faculty in higher education for the public good. Currently, these faculty are often occupied with large general education courses instead of specialized, advanced coursework or service-learning experiences (Baldwin & Chronister, 2001). In this position, though, they have a unique ability to convey the importance of and opportunities for public service to undergraduate students.

Interdisciplinary Work

The expectations for faculty—tenure-track and otherwise—can be quite ambiguous (Tierney & Bensimon, 1996). But what about for those faculty who conduct interdisciplinary research and/or have joint appointments in multiple departments? Given the rigid departmental structures and disciplinary socialization at most colleges and universities, it is extremely difficult for faculty to work across disciplinary boundaries, with promotion and tenure proving to be a particularly vexing problem (Damrosch, 1995). Who can provide an unbiased judgment about the intellectual worth of an interdisciplinary scholar's work? Who *should* be enlisted to do so? Since graduate students and early-career faculty perceive interdisciplinary research as being devalued or discounted in the academic community, what can be done to provide incentives for such research? Fortunately, some institutions are beginning to reassess their reward structures for working across disciplinary boundaries (O'Meara, 2005).

Despite a seeming lack of appreciation for interdisciplinarity in the promotion and tenure process, such approaches are vital for effectively exploring higher education for the public good. Since higher education is a field of study, not a discipline (Hearn, 1997), it must draw upon various disciplinary and interdisciplinary approaches whenever appropriate. This need for flexible approaches becomes even more pressing when the scope of higher education research is expanded from colleges and their students to include societal forces, such as communities, businesses, legislation, and public pressures. The recent proliferation of K–16 research and policy perspectives (e.g., Kirst & Venezia, 2004) suggests a willingness to expand our view of what is important to higher education, but a similar disciplinary expansion must also follow.

Internationalization

According to Schoorman (2000), internationalization is defined as "an educational process that acknowledges and reflects an international context of knowledge and practice where societies are viewed as subsystems of a larger, inclusive world" (p. 4). Despite the growing impact of globalization on the United States and its colleges and universities (Tierney, 2004), internationalization remains a relatively peripheral part of most college curricula (Goodwin & Nacht, 1991; Hayward, 2000). For example, fewer than half of undergraduate students (44%) take any foreign language courses during their academic careers (Lambert, 1989), and only 3% participate in study abroad programs (Hayward, 2000). College presidents strongly endorse the need to prepare students to function effectively in the context of an internationalized environment, but they are unable to articulate clearly what this education would entail (Lambert, 1989).

In reviewing the existing literature for the American Council on Education (ACE), Hayward (2000) concluded that students' participation in international education had not improved since the last ACE assessment in 1986–1987. However, these findings about the lack of progress in the United States' international education do not imply a lack of international representation; in fact, over 475,000 undergraduate and graduate international students attended American colleges and universities in 2001 (Sen, Partelow, & Miller, 2005).

Pertaining to higher education for the public good, this trend begs the question: Who is "the public"? Is it residents of the United States? The world? In this volume, Dolby addresses how study abroad can lead students not only to understand and appreciate "other cultures," but also to form one's own identity as an American. However, the degree to which the analyses of the various issues addressed in this volume—college access and persistence, college outcomes, civic engagement, campus partnerships with communities and industry, and public conceptions of admissions policies—apply to other countries and systems of higher education is an open question. Future research should explore not only issues of higher education internationally, but also the complex relationships between higher education and societies in various countries.

Conclusion

Working with and learning from this collection of early career scholars has been very rewarding and hopeful. From their scholarly commitments, it is easy to internalize a sense of optimism about higher education's role in the improvement of society on many levels. This chapter, as well as the entire book, is an attempt to express current conceptions, questions and thought surrounding higher education's many ways of exploring its role relative to society's needs. Further, the book explored both future directions for scholars to engage in inquiry regarding the pubic roles and responsibilities of higher education, and the various challenges on the horizon for these scholars to do their important work.

Where do we go from here? In order for early career scholars (and scholars generally) to successfully navigate the tensions between personal, institutional and disciplinary notions of socially and professionally viable research, several conditions must prevail. In addition to attending to the need for professional validation of "public good" scholarship, institutions, higher education systems, and communities need to undertake activities that can advance a higher level of understanding about the social and educational benefits of strengthened relations between higher education and society. Included among these activities are:

- **Further Examination and Dissemination** of current policy, practices, and driving issues within and between higher education and society. Exploratory efforts should be transparent and accessible to a wide range of stakeholders. Possible exploratory approaches could include joint (community and institutional) impact analyses of specific efforts, institutional and/or community self-assessments, collaborative research and assessment between social and institutional entities, and presentations and participation of representatives from higher education and social entities at each other's key meetings and gatherings to exchange mutually important insights and concerns.

+ **Dialogue** needs to be cross-sectorial; thematic; outcomes-based; "sustained" over regular and adequate time periods; representative of stakeholder populations; respectful of cultural values and ways of being; and "elastic" enough to contain multiple perspectives, yet bounded by the rules of respectful, focused discourse.

+ **Institutional Engagement** that involves various forms of interaction within and between levels of leadership in higher education institutions and systems, including students, faculty, staff, governing boards and alumni. Engagement within institutions should be targeted for specific change and understanding. Aligning the aims of institutional engagement and scholarship with the aims of public needs is critical in order to optimize broad learning and social impact.

+ **Public Engagement** that entails multiple forms of exchange between higher education communities and various publics about the larger purposes of higher education and the assets and needs of communities, assessment of public thought and opinions regarding higher education, and collective identification and strategic planning regarding challenges and mutually beneficial outcomes for higher education and society.

+ **Forming Strategic Alliances** between higher education institutions and community entities, which should seek and nurture broader relationships, including those outside of their traditional ones. Building alliance clusters requires strategic thought and action on the part of all those in the relationship and demands clarity of purpose and specific responsibilities among those in the alliance.

+ **Developing Public Policy** that translates a collective community and institutional understanding about the origins, impact, and potential solutions to social challenges into codified procedures and practices. Institutions and social entities should work together to shape and shepherd meaningful public policy that reflects collective values and reinforces mutually beneficial outcomes.

♦ **A Consciousness and Culture Shift** must occur within and outside of the academy. Perhaps the most difficult of all necessary actions is a transformation in the ways higher education and parts of society view themselves and act on those views. Additionally, the ways in which institutional and community values are reflected in behaviors, practices, policies, traditions, and relationships will need to be examined to assure alignment between cultural and environmental realities, institutional and community rhetoric, commitments of scarce resources, and conclusions made about the impact of collective efforts.

At the end of the day, it is our hope and desire that this edited book will contribute to scholarly discourse and practice in order to better understand the role of higher education in a changing society.

References

Association of University Professors and the Association of American Colleges. (1940). *The 1940 Statement of Principles on Academic Freedom and Tenure*. Washington, DC: Authors.

Baldwin, R. G., & Chronister, J. L. (2001). Teaching without tenure: Policies and practices for a new era. Baltimore: Johns Hopkins University Press.

Benjamin, E. (1997, January 29). Changing distribution of faculty by tenure status and gender. Memorandum to the Executive Committee of the American Association of University Professors.

Bok, D. (2003). Universities in the marketplace: The commercialization of higher education. Princeton, NJ: Princeton University Press.

Chambers, T. C. (2005). Pondering the social charter: Critical reflection for leaders. In A. J. Kezar, T. C. Chambers, & J. C. Burkhardt (Eds.), Higher education for the public good: Emerging voices from a national movement (pp. 326–330). San Francisco: Jossey-Bass.

Clark, B. R. (1987). *The academic profession: National, disciplinary, and institutional settings*. Berkeley, CA: University of California Press.

Copeland, J. D., & Murry, J. W., Jr. (1996). Getting tossed from the ivory tower: The legal implications of evaluating faculty performance. *Missouri Law Review, 61*, 233–327.

Damrosch, D. (1995). *We scholars: Changing the culture of the university*. Cambridge, MA: Harvard University Press.

Goodwin, C. D., & Nacht, M. (1991). *Missing the boat: The failure to internationalize American higher education*. New York: Cambridge University Press.

Gregorian, V. (2004, June 6). Colleges must reconstruct the unity of knowledge. *Chronicle of Higher Education. 50*(39), B12.

Hayward, F. M. (2000). *Internationalization of U.S. higher education: Preliminary status report 2000.* Washington, DC: American Council on Education.

Hearn, J. C. (1997). Research on higher education in a mass and diversified system: The case of the United States. In J. Sadlak, & P. J. Altbach (Eds.), *Higher education research at the turn of the century: Structures, issues, and trends* (pp. 271–319). New York: UNESCO and Garland Publishing.

Jones, G. A. (2006). The restructuring of academic work: Themes and observations. *Higher Education in Europe, 31,* 317–226.

Jones, G. A., McCarney, P. L., & Skolnik, M. L. (2005). Introduction. In G. A. Jones, P. L. McCarney, & M. L. Skolnik (Eds.), *Creating knowledge, strengthening nations: The changing role of higher education* (pp. 3–20). Toronto: University of Toronto Press.

Kirshstein, R. J., Matheson, N., & Jing, Z. (1997). *Instructional faculty and staff in higher education institutions: Fall 1987 and Fall 1992* (NCES 97-470). U.S. Department of Education, National Center for Education Statistics. Washington, DC: U.S. Government Printing Office.

Kirst, M. W., & Venezia, A. (Eds.). (2004). *From high school to college: Improving opportunities for success in postsecondary education.* New York: John Wiley & Sons.

Lambert, R. D. (1989). *International studies and the undergraduate.* Washington, DC: American Council on Education.

Lather, P. (2003). Issues of validity in openly ideological research: Between a rock and a soft place. In Y. Lincoln, & N. Denzin (Eds.), *Turning points in qualitative research* (pp. 185–215). New York: Rowman & Littlefield. (Original work published 1986).

O'Meara, K. A. (2005). Encouraging multiple forms of scholarship in faculty reward systems: Does it make a difference? *Research in Higher Education, 46,* 479–510.

Pascarella, E. T., & Terenzini, P. T. (1991). *How college affects students: Findings and insights from 20 years of research.* San Francisco: Jossey-Bass.

Pascarella, E. T., & Terenzini, P. T. (2005). *How college affects students: A third decade of research.* San Francisco: Jossey-Bass.

Pasque, P. A., Smerek, R. E., Dwyer, B., Bowman, N., & Mallory, B. (2005). *Higher education collaboratives for community engagement and improvement.* Ann Arbor, MI: National Forum on Higher Education for the Public Good.

Rudolph, F. (1962/1990). *The American college and university.* Athens, GA: University of Georgia Press.

Sabin, P. (2002, February 8). Academe subverts young scholars' civic orientation. *Chronicle of Higher Education, 48*(22), B24.

Schoorman, D. (2000). *How is internationalization implemented? A framework for organizational practice.* (ERIC Document Reproduction Service No. ED444426).

Sen, A., Partelow, L., & Miller, D. C. (2005). *Comparative indicators of education in the United States and other G8 countries: 2004* (NCES: 2005-021). U.S. Department of Education, National Center for Education Statistics. Washington, DC: U.S. Government Printing Office.

Slaughter, S., & Rhoades, G. (2004). *Academic capitalism and the new economy: Markets, state, and higher education.* Baltimore: Johns Hopkins University Press.

Tierney, W. G. (2004). Globalization and educational reform: The challenges ahead. *Journal of Hispanic Higher Education, 3,* 5–20.

Tierney, W. G., & Bensimon, E. M. (1996). *Promotion and tenure: Community and socialization in academe.* Albany, NY: State University of New York Press.

Ward, K. (2005). Rethinking faculty roles and rewards for the public good. In A. J. Kezar, A. C. Chambers, & J. C. Burkhardt (Eds.), *Higher education for the public good: Emerging voices from a national movement* (pp. 217–234). San Francisco: Jossey-Bass.

Contributors

Alexander W. Astin is Allan M. Cartter Professor Emeritus of Higher Education and Founding Director of the Higher Education Research Institute at UCLA. He is also the Founding Director of the Cooperative Institutional Research Program and the author of 21 books and some 400 other publications in the field of higher education. He is currently principal investigator (with H. S. Astin) on a national study of spiritual development among undergraduates at 150 higher education institutions. His latest book is *Mindworks: Becoming More Conscious in an Unconscious World* (Information Age Publishing, 2007).

Helen S. Astin, a psychologist, is Professor Emeritus and Senior Scholar at the Higher Education Research Institute at UCLA. Her research and writing have been on issues of gender, ethnic diversity, leadership, and more recently on spirituality in higher education.

Nicholas A. Bowman is a postdoctoral research associate in the Center for Social Concerns at the University of Notre Dame. He received a Ph.D. in Psychology and Education from the University of Michigan. His research interests include college diversity experiences and student development, the assessment of college student outcomes, and the effects of college rankings on various higher education constituencies. His work has appeared or is scheduled to appear in *Research in Higher Education, The Journal of Higher Education, Review of Higher Education, Journal of College Student Development, American Journal of Education*, and *Personality and Social Psychology Bulletin*.

Bryan McKinley Jones Brayboy is President's Professor of Education at the University of Alaska Fairbanks and Borderland's Associate Professor of Educational Leadership and Policy Studies at Arizona State University. His scholarship, teaching, and service are broadly centered on underrepresented students and faculty in higher education. More specifically, his research focuses on the strategies used to achieve academic success by American Indian college students, as well as the cultural, emotional, psychological, political, and financial costs and benefits of this academic success. Most recently, he has been engaged in exploring the role of Indigenous epistemologies, ontologies, and pedagogies in the academic experiences of Indigenous students, staff, and faculty.

John C. Burkhardt is Clinical Professor of Higher and Postsecondary Education at the University of Michigan and Director of the National Forum on Higher Education for the Public Good, an effort to make higher education more responsive to the needs of a changing society. He also holds the title of Special Assistant to the Provost for University Engagement at the University of Michigan. He came to Michigan after serving eight years as a program director at the W.K. Kellogg Foundation where he coordinated leadership grant making and projects in education and leadership development around the world.

Anthony Chambers is a member of the faculty and founding Director of the Centre for the Study of Students in Postsecondary Education in the department of Theory and Policy Studies in Education at the University of Toronto in the Ontario Institute for Studies in Education (OISE). He also serves as Associate Vice-Provost, Students at the University of Toronto. Tony was formerly Associate Director of the National Forum on Higher Education for the Public Good where he created and directed the Rising Scholars Program to Advance Research on Higher Education for the Public Good. He has published widely, serves on several editorial boards, including the Michigan Journal of Community Service-Learning, and co-edited the recent book, *Higher Education for the Public Good: Emerging Voices from a National Movement* (Jossey-Bass Publishers, 2005).

Nadine Dolby is Associate Professor of Curriculum Studies at Purdue University. Her most recent book, *Youth Moves: Identities and Education in Global Perspective* (edited with Fazal Rizvi) was published by Routledge in 2007. Her other publications include *Constructing Race: Youth, Identity, and Popular Culture in South Africa* (State University of New York Press, 2001) and *Learning to Labor in New Times* (edited with Greg Dimitriadis, Routledge, 2004). She has also published in numerous journals including *Harvard Educational Review, African Studies Review, Comparative Education Review, Qualitative Inquiry, Journal of Studies in International Education, Australian Education Researcher, Educational Researcher, British Journal* *of Sociology of Education*, and *Teachers College Record*. She has conducted research in South Africa, Australia, and the United States. Her areas of research interest include international education, higher education, and global youth culture.

Lamont A. Flowers is the Distinguished Professor of Educational Leadership in the Department of Leadership, Counselor Education, Human and Organizational Development and the Executive Director of the Charles H. Houston Center for the Study of the Black Experience in Education in the Eugene T. Moore School of Education at Clemson University. He has authored and/or co-authored more than 65 scholarly publications in the areas of academic achievement, student retention, and educational leadership. He also serves as a Senior Associate Editor for the *College Student Affairs Journal* and the Editor-in-Chief of the *Journal of the Professoriate*.

Julia Garbus, a researcher, freelance writer, and writing tutor, received her Ph.D. in rhetoric and composition from the University of Texas–Austin and taught at the University of Northern Colorado. Her articles on Scudder's rhetorics and pedagogies have appeared in *College English* and in *Local Histories: Reading the archives of composition*, and another is forthcoming in *College Composition and Communication*. She's also written about tutoring nontraditional students, including a piece in a soon-to-be-published Fountainhead Press collection on teaching writing to students with disabilities. She has a book about Scudder in the works.

Sara Goldrick-Rab is Assistant Professor of Educational Policy Studies and Sociology at the University of Wisconsin–Madison, and Scholar at the Wisconsin Center for the Advancement of Postsecondary Education. She earned her Ph.D. in sociology at the University of Pennsylvania. Dr. Goldrick-Rab was a 2006–2007 postdoctoral fellow of the National Academy of Education/Spencer Foundation. Her research on inequality in postsecondary transitions has been published in *Sociology of Education*, *Educational Evaluation and Policy Analysis*, and *Teachers College Record*, and she is the co-author of *Putting Poor People to Work* (Russell Sage, 2006), which was a finalist for the C. Wright Mills award.

Denise O'Neil Green, at the time of writing, was assistant professor of educational psychology and senior associate of the Office of Qualitative and Mixed

Methods Research in the College of Education and Human Sciences at the University of Nebraska–Lincoln. Her research focuses on the development and implementation of qualitative research designs that aid social science and education researchers, policymakers, and administrators in understanding diversity issues and diverse populations in public policy, higher education, and K–12 education. Currently she is Associate Vice President for Institutional Diversity at Central Michigan University.

Seanna M. Kerrigan brings a decade of experience to her current position as the Capstone Program Director at Portland State University. In this role, she works collaboratively with community-based organizations and faculty to develop over 220 service-learning courses which engage over 3,300 students each academic year. She also assists faculty in the design, implementation, reflection, and assessment of these courses, works on an administrative level within the University to ensure the ongoing success of this cutting-edge program, and promotes the concept of service-learning to faculty, students, and staff locally and nationally. Her scholarship focuses on the assessment of Capstone courses with a special interest in expressing the voices of the students and the community member involved.

Jennifer E. Lerner holds a Ph.D. in Sociology from the University of Michigan and is currently Assistant Dean of Social Sciences and Assistant Professor of Sociology at the Loudoun Campus of Northern Virginia Community College. Her research interests include education, culture, stratification, work/family conflict, diversity and multiculturalism, and pedagogy. Jennifer has published work in *Teaching Sociology*, *The Sociological Quarterly*, *College Teaching*, and the *Journal of College Student Development*.

Magdalena Martínez is an education consultant. Currently she is working with the Nevada System of Higher Education where she is focusing on issues of access, equity, and student success for under-represented student populations. She received her Ph.D. from the Center for the Study of Higher Education at the University of Michigan, M.Ed. from Harvard Graduate School of Education, and B.S. from the University of Nevada Las Vegas.

Michele S. Moses is Associate Professor of Educational Foundations, Policy and Practice at the University of Colorado–Boulder. She specializes in philosophy and education policy studies. Her research centers on issues of educational equality and social justice within education policies related to race and class, such as affirmative action. Recent articles have appeared in *Educational Researcher, Harvard Educational Review, Journal of Social Philosophy, Journal of Philosophy of Education, Philosophy and Public Policy Quarterly,* and *Educational Policy.* In addition, she is the author of *Embracing Race: Why We Need Race-Conscious Education Policy* (Teachers College Press, 2002).

Richard L. O'Bryant took leave from his tenure track position at Northeastern University to become director of the John D. O'Bryant African American Institute—named in remembrance of his father. Richard O'Bryant joined the Northeastern family as an assistant professor of political science and a senior research fellow at the Center for Urban and Regional Policy. He oversees educational and cultural programs, research, services, and activities focused on African American students. His recent publications include *ICT as a Public Good: Community Building and Expanding U.S. Self-Sufficiency Policy* (2008) and a review of *Media Access: Social and Psychological Dimensions of a New Technology Use,* published in February 2005 in the *New Media and Society Journal.* He received his Ph.D. in urban and regional studies from MIT in 2004.

Penny A. Pasque is Assistant Professor of adult and higher education in the Department of Educational Leadership and Policy Studies and Women's and Gender Studies at the University of Oklahoma. Her research includes strengthening the connections between higher education and society, addressing in/equities in higher education, and qualitative methodologies. Her latest research project is a longitudinal study on women leaders in higher education. She received a Ph.D. from the Center for the Study of Higher and Postsecondary Education at the University of Michigan. Penny has published in the *Journal of College Student Development* and the *Review of Higher Education* and her forthcoming publication is *American Higher Education, Leadership, and Policy: Critical issues and the Public Good* with Palgrave Macmillan (in press).

Joshua Powers is an Associate Professor and Chair of the Educational Leadership Department at Indiana State University. His research focuses on the commercialization of academic science and factors that explain technology transfer performance differences among universities as well as the ethical and financial implications of academic entrepreneurship. Most recently, he has been engaged

285

in a NIH sponsored project investigating the effects of particular U.S. licensing practices on the pace of follow-on innovation. He has published in *The Journal of Business Venturing, Research Policy, The Journal of Higher Education*, the *Chronicle Review*, and *Health Affairs* among other outlets.

Luis Urrieta, Jr. is Assistant Professor of Cultural Studies in Education and Fellow in the Lee Hage Jamail Regents Chair in Education at the University of Texas–Austin. Urrieta's general research interests are on issues of identity, agency, and social movements in education with a strong focus on Chicana/o identity and activism, and more recently on U.S.-Mexico migration issues. Urrieta was born and raised in Los Angeles, CA, and is the son of Mexican immigrants from Michoacán.

David J. Weerts is Assistant Professor of higher education in the Department of Policy and Administration at the University of Minnesota and faculty affiliate at the Wisconsin Center for the Advancement of Postsecondary Education, University of Wisconsin–Madison. His teaching and scholarly interests include state financing of higher education, university-community engagement, and alumni philanthropy and volunteerism. His research has been published in various scholarly outlets including *The Journal of Higher Education, New Directions for Institutional Research*, and the forthcoming issue of *Research in Higher Education*. Weerts holds a Ph.D. in higher education from the University of Wisconsin–Madison.

LaVergne, TN USA
27 July 2010
191151LV00002B/128/P